Celluloid Vampires

Celluloid Vampires

Life After Death in the Modern World

STACEY ABBOTT

University of Texas Press ✦ *Austin*

Chapter 2, "The Cinematic Spectacle of Vampirism: *Nosferatu* in the Light of New Technology," originally appeared in *Horror Film: Creating and Marketing Fear*, edited by Steffen Hantke. This material is reprinted with permission from the University of Mississippi Press.

Requests for permission to reproduce material from this work should be sent to Permissions, University of Texas Press, P.O. Box 7819, Austin, TX 78713-7819.
www.utexas.edu/utpress/about/bpermission.html

⊚ The paper used in this book meets the minimum requirements of ANSI/NISO z39.48-1992 (R1997) (Permanence of Paper).

LIBRARY OF CONGRESS CATALOGING-IN-PUBLICATION DATA
Abbott, Stacey.
　　Celluloid vampires : life after death in the modern world / Stacey Abbott.—
1st ed.
　　　　p. cm.
　　Filmography: p.
　　Includes bibliographical references and index.
　　ISBN 978-0-292-71695-7 (cloth : alk. paper)—ISBN 978-0-292-71696-4
(pbk. : alk. paper)
　　　1. Vampire films—History and criticism.　I. Title.
　　PN1995.9.V3A23 2007
　　791.43′675—dc22　　　　　　　　　　2007005470

For Simon, with love

Contents

Acknowledgments

This book is the product of many years research and writing and as such there are a great many people to whom I owe a debt for their assistance, contribution, and interest in my work, but also for occasionally bringing me into the light of day and reminding me that there is more to life than vampires. This book began as my PhD thesis and so my biggest debt is to my supervisor Roger Luckhurst, who offered guidance, insight, and always knew just the right thing to say to help me through the difficulties of PhD research. He continues to offer his support and guidance. Thank you for being supervisor, mentor, and occasional therapist. I would also like to thank Karen Myers, Markman Ellis, and Steve Neale, who offered insightful comments, corrections, and encouragement to find a publisher while the book was in its PhD form. Thank you to Steffen Hantke for his interest in my work upon hearing my first conference paper on *Nosferatu*, for expressing a desire to publish it as an article, and for all of his useful editorial comments. I am particularly grateful to readers Professor Tony Williams and Professor Joan Hawkins for their insightful observations and for recommending the publication of this book.

In turning the thesis into a book, I would like to thank those at the University of Texas Press for their support and assistance. In particular I owe a debt to Wendy Moore for her belief in the project and to Laura Griffin for her superb work as an editor. At Roehampton University, I would like to thank the School of Arts' Research Committee for providing me with a sabbatical to complete the book and my colleagues in the Film and Television department for their unending support and enthusiasm for my research. Thank you to Ken Lyndon at TV Roehampton, Mike Allen at Birkbeck College, and Tom Cabot at the British Film Institute for their help in producing the stills included here. I couldn't have done it without them. To my office partner Deborah Jermyn I express my appreciation for her friendship and encouragement. I would also like to thank those students who have taken my Modern Vampire module. You helped me to view these films with fresh eyes.

The staff at the following libraries was of great assistance in facilitating my research: Roehampton University Library, the University of London Library, Birkbeck College Library, and the British Library. I would in particular like to express my appreciation to the staff of the British Film Institute Library for creating a friendly and welcoming environment in which to work. My friend Donato Totaro was of great assistance as his shared interest in the horror genre meant that he could often recommend interesting vampire films for me to see and I am particularly indebted to him for sending me the tape of Larry Fessenden's *Habit* which proved quite key to my research. Thank you to Larry Fessenden for his interest in my work and his patience in answering all of my questions about his film.

Of course it is to my parents Stanley and Joan Abbott that I owe the greatest debt for I am a product of their limitless love and support, without which I would not have had the strength of will and character to persevere through this research. To my siblings, Glenn, Leslie, Jeff, and Joanne, I thank them for their daily emails which not only kept me in touch with family, made me laugh, and occasionally brought me down to earth, but also made me feel that the distance between us was not that wide after all.

To my husband, Simon Brown, I cannot hope to express the thanks that he deserves. Since I began this research, Simon has been by my side, offering advice, encouragement, and emotional support when needed. He has always been there to listen to my thoughts and ramblings and has never hesitated to challenge my ideas, always bringing a new perspective to every issue. Our discussions have helped me work through countless problems or stumbling blocks and he deserves particular thanks for watching an endless stream of good and bad vampire films.

Finally, this book isn't about favorites, but here is my chance to thank those filmmakers, writers, and actors who brought me some of my favorite vampire stories, films, television series, and simply my favorite vampires. These are the creative artists who have made this such a rewarding project and who have shown that a vampire can be so much more than a monster: Sheridan LeFanu, Bram Stoker, F. W. Murnau, Tod Browning, Terence Fisher, George Romero, Anne Rice, Dan Curtis, Kathryn Bigelow, Tom Holland, Larry Fessenden, Francis Ford Coppola, Joss Whedon, Max Schreck, Bela Lugosi, Christopher Lee, Barbara Shelley, John Amplas, Bill Paxton, Wesley Snipes, Gary Oldman, James Marsters, David Boreanaz, Julie Benz, and Juliet Landau.

Celluloid Vampires

Introduction: A Little Less Ritual and a Little More Fun

In 1896, one year before the publication of Bram Stoker's *Dracula*, French magician and filmmaker George Méliès brought forth the first celluloid vampire in his film *Le manoir du diable* (*The Haunted Castle*). In this film, a bat flies into a Gothic castle, transforms into a man who then conjures up numerous visions to horrify the other inhabitants of the castle. He is vanquished by a man brandishing a crucifix. In the century that has followed, the vampire continues to be one of the most popular Gothic monsters to haunt our cinema and television screens with hundreds of films that both draw from classic vampire folklore and literature and break away from this tradition to reinvent the vampire myth. Today, more people are familiar with the vampire genre through film and television than through classic literature.[1] How has this legacy of celluloid vampires affected our understanding of vampire mythology? Has the vampire changed from its folkloric and literary origins?

Vampires have traditionally been associated with the past through their perceived relationship with primitive desires, folklore, or Gothic fiction. To imagine a modern vampire seems almost contradictory. The vampire emerged in literature in the nineteenth century as part of the Gothic genre and therefore has traditionally been defined by its conventions. The Gothic, in literary terms, is a genre of fiction written in the eighteenth and nineteenth century that celebrates the irrational, the fantastic, and the supernatural. The writing style of Gothic fiction is usually excessive, emphasizing, through detailed description, gloomy and unsettling atmospheres and settings. Narratively, the novels often focus upon a conflict between past and present.[2] Fred Botting describes Gothic atmospheres as signaling "the disturbing return of pasts upon presents" and explains that "in the twentieth century, in diverse and ambiguous ways, Gothic

figures have continued to shadow the progress of modernity with coun-
ternarratives displaying the underside of enlightenment and humanist
values."[3] Similarly, David Punter argues that

> Gothic stood for the old-fashioned as opposed to the modern; the bar-
> baric as opposed to the civilised; crudity as opposed to elegance . . .
> Gothic was the archaic, the pagan, that which was prior to, or was
> opposed to, or resisted the establishment of civilised values and a well-
> regulated society.[4]

That the vampire is a key proponent of the genre is demonstrated by
David Punter's description of Gothic fiction as "the fiction of the haunted
castle, of heroines preyed upon by unspeakable terrors, of the blackly
lowering villain, of ghosts, vampires, monsters and werewolves."[5] The
vampire, drawn as it was from folklore and mythology, came to represent
the barbaric and archaic world that resists the civilized and the modern.
As the vampire is immortal, it is seen as stretching back into far reaches
of the past. For instance, in Bram Stoker's classic vampire novel *Dracula*,
the vampire draws attention to his antiquity by describing the people and
events of centuries' worth of national and family history to the young
solicitor Jonathan Harker "as if he had been present at them all."[6] Harker
clearly articulates a distinction between the vampire and the modern world
when he claims that his use of shorthand to describe his mysterious surroundings and the strange events that befall him is "nineteenth century
up-to-date with a vengeance" (36). The events and images that confound
his sensibilities while he is in Castle Dracula pre-exist modernity and his
rationalist understanding of the world. Harker views Count Dracula and
his vampire brides as premodern and supernatural, oppositional forces
threatening modernity. Brian W. Aldiss sees the relocation of the vampire
into a modern setting as signaling the infection of the modern with the
vampire's barbarity:

> In this great transitional novel, we are not to remain among ancient
> things, whose distance brings comfort along with terror. The strength of
> Stoker's novel is that his evil Count, for all the world like a disease that
> cannot be checked, arrives in London. A barrier has been crossed; the
> infection has entered the modern vein.[7]

While Dracula's arrival in modern London does mark the relocation of
the vampire from the Gothic past into a recognizably up-to-date location,

the vampire has come to represent so much more, particularly in the years that have followed Stoker's novel. An alternate interpretation of the vampire's immortality is that it not only stretches into the past, but also pushes forward into the future, and many vampires in film and television embrace the future rather than wallow in the past.

The difference between old- and new-world vampires is demonstrated by the violent transfer of power across generations on the American television series *Buffy the Vampire Slayer* (1997–2003), most notably by the punk rock vampire Spike. While the series takes place in a contemporary setting rather than in an exotic past, the vampires of seasons one and two, led by an old-world vampire, the Master, and his second-in-command, the Anointed One, are initially presented as members of a tradition-based society ruled by prophecy, superstition, and ritual. Describing themselves as the Brethren of Aurelius, the vampires maintain their association with the premodern using poetic language as well as a ruined church, buried within the mouth of hell, as a lair. However, the introduction of a new vampire, Spike, demonstrates that the vampire can be presented as a modern figure, more inherently linked to its contemporary setting than to the past.

Spike evokes a modern sensibility with his contempt for tradition and ritual, feelings that are established from the moment of his irreverent entrance into the vampires' lair ("School Hard," season 2: episode 3). His sneering attitude and physical appearance—bleached-blond, punk-style haircut, leather jacket, cigarettes, jeans, and t-shirt—elicits an image of rebellion. As he enters the room, one of the vampires is proclaiming that the Night of St. Vigious, a vampire holy day, will be as glorious as the Crucifixion, which he claims to have witnessed. Spike dismisses this remark by pointing out that if "every vampire who said he was at the Crucifixion was actually there, it would have been like Woodstock. I was actually at Woodstock. That was a weird gig. Fed off a flower person and I spent the next six hours watching my hand move." Spike challenges the vampire's authority and demonstrates his own preference for the contemporary by comparing the Crucifixion to a twentieth-century pop culture event. In this case, the vampire is presented as shedding any association with the ancient in favor of the modern.

Spike mocks and dismisses the prayers and superstitions performed by the other vampires, describing his contribution to their rituals as "going up and getting chanty with the fellas." He also ignores his holy charge to kill the Slayer on the Night of St. Vigious by attacking Buffy and her friends two days early because he "got bored." His embodiment of a modern and secular sensibility culminates in his destruction of the Anointed One as he declares that "there is gonna be a little less ritual and a little more fun around here," setting himself up as the new head vampire in Sunnydale.

This violent usurpation of a traditional vampire by a modern one is mirrored in the film *Blade* (1998). The vampire Frost, like Spike, is portrayed as young and rebellious. He runs clandestine vampire nightclubs, lives in a modern high-rise, and ignores the orders of the vampire elders. Made a vampire rather than born one, Frost warns Dragonetti—the leader of the born vampires and their noble ruling body, the House of Erebus—that he is at risk of becoming extinct if he does not change his ways. Frost later proves his point when he defangs and destroys Dragonetti in order to take his place as leader. Both the Brethren of Aurelius and the House of Erebus equate the vampire with nobility, ancient tradition, and established rules that date back centuries, while Spike and Frost seek to break with the past and establish their own futures. They are modern, not only because of their contempt for the old ways or their passion for contemporary music, technology, and popular culture, but also because the act of destroying the traditional vampire in order to take its place, effectively replacing the old with the new, is one of the distinctive characteristics of modernity.

Spike and Frost, however, represent but two images of the modern vampire. While Stoker's *Dracula* was primarily the prototype for the cinematic vampire in the first major cycle of American horror films in the 1930s and 1940s, since the 1970s the image of the vampire has become fragmented into a diverse range. Vampires in film and television are no longer ruled by the past or tradition but rather embrace the present and its vast array of experiences. Vampires today can be good (*Blade*), evil (the Master in *Buffy the Vampire Slayer*), or both (*Angel*); European (*Revenant*), African-American (*Blacula*), or Mexican (*From Dusk till Dawn*); children (*The Little Vampire*) or grandparents (*My Grandfather Is a Vampire*); isolated (*Nadja*) or familial (*Near Dark*); rock stars (*Queen of the Damned*), philosophy students (*The Addiction*), performance artists (*Fright Night II*), or action heroes (*Blade*); gangs (*Blood Ties*) or gangsters (*Innocent Blood*); nomadic (*The Forsaken*) or urban (*Habit*); fallen priests (*Vampires*) or fallen apostles (*Dracula 2000*).

The success of the television series *Buffy the Vampire Slayer* and *Angel*, as well as late-night programs *Kindred: The Embraced* and *Forever Knight*, the Canadian children's series *Vampire High*, and the British cult series *Ultraviolet*, has caused audiences to break the primary vampire rule on a regular basis by inviting them into the home. For every new cinema release that suggests the death of the vampire genre by pushing its boundaries to their limits, there is one that follows to reset the boundaries. Nina Auerbach argues that there is a vampire for every generation and that "since vampires are immortal, they are free to change incessantly."[8] The vampire is in a constant state of disintegration and renewal, and it is through this process that it is intrinsically linked to the modern world, which is also perpetually in the throes of massive change.

The modern vampire, from Dracula to present-day vampires such as Frost and Spike, has consistently challenged its relationship to convention and tradition, gradually escaping the confines of time and space to become free of the association with the past and liberated into the expanse of the modern landscape. It is my intention to examine the relationship between the celluloid vampire and the modern world, and to argue that rather than acting in opposition to modernity, the vampire has come to embody the experience of it.

To recognize how the vampire has been redefined through the language of modernity, it is important to establish a definition of modernity. Charles Baudelaire described modernity as the here and now, a fleeting, intangible, transitory moment in time, co-existing with that which transcends time and space: the eternal.[9] He believed that the essence of modernity exists in the moment that binds time and space together before it is lost in the ever-changing landscape of the modern. Georg Simmel equally defined modernity as the perception and experience of the present moment. Simmel argued that life in the modern metropolis was so full of external stimuli that the city dweller had to protect himself by restricting social interaction to a series of self-contained and fragmented exchanges. These exchanges served to reduce all social interactions to a means to an end and to disconnect them from the past or future. According to Simmel's argument, modernity becomes the act of living in the eternal present.[10]

While nineteenth-century modernists Baudelaire and Simmel locate modernity within the experience of life in the city, contemporary theorist Marshall Berman suggests that as the moment—the essence of modernity—is fleeting and intangible, modernity must also suggest a cycle of re-creation, each fleeting moment replaced by the next. This cycle is reflected in the need to develop and modernize, where the "new" is replaced by the "newer," in a constant cycle of development and destruction. He explains that modernity "pours us all into a maelstrom of perpetual disintegration and renewal, of struggle and contradiction, of ambiguity and anguish. To be modern is to be part of a universe in which, as Marx said, 'all that is solid melts into air.'" For Berman, modernity is therefore a whirlwind of change, development, and destruction, not just of buildings or cities, but philosophies, morals, and values. Modernity is the world of self-annihilation and rebirth. More importantly, modernity is defined by the experience of this whirlwind for, he argues, "To be modern is to find ourselves in an environment that promises us adventure, power, joy, growth, transformation of ourselves and the world—and, at the same time, that threatens to destroy everything we have, everything we know, everything we are."[11] Furthermore, Anthony Giddens argues that one of the defining features of modernity is the separation of time and space, previously united in the premodern era through the definition of place. He explains that part of the experience of modernity is the process of "disembedding of social institutions" from local contexts and "their rearticulation across indefinite tracts of time-space."[12] Modernity is essentially a posttraditional order, and therefore being removed from the trappings of tradition is intrinsic to the experience of modernity.

Ambivalence toward modernity, an exciting and yet a destructive force, is mirrored in the ambivalence felt toward the vampire, an equally exciting and destructive presence. The relationship between the two is reinforced by the fact that the vampire regularly emerges amidst periods of extreme, and sometimes violent, change, such as the 1890s in Britain and the 1970s in America. According to Nina Auerbach, the vampire genre shifted from England to America between the nineteenth and the twentieth centuries because "vampires go where power is: when, in the nineteenth century, England dominated the West, British vampires ruled the popular imagination, but with the birth of film, they migrated to America in time for the American century."[13]

The migration to America, however, was also a result of a transition within the Gothic genre as one of the Hollywood studios, Universal, deliberately drew upon nineteenth-century Gothic fiction, in the form of *Dracula* and *Frankenstein*, as a source of new material for their films. The success of these films led to the development of what would become known as Hollywood Gothic.[14] Like such literary predecessors as *The Vampyre*[15] and *Carmilla*,[16] Gothic vampire films from this first cycle of American horror films, such as *Dracula* (1931), *Dracula's Daughter* (1936), and *Son of Dracula* (1943), were made in the present but were set in Gothic locations. It was, however, during key moments when Britain and America became the loci for new waves of modernization and change, such as 1890s Britain and 1970s America, that the vampire genre literally relocated into these modern settings. The vampires' migrations are therefore indicative of not only the pursuit of power, but rather an engagement with the processes of reorientation as the conditions and understanding of the modern world were being redefined.

As I discuss in Chapter 1 of this book, *Dracula* was written at the end of the nineteenth century as Britain was coming to grips with massive social, technological, and scientific changes, all of which contributed to Stoker's reworking of the vampire myth from previous literature and folklore. Furthermore, the novel is littered with references to the most up-to-date technologies of the period, such as the telegraph, the phonograph, and the typewriter. These technologies contributed to the separation of time and space described by Giddens.[17] Stephen Kern sees the late nineteenth century as a turning point in the redefinition of time and space. He explains that "the present was no longer limited to one event in one place, sandwiched tightly between past and future and limited to local surroundings. In an age of intrusive electronic communication, 'now' became an extended interval of time that could, indeed must, include events around the world."[18] For instance in a transatlantic telephone call, the here and now is different on each end of the telephone line. The impact of these new developments is felt in Stoker's novel; while the vampire hunters use the technology in their hunt for Dracula, the vampire— a reanimated corpse traditionally defined by the physicality of its body—is liberated from physical boundaries by possessing transformative qualities. The vampire hunters use the technology, but the vampire becomes the technology, able to transcend the boundaries of its body by transforming into other creatures and communicating across distances.

The association of the vampire with technology is foregrounded by the adaptation of the vampire myth for the cinema, as the vampire became the product of technological reproduction. A celluloid vampire is more than simply a film adaptation of the myth; it is the reinvention of the vampire through film technology. The technological modernization of the vampire will be addressed in Chapter 2 by exploring how *Nosferatu* (1922), the German adaptation of *Dracula*, takes the transforming and magical properties of Stoker's vampire and reinterprets them through the language of cinema, a language formed from a legacy of nineteenth-century photography and magic lantern techniques. These techniques present the vampire as a spectral, disembodied presence that, like the cinema itself, seems both supernatural and modern.

Finally, to complete my discussion of *Dracula*, in Chapter 3 I focus on the standardization of the vampire myth in cinema through director Tod Browning's adaptation of Stoker's novel for Universal Studios in 1931, its subsequent sequels, Paul Landres' *Return of Dracula* (1957), and the release of Hammer Studios' version *The Horror of Dracula* in 1958. I address how these films present an ambivalent relationship with modernity as they both embrace many characteristics of the modern while fundamentally associating the vampire with a nostalgic representation of a fictional nineteenth-century past.

In Chapter 4 I address how the modern vampire reappears in the cinema of the United States during a cultural crisis in the 1970s, similar to that of 1890s Britain. I explore how, in this period, the vampire became embroiled in both a national identity crisis and a transition in the concept of modernity. This occurred as the icons of nineteenth-century modernity were being replaced by new images of the modern, and America made the transition from an industrial to a post-industrial nation. There are, therefore, distinct parallels between Stoker's *Dracula* and the plethora of vampire films produced in the United States in the 1970s. The vampire narratives from both periods focus upon a westward movement of the vampire from the premodern world to the modern world. At first glance, the vampire seems to personify a force opposing civilization, but in fact the vampire is born out of the processes of change within the modern world. A case study of George Romero's *Martin* in Chapter 5 demonstrates that the vampires embody these processes by breaking from their previous representations and reinventing the conventions traditionally associated with the vampire, specifically through the language and icons of the newly emerging experience of modernity. They become more modern than the vampire hunters who pursue them.

For his novel, Stoker had to rethink the superstitions from folklore as well as conventions established through earlier Gothic fiction; the filmmakers of the 1970s had to enter into a dialogue with the traditions established from the success of *Dracula* on page and screen. As Gregory A. Waller points out,

> Rather than being a footnote to or an imitation of *Dracula*, the story of the living and the undead as it develops in the twentieth century is an ongoing process of retelling and revisioning Stoker's narrative and in various ways modifying, reaffirming, or challenging the assumptions that inform *Dracula*.[19]

He further argues that at first glance the intrusion of the vampire into America in the 1970s, represented by an outmoded Count Dracula in films such as *Blood for Dracula* (1973) or *Love at First Bite* (1979), seemed to "defang the aristocratic vampire and suggest in one fashion or another that the undead pose no threat to the modern world." What these films really suggest is that there is no place in the modern world for old-world vampires, while books and films, such as Richard Matheson's *I Am Legend* (1957), Stephen King's *Salem's Lot* (1976), and George A. Romero's *Night of the Living Dead* (1968) and *Dawn of the Dead* (1979), all "bring the undead into present day America," reinventing the vampire so that they are no longer exotic and aristocratic intruders, but rather average people, such as neighbors, family, and friends. In this manner, Waller asserts, they "expand rather than diminish the threat posed by the undead . . . Extend[ing], and at times subvert[ing] the conventions of the genre and thereby forc[ing] us to assess our understanding of the story of the living and the undead."[20] This shift in the genre enabled the vampire myth to capture the turbulent internal tensions and social crises within America in the 1970s.

The discussion of the 1970s is followed in Chapters 6 and 7 by a return to the subject of film technology, and a look at how the special effects technologies of the 1970s and 1980s reinforced the cultural reinterpretation of the vampire myth. While the vampire transcended the body's physical boundaries in *Nosferatu*, the low-budget, independent filmmaking techniques used in Romero's *Night of the Living Dead* (see Chapter 6), influenced the vampire film of the 1970s by binding the vampire once again to the body, more specifically the abject corpse. Chapter 7 furthers this discussion by exploring how the rise of sophisticated makeup effects in the 1980s captured the decade's obsession with both physicality and the abject by puncturing and perforating the body's boundaries through graphic transformation. The spectrality of the early film vampire gave way to the carnality of its followers.

Another way in which the vampire engages with the issues of modernity in the novel *Dracula* and in the vampire films from *Martin* (1977) to *Blade* (1998) is through its relocation to the city, the subject of Chapters 7, 8, and 9. The vampire not only migrates to the New World but also emerges within the heart of its great cities. Rather than simply injecting the modern with an infection of the barbaric, as suggested by Aldiss, the modern vampire is shaped by its new relationship to the urban. As Giddens argues, to be modern is to be disembedded from the restrictions imposed by tradition, while Zygmunt Bauman suggests that mobility and freedom from spatial boundaries defines modern existence.[21] He explains that "all of us are willy-nilly by design or default on the move. We are on the move even if, physically, we stay put: immobility is not a realistic option in a world of permanent change."[22] Within the cities, the vampire joins modern networks of movement and begins to gain access to these new freedoms. Dracula's arrival in London in 1897 launches this process of release for the vampire, a process which continues with the arrival of a young vampire in Pittsburgh in 1977 (*Martin*), and culminates in the vampire films of the 1980s and 1990s, when the vampire makes a transition from an outsider settling in the city to a vampire fully integrated within the urban landscape. With this process the vampire gradually sheds spatial and temporal boundaries, along with the traditions that link it to the past, allowing the vampire to access this increased freedom of mobility. As a result, from the 1970s through to the end of the twentieth century, the vampire's image has gradually evolved and fragmented into a wide range of different types of vampires, here represented in Chapter 8 with my analysis of the lone female vampire of New York, in Chapter 9 in the vampire road movie, and in Chapter 10 in the multiracial gangs of postmodern Los Angeles.

Just as the freedom of mobility in urban space liberates the vampire from spatial boundaries, the reinterpretation of the vampire through the language of science and technology liberates it from the confines of the body. This reinterpretation, as discussed in Chapter 11, takes two forms. The first is through the iconography of the genre as both vampires and vampire hunters are increasingly portrayed as cyborgs, replacing conventions and traditions of the genre with scientific rationale and technological weaponry. The second form of reinterpretation involves special effects. The rise of computer-generated images in the 1990s returns spectrality to the vampire—no longer to transcend the physical but to redefine the shape, form, and makeup of the body through the new technology. The cinematic vampire—the sum of the cinema's technological makeup and capabilities—charts in its evolution the transition of twentieth-century technologies from the wonder of the modern world to the wonder of the cyberworld. Finally, in Chapter 12, the book culminates with a questioning of where the vampire, at the beginning of the twenty-first century, goes from here. I suggest that perhaps the vampire, like the technological, industrial, and economic world that surrounds it, has undergone another liberation, this time from national boundaries. Has the modern vampire gone global?

My aim in this book, therefore, is to demonstrate that the vampire, from *Dracula* to *Blade* and beyond, does not singularly embody the primitive and the barbaric, but rather is shaped both by the changing world into which it emerges as well as by the medium through which it is represented. Its history demonstrates a self-conscious awareness of tradition by continually reinventing itself for new audiences. The vampire is timeless but, through the process of renewal, it is completely in tune with the present. As a result, it captures in its immortality the essence of modernity as the world shifts and transforms from generation to generation. While Harker's modern businessman is the essence of nineteenth-century professionalism, his modernity is fleeting. Instead, the vampire's spirit of disintegration and renewal means that it is the vampire that remains "up-to-date with a vengeance" (36).

PART ONE

BRAM STOKER'S *DRACULA* FROM NOVEL TO FILM

CHAPTER ONE

Dracula: A Wonder of the Modern World

And the vampire lunged at me, that strangled cry rising again as the stench of fetid breath rose in my nostrils and the clawlike fingers cut into the very fur of my cape. I fell backwards, my head cracking against the wall, my hands grabbing at his head, clutching a mass of tangled filth that was his hair . . . I realized, through my frantic sobbing breaths, what it was I held in my arms. The two huge eyes bulged from naked sockets and two small, hideous holes made up his nose; only a putrid, leathery flesh enclosed his skull, and the rank, rotting rags that covered his frame were thick with earth and slime and blood. I was battling a mindless, animated corpse.

INTERVIEW WITH THE VAMPIRE [1]

When the vampires Louis and Claudia search eastern Europe for other vampires in Anne Rice's *Interview with the Vampire*, they find only "mindless, animated corpses" haunting graveyards, ancient monuments, and tombs. In presenting a confrontation between new-world and old-world vampires, Rice draws upon the essential differences between literature and folklore. According to Paul Barber, the typical vampire of folklore would have most likely been plump, "with long fingernails and a stubbly beard, his mouth and left eye open, his face ruddy and swollen." He was not an elegant gentleman like his literary cousin, but a "dishevelled peasant." [2] Christopher Frayling explains that, when nineteenth-century romantic fiction adopted vampire folklore, these peasant vampires became aristocratic hero-villains, "fashionably pallid and clean-shaven, with seductive voices and pouting lips, and they were always sexually attractive." [3]

Nineteenth-century vampire fiction, however, does share certain things with folklore, most notably the equation of vampires with primal and barbaric primitive forces. Stories such as "Ken's Mystery" [4] and "Vampire

Maid"[5] focus upon hapless men who are lured by beauty and romance to a place of timeless isolation only to be fed upon by monstrous female vampires who draw their strength from the men's blood. Even the aristocratic Lord Ruthven in John Polidori's *The Vampyre* seems untouched by the modern world and is fuelled primarily by his desire for the blood of innocent girls.[6] When Jonathan Harker first encounters the vampire in Bram Stoker's *Dracula* and is confronted by much that he cannot understand, he rationalizes that the forces are ancient and supernatural, stating that "unless my senses deceive me, the old centuries had, and have powers of their own which mere 'modernity' cannot kill" (36). Jonathan separates that which he understands to be modern from that which Dracula seems to represent: a supernatural and primitive other. To Jonathan, although Dracula is charming and well educated, he is still no different from the vampires of folklore except that his education and ambition make him more dangerous.

Bram Stoker's concept of the vampire, however, is much more complex than initially suggested by Harker's observations. The novel demonstrates a break with conventional vampire fiction by carefully situating its story within a specific time and place and by reconfiguring the vampire myth through the language of modernity. While this novel is not the only vampire story of the period to locate the vampire within a modern setting, Stoker's novel demonstrates a more comprehensive engagement with the concept of modernity and marks an attempt to equate the vampire itself with the modern world. The novel clearly locates the narrative within Stoker's contemporary London and is littered with icons of modern living, such as new technologies, sciences, transportation networks, bureaucracy, and urbanization, all of which would have been instantly recognizable to his late-nineteenth-century readers. Rather than simply establish a structural opposition between a premodern vampire and the modern scientific community, the novel places their conflict, and the vampire itself, at the center of a whirlwind of social and technological change, and emphasizes the ambiguous distinction between the two. In *Dracula*, the conflict between the vampire and the vampire hunters becomes the site for an exploration of the complexities of modernity. It does this in three ways. First, the novel relocates the vampire narrative to contemporary London, capturing the modern perception of this growing urban space and demonstrating how the characters (vampires and vampire hunters alike) negotiate and command the landscape. Second, Stoker eschews traditional methods of vampire hunting in favor of highlighting modern systems of bureaucracy and professionalism to coordinate and compartmentalize the vampire hunters' investigation, as well as the vampire itself, as a means of tracking and defeating Dracula. Third, Dracula is represented as a creature that eludes these attempts at categorization, just as he defies nineteenth-century concepts of time, gravity, and physics, by personifying the changing definitions of these accepted scientific principles. Stoker, drawing upon the language of modern technology, has rewritten the characteristics of the vampire to embody the increasingly ambiguous relationship between science and the occult. The clash between vampire and vampire hunters in the novel, rather than suggesting an opposition between the primitive and the civilized, is really a clash of modernities. As the world continues to progress, a new form of modernity—the hypermodern world of electricity, hypnosis, telepathy, telecommunications, and the disintegration of time and space—gradually overturns the form of modernity exemplified by rational thought, scientific analysis, and bureaucracy. Dracula's entrance into the modern landscape conveys the belief that modernity is ever-changing, the new is replaced by the newer.[7]

Navigating the Metropolis

The growth and development of the metropolis is one of the primary images of nineteenth-century modernity. The city was the center of modern industrialization, capitalism, and trade, as well as developments in modern science and technology. As a result, the city increasingly became equated with modernization and progress as illustrated by Elisée Reclus who argued in 1895 that "where the cities increase, humanity is progressing; where they diminish, civilization itself is in danger."[8] While Reclus saw the city as the center of progress, Georg Simmel discussed modernity in terms of the subjective experience of the metropolis in which humankind was under threat of being overwhelmed by external stimuli.[9] For Baudelaire, however, the city, with its crowded streets, evolving fashion, and heightened circulation, was the epicenter of modern life; the city's emphasis upon change and constant movement evoked the transitory quality of the modern.[10]

It was within this cultural milieu that Stoker wrote *Dracula* and chose to locate his narrative in the heart of the most modern of cities: London. At the time Stoker wrote the novel, London was experiencing massive growth. Not only was there a rise in population, but with the improvement in railroads and underground transport, there was an increase in the number of people moving from the inner ring to the developing suburbs, causing London to expand in size as well as population.[11] This development of London into Greater London was met with both positive and negative responses, as illustrated by the following descriptions of the city printed in the *Contemporary Review* and the *Quarterly Review* in 1895.

> London, compact as it is in its central districts, is a splendid example of this dispersion of the urban population among the fields and forests for a hundred miles round, and even down to the seaside . . . The very heart of London, "the City" properly so-called, is little but a great Exchange by day, depopulated by night; the active centres of government, of legislation, of science and art, cluster round this great focus of energy, increasing year by year, and elbowing out the resident population into the suburbs.[12]

Where *Contemporary Review* emphasized the growth and development of the city, the *Quarterly Review* responded primarily to the decay and neglect of the city and its population.

> London is perhaps the most eccentric wonder in the history of the world. Its vast extent of sordid, inartistic buildings, and its enormous migratory lodger population; its abundant evidence of wealth, and yet its wide-spread areas of local poverty; its feeble minded native occupants, and the energy of its foreign and provincial immigrants; the sumptuousness of its western mansions, and its unlimited extent of squalid homes; its ill-arranged, ill-kept, and dirty streets, and its polluted atmosphere, are all exceptional, and most of them are in their various ways superlative. Moreover London, all its gifts considered, is perhaps the least efficient and least influential aggregate of people on the globe.[13]

It is this cocktail of images of the modern city, the squalid and the beautiful, the poverty-stricken and the urban crowds of commuters and businessmen, that attracts Dracula to London. Dracula informs Jonathan Harker, the young solicitor hired to facilitate his move to London, "I long to go through the crowded streets of your mighty London, to be in the midst of the whirl and rush of humanity, to share its life, its change, its death, and all that makes it what it is" (20). These words evoke Baudelaire's own description of the modern "man of the crowd," the flâneur, whose

> passion and his profession are to become one flesh with the crowd. For the perfect flâneur, for the passionate spectator, it is an immense joy

to set up house in the heart of the multitude, amid the ebb and flow of movement, in the midst of the fugitive and the infinite. To be away from home and yet to feel oneself everywhere at home; to see the world, to be at the centre of the world, and yet to remain hidden from the world.[14]

In other words, like Dracula's dream of life in London, the flâneur must circulate unnoticed within the crowds of the city and feed off the life around him.

Stoker's decision to set his story in modern London was, however, not unique in late nineteenth-century Gothic fiction. The narratives, characters, and settings of Gothic fiction were transforming. While eighteenth-century Gothic focused upon the past's intrusion on the present in the form of an external threat or monster, nineteenth-century Gothic was increasingly defined by internal threats and anxieties. By the late nineteenth-century, any external Gothic forms still present in the genre came to embody a psychological disturbance and suggested an increasing uncertainty around individual subjectivity. Settings of old castles, monasteries, churches, and graveyards were no longer appropriate and were abandoned in favor of contemporary urban locations. Fred Botting explains that "the modern city, industrial, gloomy and labyrinthine, is the locus of horror, violence and corruption. Scientific discoveries provide the instruments of terror, and crime and the criminal mind present new threatening figures of social and individual disintegration."[15] Nineteenth-century Gothic fiction blurs the distinction between fantasy and reality, integrating the Gothic within the familiar. As anxieties about the modern world continued to evolve, there was an increasing diffusion of Gothic traces throughout fiction, particularly in representations of the modern city. From the press coverage of the Jack the Ripper murders in 1888 to such Gothic novels as *Dr. Jekyll and Mr. Hyde* (1886), *The Three Impostors* (1895), and *The Beetle* (1897), the very real and recognizable streets of Whitechapel, Bloomsbury, and even the developing suburbs were increasingly portrayed as dark and menacing enclaves for the monstrous and the macabre.[16]

Although Stoker's London is similarly the locus of horror, Stoker does not present the city in *Dracula* in the same manner as Stephenson, Machen, and Marsh, authors of *Dr. Jekyll and Mr. Hyde*, *The Three Impostors*, and *The Beetle*, respectively. Those novels imbue the city with supernatural qualities, transferring the narrative from a Gothic medieval castle to a Gothic city, while at the same time fixing their narrative within specific locations and recognizable city streets. In *Dracula*, on the other hand, Stoker maintains a distance from the urban landscape, and rather than having the vampire project his uncanniness upon the city, Stoker imbues Dracula and his hunters with the modern qualities of the city. This is achieved by offering a panoramic view of London, following the characters as they board established networks of transport, and emphasizing their smooth movement through the city. Stoker uses selective snapshots of the characters in recognizable locations to capture the presence of the city, but draws upon modern transport to emphasize the perception of space as unified and interconnected.

For instance, when Seward and Van Helsing return to the Berkeley Hotel after destroying the vampiric Lucy in a Hampstead cemetery, Van Helsing finds a telegram from Mina Harker waiting for him. She announces that she is on her way to London from Exeter. Upon reading this, Van Helsing states that, despite her arrival, he must be on his way to Amsterdam via Liverpool Street Station, and asks that Seward pick Mina up at Paddington and bring her to his home in the asylum in Purfleet. These plans provide little detail for they do not describe the locations, the city streets, or the means of transport across the city. They do, however, offer a keen impression of navigation across the urban landscape with the only points of reference being the two railway stations, Liverpool Street and Paddington, and the only snapshot of the city offered is Seward's brief observations while waiting for Mina: "I took my way to Paddington, where I arrived about fifteen minutes before the train came in. The crowd melted away, after the bustling fashion common to arrival platforms" (219).

It is the use of train travel within the novel that encapsulates a major change in modern perception of landscape. Wolfgang Schivelbusch argues that the transition from coach to rail travel led to the development of a new kind of perception, "one which did not try to fight the effects of the new technology of travel but, on the contrary, assimilated them."[17] Schivelbusch suggests that the speed at which the train traveled through the landscape caused the views from the window to become blurred and indistinct. The modern traveler, however, began to recognize that this speed served to shrink space and bring various elements from different locations together into the same frame, creating a new way of seeing the world. This form of perception enabled the traveler to "grasp the whole, to get an overview" of his or her landscape.[18]

Stoker's novel offers a similar view of the city. The city is no longer confined to a series of streets within which the characters live or along which they walk for it has grown to engulf all of the surroundings within reach of the train. The characters are constantly traveling between distant locations as they circulate from Purfleet to Piccadilly to Hampstead and rather then move through the city along the dark, winding streets of London, as do the characters in *The Three Impostors*, they traverse the city with the speed and precision of the railway. Although initially conceived as a form of intercity transport, it was not long before the potential for an increase in commuter traffic encouraged the construction of a plethora of railways crisscrossing the city and suburbs in a maze of commuter lines. Between 1855 and 1895 the number of railroad lines in and around the city had more than tripled.[19] Stoker's characters are at the center of this complex system of transport networks that binds the city together. Although there are no direct references to Dracula using the railway, Jonathan does find Dracula lying on the sofa in his library in Transylvania studying train timetables (22). This fact along with the speed with which he maneuvers through the city does suggest that Dracula has come to embody the railway's redefinition of time and space. When Dracula discovers that Van Helsing and his men have tampered with his coffins in Carfax Abbey, he leaves Purfleet to inspect his residences in Mile End, Bermondsey, and Piccadilly. As this takes place during the day, while Dracula is trapped in his human form, we must infer that he either takes the train or he moves around the city with the speed of a train. The ease with which both Dracula and Dr. Seward shuttle back and forth between Purfleet, Seward to his asylum and Dracula to Carfax Abbey, and Hillingham to meet Lucy, illustrates the expanse of the city is no obstacle to them. Dr. Seward opens his 18 September diary with the words "just off for train to London" (142) as he prepares to go to Hillingham with a premonition of the doom that awaits him. One can only assume that Dracula caught the train the night before and that Seward is going into the city in his wake.

The snapshots of the city that are presented in the novel capture a complex exploration of the modernization of the city and the evolving relationship between humanity and its spatial landscape. Schivelbusch suggests, when describing the views from the train windows, that "the depth perception of the pre-industrial consciousness was, literally, lost: velocity blurs all foreground objects, which means that there no longer is a foreground" creating a barrier between the landscape and the passenger.[20] The glimpses of London offered in *Dracula* suggest a similar lack of foreground. The narrators do not locate themselves within the scene they are describing but rather describe the vista before them. Two accounts of action taking place upon the street, one from *The Three Impostors* and the other from *Dracula*, demonstrate this distinction.

Mr. Dyson, walking leisurely along Oxford Street, and staring with bland
inquiry at whatever caught his attention, enjoyed in all its rare flavours
the sensation of mankind, the traffic, and the shop windows tickled his
faculties with an exquisite bouquet . . . He had narrowly escaped being
run over at a crossing by a charging van, for he hated to hurry his steps,
and indeed the afternoon was warm; and he had just halted by a place
of popular refreshment, when the astounding gestures of a well-dressed
individual on the opposite pavement held him enchanted and gasping
like a fish. A treble line of hansoms, carriages, vans, cabs, and omnibuses
were tearing east and west, and not the most daring adventurer of the
crossings would have cared to try his fortune; but the person who had
attracted Dyson's attention seemed to rage on the very edge of the pavement, now and then darting forward at the hazard of instant death, and
at each repulse absolutely dancing with excitement, to the rich amusement of the passers-by.[21]

In the above passage, the protagonist walks through the London streets,
looking both left and right, observing all of the action around him. Dyson appears to have adopted Baudelaire's persona of the flâneur, the man
of the crowd.[22] His pace is leisurely and his aim is observation but from
within the crowd and not from outside. Although the narration is in the
third person, the descriptions express Dyson's subjective experience of the
city. The location is described in detail and the atmosphere that is captured is one of a whirlwind of activity around the observer. His encounter
with the young man across the street illustrates the perception of depth
as the action moves from the background to the foreground of the scene
as he struggles to cross the street and run toward Dyson to speak to
him. The protagonist is a part of the scene rather than simply observing
from an objective distance. Now compare the following passage of Mina
recounting Jonathan's first sighting of Dracula in London:

[Jonathan] was very pale, and his eyes seemed bulging out as, half in
terror and half in amazement, he gazed at a tall, thin man, with a beaky
nose and black moustache and pointed beard, who was also observing
the pretty girl. He was looking at her so hard that he did not see either
of us, and so I had a good view of him. His face was not a good face; it
was hard, and cruel, and sensual, and his big white teeth, that looked all
the whiter because his lips were so red, were pointed like an animal's.
Jonathan kept staring at him, till I was afraid he would notice . . .
[Jonathan] kept staring; a man came out of the shop with a small parcel,

and gave it to the lady, who then drove off. The dark man kept his eyes fixed on her, and when the carriage moved up Piccadilly he followed in the same direction, and hailed a hansom. (172)

This demonstrates a very different spatial model. Mina's description is emblematic of the panoramic gaze of the novel. She describes a series of looks, Jonathan staring at Dracula and Dracula staring at the young woman, while Mina observes the whole event. As with the panoramic gaze described by Schivelbush, a barrier exists between the gazer and the object of the gaze while both remain unaware of the gaze directed at them. In her description of the event, Mina does not include herself in the scene but stands back impartially until she finally breaks Jonathan from his reverie. The scene lacks any in-depth description of the setting, the atmosphere, the crowds around them, or any sense of movement from foreground to background that would serve to link the characters within the same space. Instead, the sequence captures a fleeting series of looks with each observer locked within their own panoramic space. The spectatorial quality of these gazes also suggests a cinematic quality. Although Stoker does not mention the cinema in the novel—it is one of the few developing technologies he excludes from his text—the cinematograph had been invented and premiered in France, the US, and Great Britain by the time the book was published. It could almost be an implicit reference within this sequence.[23]

It is a rare moment in the novel for Mina and Jonathan to pause in their work and look at the city around them. Unlike Dracula, with his desire to feed off the life of the urban crowds—like Baudelaire's flâneur—Stoker's vampire hunters do not share the flâneur's leisure time. Instead, Stoker's characters operate with an efficient work ethic that dictates the focus and purpose of each of their actions and movements. The image of the city glimpsed in these brief snapshots is, therefore, a modern city of business and professionals. Stoker's London is populated by professionals who, like his vampire hunters, do not look at the city around them but simply accept proper professional behavior, thus offering a veil of invisibility and security within the crowded streets to those who know how to manipulate the system. Recognizing the modern city's blindness to illicit behavior concealed by an air of authority, Van Helsing surmises that Dracula is using his Piccadilly house as the central point of his network of hideaways as it is concealed within the vast traffic of central London. Van Helsing manipulates the system when he advises Jonathan and the others to break into Dracula's home in broad daylight, for as long as they "do it as such things are rightly done, and at the time such things are rightly done, no one will interfere" (293).

Similarly, Dracula understands the need to join the flow of the professional crowd. This is why he keeps Jonathan in Transylvania: to help him prepare for his journey by practicing his English and asking Jonathan questions on British law. Dracula knows that in order to survive unnoticed in London, he must be able to handle his own affairs with the air of a professional, as well as command the language like a native. As he explains to Jonathan, "Well I know that, did I move and speak in your London, none there are who would not know me for a stranger . . . I am content if I am like the rest, so that no man stops if he see me, or pause in his speaking if he hear my words, to say, 'Ha, ha! a stranger!' " (20)

Stoker's novel emphasizes the importance of the business sector within the modern city and suggests that the mechanization of the city stretches beyond travel, to accepted codes of behavior. Marshall Berman suggests that the end of the nineteenth century saw a transition in the characteristics of the modern city. He explains that "for a little while the chaotic modernism of solitary brusque moves gives way to an ordered modernism of mass movement."[24] The nineteenth-century man in the crowd transformed into the twentieth-century man in traffic, and the way Stoker situates his characters within the panoramic conception of the urban landscape places the vampire narrative at the cusp of this transition.

Professional Investigators and Archivists

Stoker relocated the vampire story to modern London, enabling him to embed the vampire in a modern reconception of the urban landscape. Further, Stoker structured the actual hunt for Dracula in a manner that captures another nineteenth-century transformation: that of administration and communication networks into an efficient bureaucratic mechanism.

In 1879, Stoker published his first book, *The Duties of Clerks of Petty Sessions in Ireland*, the result of his appointment as Inspector of Petty Sessions at Dublin Castle. In this position, "Stoker read through documents accumulated since 1851, writing extracts on how clerks should deal with pawnbrokers and paupers, peddlers and lunatics."[25] Stoker encouraged the development of modern and efficient bureaucracy by advocating uniformity and systematic procedures for recording and filing all documents within the Irish civil service. He later wrote *Dracula*, after London underwent a major transition period; the bureaucratic systems of administration, hitherto used within the businesses in the City (the economic center of London), and to coordinate the constituent elements of the empire, were implemented to regulate and control the growth of Greater London.[26] The novel draws upon these new developments in bureaucracy and the unification of the city—as well as certain characteristics of Stoker's own attempts to systematize bureaucratic operations of the Irish civil service—in creating the methods and techniques adopted by the vampire hunters in their search for Dracula. As a result, what Gregory A. Waller described as the "Power of Combination"—strength derived from community and shared purpose—in *Dracula* was transformed from a holy crusade into an administrative machine.[27]

These changes to nineteenth-century bureaucracy were a response to an increased demand for administration to be handled with the speed and precision of the machine, transforming the bureaucrat into what Max Weber described as "a single cog in an ever-moving mechanism which prescribes to him an essentially fixed route of march."[28] The modern bureaucracy, therefore, used a complex system of administration and organization to successfully coordinate its responsibilities and to negotiate the modern landscape. The modernism of mass movement of the nineteenth century, as described by Berman, therefore includes the synchronized and compartmentalized operation of the bureaucratic machine, which provides the modern inhabitant of the urban landscape with a means of linking his or her existence with his or her fellow city dwellers. The interconnectedness of society was further synchronized by the development of what has come to be known as the Taylorized workforce, named after Frederick Winslow Taylor, the pioneer of ergonomics, whose *Principles of Scientific Management* (1911) revolutionized the twentieth-century industrial workplace by reducing all production to series of sequential, standardized, and mechanized actions that would increase productivity and efficiency. Like Weber before him, Taylor advocated the removal of individuality from business but extended this practice to the factory in order to transform the industrial workforce into an efficient and productive human mechanism.

The vampire hunting team in *Dracula* represents these new modern workers, as they are a microcosm of the modern bureaucratic machine and a foreshadowing of the new Taylorized social order. In the novel, the act of hunting the vampire is broken down into a series of individual tasks that are undertaken by specialized members of the team with Mina Harker acting as the centralized brain, sending out instructions to all of its individual parts. Dracula, no longer the primitive vampire of old, mirrors

Mina's embodiment of the modern administrative machine as he controls his own team of administrators who facilitate his infiltration into and escape from England.

Stoker constructs this bureaucratic machine from the products and ideals of the nineteenth-century professional class. Professionalism was a growing movement that encouraged specialization in training and education, creating a market for specialized services such as medicine, dentistry, law, accounting, and engineering.[29] Stoker himself was born into a professional family. His grandfather and father were civil servants, a path that Stoker would follow for a time before joining Henry Irving at the Lyceum Theatre. Abraham Stoker Sr. and his wife raised their children to be educated professionals, working in medicine, law, or the civil service. Stoker therefore chose trained, educated men to hunt down his vampire rather then the superstitious peasants of vampire folklore or the vengeful father figure of Sheridan LeFanu's *Carmilla*.[30] Jonathan Harker is a solicitor, Dr. Seward is a psychiatrist, and Van Helsing is a physician as well as a lawyer. Arthur Holmwood and Quincey Morris are not trained professionals but they do possess skills and experiences that they utilize with the expertise of a professional. Quincey is a financially independent adventurer and hunter and he draws upon these experiences in the pursuit and eventual destruction of Dracula. He acquires the weapons, organizes their plan of attack, and delivers one of the fatal blows to Dracula with his bowie knife. Arthur relinquishes the formality of his aristocratic title and acts as an investor in the activities of the vampire-hunting team.[31] In the search for the vampire, Stoker relies on the professional to offer both objective scientific observation as well as respectable ethics that enable the team to avoid unnecessary attention. When Jonathan meets with the clerk in Piccadilly, he informs the clerk that he is a fellow professional man and shows an identification card. This introduction immediately precludes suspicion and gains him access to the privileged information he seeks.

In relocating to the West, Dracula himself appears to have relinquished his aristocratic title in favor of professionalism. In Transylvania he was a Count, while in London his sole desire is to blend into the professional community. His library in Transylvania, made up of books of the "most varied kind—history, geography, politics, political economy, botany, geology, law—all relating to England" (19), suggests that, like the self-educated archaeologist and historian Abel Trelawny in *The Jewel of the Seven Stars*, Dracula is a self-taught man. He uses Jonathan to learn about the intricacies of English law and the detailed paperwork involved in shipping and handling his own affairs while in London. It is Jonathan's opinion that the Count "would have made a wonderful solicitor . . . his knowledge and acumen were wonderful" (31). Once Dracula arrives in London, he coordinates all of his real estate transactions himself and arranges his own transportation. The appearance of professionalism enables Dracula to move throughout the city invisibly; like Jonathan, this gives him the air of respectability and normality.

Mina Harker, wife to Jonathan Harker and secretary to the vampire hunting team, is at the center of this team of professionals. Described by Van Helsing as "one of God's women fashioned by His own hand to show us men and other women that there is a heaven where we can enter, and that its light can be here on earth" (188), Mina is the inspiring light behind the vampire hunters' pursuit of Dracula. Gail B. Griffin describes Mina's role within the group as that of the "archetypal Good Woman." Asexual and nurturing, Mina acts in opposition to Lucy's archetype of fallen woman, and the men gather around her.[32] Once Mina is contaminated by Dracula's blood, the men must save her to preserve their ideal of a woman as an asexual figure of adoration.

Friedrich Kittler suggests, however, that in addition to her inspiring presence, the men are drawn to Mina and form their circle around her because of her role as secretary.[33] A self-trained but thoroughly professional clerk, Mina becomes the chief coordinator of the investigative machine and establishes the means of tracking Dracula. Once Mina reads Jonathan's diary, she recognizes its importance and sets about translating and transcribing the stenographic text with her typewriter to make it accessible for the others to read. Upon meeting Van Helsing and ascertaining that Jonathan's account of his encounter with Dracula is true, she immediately applies her administrative skills to the mission of discovering the vampire. She collates all of the documents, including the vampire hunters' personal diaries and letters, carefully chosen newspaper accounts, telegrams, and business papers, and in doing so, the texts become a product of a nineteenth-century business discourse. Mina turns the paper trail into a filing system that is not only used as part of the team's investigation but also comprises the entire narrative of Dracula itself. Jonathan notes at the end of the novel that nothing is left of their adventure except "a mass of typewriting" and "hardly one authentic document" (378). Rather than simply a mass of typewriting, Mina has constructed the documents into an archived narrative; what Michel Foucault describes as a system designed to draw out relations and connections between the documents and determine the meaning of the collection.[34] Mina's bureaucratic archive of material evidence against Dracula gives her the power to read the narrative between the lines. She and Jonathan regularly examine the texts for evidence, tracing Dracula's movement through Renfield's mood swings and finding clues as to the whereabouts of Dracula's coffins. For instance, Jonathan keeps journal entries recounting his meetings with customs officers, stationmasters, and drivers, as he attempts to trace the transportation of Dracula's coffins from Whitby to Carfax and beyond. He later examines the records of his meetings in order to locate the Count's house in Piccadilly. As the characters continue to keep a record of their investigation, each new entry to the archive leads to further clues.

Mina controls the search for Dracula through her systematic ingestion of the details of the case and her ability to analyze the information like a computer, producing the results of her analysis and instructing the men thusly. Mina's technological synthesis of information begins with her ability to memorize train timetables, which proves to be instrumental in her methodical investigation. For example, the first meeting between Mina and Van Helsing, while Mina is still based in Exeter, is described in a collection of various telegrams, letters, and journal entries wherein Mina informs Van Helsing about the train schedules and recommends the times that would best suit his needs. The exchange begins with the following instruction from Mina, "25 September—Come to-day by *quarter-past ten train* if you can catch it" (180, my emphasis). Later, Mina informs Van Helsing that "Jonathan will be here at half-past eleven, and you must come to lunch with us and see him then; you could catch the quick *3.34 train, which will leave you at Paddington before eight.*" (186, my emphasis). Later that same day, Mina sends a letter to Van Helsing informing him that

> I have this moment, whilst writing, had a wire from Jonathan, saying that he leaves by the *6.25 to-night* from Launceston and will be here at *10.18,* so that I shall have no fear to-night. Will you therefore, instead of lunching with us, please come to breakfast at eight o'clock, if this be not too early for you? You can get away, if you are in a hurry by the *10.30 train, which will bring you to Paddington by 2.35* (187, my emphasis).

In the nineteenth century, the telegraph was responsible for transforming the railway from a disparate and uncoordinated collection of independent railway lines into a uniform and reliable system of transport.[35] Mina, similarly, with her knowledge of the train schedules, operates as the link between the investigators, and controls the investigation by monitoring their actions, disseminating information between them, and operating as the nerve center for the team. Mina is no longer just a transmitter, typewriter, and database, but also a telegraph office.

All information in the text must be channeled through Mina before a conclusion can be reached. When Van Helsing explains his theory as to why he believes that Dracula would be returning to Transylvania, he provides the details but asks Mina to draw the evidence together and make the obvious conclusion (303). Following a lengthy period of communication silence when Mina is excluded from the ministrations of the group for fear of her psychic link with the Count, she pores over all of the records previously withheld from her, including Dr. Seward's transcription of her own statements under hypnosis, in order to locate Dracula's route home. Her analysis is swift and efficient as she examines all of the facts, considers all of the potential courses of action open to Dracula in his escape, and logically deduces the route he has chosen. She explains, "I have examined the map, and find that the river most suitable for the Slovaks to have ascended is either the Pruth or the Sereth. I read in the typescript that in my trance I heard cows low and water swirling level with my ears and the creaking of wood. The Count in his box, then, was on a river in an open boat—propelled probably either by oars or poles, for the banks are near and it is working against stream" (353). The result of her analysis renews the vampire hunters' pursuit of Dracula.

While the methods of the vampire hunters may seem to ground the characters within the modern, they also serve to overturn their own definition of modern in favor of a new form of modernity. Marshall Berman argues that to be truly modern means to "experience personal and social life as a maelstrom, to find one's world and oneself in perpetual disintegration and renewal" for inherent in modernity is the need to destroy itself in favor of the even more modern.[36] For Mina this means that while she uses her administrative skills to destroy Dracula, her skills also work to recreate herself in his image. Mina's use of business technologies to construct the archive of evidence against Dracula also serves to remove the distinct quality of the original texts—the idiosyncratic personality of the author—by transforming them into uniform records for analysis. Thus, like Dracula does to his victims, Mina robs the accounts of their soul. For instance, one of the primary characteristics of the modern typewriter, Mina's most valued tool in the hunt for Dracula and the construction of the archive, was its ability to "create uniformity in business matters and communications" and standardize the presentation of professional documents.[37] Mina uses this machine to transcribe Dr. Seward's phonograph diary, later informing him that it is "cruelly true. It told me, in its very tones, the anguish of your heart. It was like a soul crying out to almighty God. No one must hear them spoken ever again! See, I have tried to be useful. I have copied out the words on my typewriter, and none other need now hear your heart beat, as I did" (222). Mina's transcription serves to remove the immediacy and raw emotion of the text that has, according to Jennifer Wicke, already been stripped to a degree by the mechanization of the recording device. She suggests that, as readers, "we are not dealing here with pure speech in opposition to writing, but instead with speech already colonized, or vampirized, by mass mediation." [38]

Stoker exploits nineteenth-century bureaucracy and professionalism as a modern means of systematizing the vampire hunters' investigation and pursuit of Dracula, while also suggesting a correlation between the dehumanizing characteristics of bureaucracy and vampirism. In the way that Dracula consumes blood, Mina uses her typewriter to consume, reproduce, and transform information. While it is her embodiment of the typewriter [39] and the telegraph that allow Mina to control the vampire hunters' investigation, it also gradually transforms her into a reflection of Dracula.

Transformation of Science and Technology

Mina's vampirism is evoked through her absorption of nineteenth-century bureaucracy and business discourses, while Dracula's vampirism is defined by the essence of modernity itself: change. The manner in which Stoker's vampire differs from vampires from folklore and earlier literary sources suggests that Dracula is a physical embodiment of the changing face of science and technology. As a result, the scientific rationality and technological innovation that initially seemed to be introduced in the novel as a means of grounding the narrative within the modern and the rational, actually transforms the novel's evocation of the modern into a new evolving form of modernity, one that recognizes the increasing ambiguity between the natural and supernatural worlds.

This ambiguity was suggested by the development of a number of new technologies, described by Pamela Thurschwell as teletechnologies, including the telephone, telegraph, and phonograph. These technologies collapsed distance and facilitated communication across spatial, temporal, and even spiritual boundaries. [40] For instance, nineteenth-century writers and critics who praised the phonograph for its "practical utility" and recognized its potential as a tool for dictation and letter writing, also saw the machine as quite magical. William Lynd points out how, earlier in the century, the suggestion that a machine that could record the sound of a voice would have been perceived as unscientific, merely a flight of fancy, and yet "Edison made those so-called flights of imagination established fact."[41] The machine was credited with a redefinition of time and space. Recordings made on a phonograph could be reproduced and sent around the world for loved ones or colleagues in other nations to hear. It was also able to trace the vocal evolution of a person from childhood to old age and "hear the early prattle, the changing voice, the manly tones, the varying manner and moods of the speaker, so expressive of character—from childhood upwards."[42]

The phonograph was also perceived by many critics at the time as a means of overcoming death through the preservation of the voice. F. J. Garbit described the phonograph as the "scientific and acoustic miracle of the nineteenth century," and wondered at its ability to "reproduce and hear at pleasure the voice of the dead!"[43] Arthur Conan Doyle's "The Story of the Japanned Box" tells a ghostly tale of a wealthy estate being haunted by the disembodied voice of its deceased mistress who has, unbeknownst to the servants, recorded a dying message on the modern phonograph to remind her husband to live a respectable life in her absence. Superstitious rumors abound, as the staff concocts fantasies about the origins of the ghostly voice that emanates from their master's room. The phonograph grants the wife a nightly visitation from beyond the grave, suggesting a close relationship between the phonograph and the spirit world.[44]

Steven Connor has suggested that the spirit world and the real world of science became increasingly intertwined as the progress of spiritualism— the belief in the spirit world and the ability to communicate with it through a medium—in the nineteenth century involved a "twinning or ghosting of the development of communications technology."[45] As communications technologies became increasingly sophisticated, the spiritualist developed parallel innovations, from alphabetic knocks to automatic writing to direct voice.[46] These developments demonstrated an increasing separation between the medium and the spirit world as the medium gradually shifted from acting as an interpreter of messages to an operator facilitating communication. The spiritual message was no longer received through their body but channeled through technical apparatus such as the speaking trumpet or megaphone.[47] The practicality and the potential for more supernatural uses of the technology increased during this period of change and willingness to make associative leaps between accepted science and less conventional beliefs.

This willingness to explore the correlation between seeming "flights of imagination" and science is symptomatic of a movement from a period of normal science into a phase of extraordinary science. Thomas Kuhn argues that normal science is the establishment of a set of accepted principles, based upon "past scientific achievements" to which all further scientific developments must apply.[48] When anomalies are discovered, science undergoes a period of revolution where these anomalies are either disproved, made to conform to the rules of normal science, or serve to establish a new scientific paradigm. If the latter action takes place, the perception of the natural world undergoes a period of what Kuhn labels "extraordinary science" as the scientific community attempts to establish, through association and experimentation, the rules of this new paradigm. This period is marked by "a willingness to try anything" and a return to fundamentals.[49] In other words, once the door to new possibilities is open, science must contend with a flood of related subjects and phenomena, previously viewed as unscientific or mystical that may now be viewed as scientific.

The nineteenth century witnessed such a revolution between positivism—"a philosophical approach that rejects metaphysics and confines itself to the facts of experience" to collapse all natural phenomenon into a unifying theory of natural law—and newly evolving paradigms of science sparked by the explosion of developments within teletechnology, electrical sciences, and psychic research.[50] This dependence upon the material and observable was undermined by the evolution in the nineteenth and early-twentieth centuries of sciences that relied upon unseen transmissions, invisible sound and light waves, and electrical impulses and currents. Although positivism did seek to reconcile these startling innovations within its area of study, these new technologies suggested new possibilities and unexplored areas in science that could not be explained or contained by positivism. As a result, a period of extraordinary science, questioning the rigors of nineteenth-century materialism, was inaugurated. Stoker exploited this period of experimentation, creating a supernatural tale that subverts rationalism and materialism and draws out the ambiguity between science and the supernatural by linking the extraordinary world of vampires to the changing realm of teletechnologies and electrical sciences. Stoker's novel suggests that the supernatural is not only possible but also a natural product of the modern world.

Van Helsing articulates the fundamental principle of extraordinary science when he rebukes Seward for his narrow-mindedness by asking, "Am I to take it that you simply accept fact, and are satisfied to let from premise to conclusion be a blank? No? Then tell me—for I am student of the brain—how you accept the hypnotism and reject the thought-reading" (191). For Van Helsing, once science accepted hypnotism as scientific, it opened the door to a stream of related fields such as thought transference, astral projection, and materialization. Therefore, Van Helsing is able to accept the possibility that vampirism is equally explainable. Van Helsing further points out to Seward that "there are things done to-day in electrical science which would have been deemed unholy by the very men who discovered electricity—who would themselves not so long before have been burned as wizards" (191). Like William Lynd, he recognizes that new ideas are often dismissed as impossible or rejected as supernatural, and that science is constantly in a state of flux between established facts and new discoveries. In the novel, the characters' use of technology and bureaucracy is an attempt to ground everything they encounter within the modern, scientific, explicable world, but Stoker's choice of particular types of sciences and technology also challenges the material aspects of science and are indicative of a scientific revolution. The new technologies undermine the characters' perception of normality by suggesting the possibility of new forms of normality.

The novel, initially, establishes a rational and positivist framework through the journal entries of Jonathan Harker, the first narrator of the novel. Jonathan writes his journal like an anthropological record, recounting his observations on his way to Transylvania and the castle of Count Dracula. At the beginning of his journey, his diary consists of descriptions of the local population, the countryside, recipes, and superstitions. His first response is to dismiss all of these superstitions as unfounded and irrational. This rational framework, in both the style of the novel and in Jonathan's perception, comes under attack as Jonathan encounters increasingly supernatural events and phenomena on his approach to the castle, including howling wolves, magic blue flames, and a driver who seems to be able to command the forces of nature with a wave of his hands (12–13). Upon his arrival at the castle, normality seems to be restored as Jonathan is immediately met with all of the comforts of home, a warm dinner, a comforting fireplace, and a generous host. This is reinforced later in the evening when he makes his way into the Count's library and he finds a familiar collection of English publications, including the *London Directory*, the "Red" and "Blue" books, *Whitaker's Almanac*, the Army and Navy Lists and the Law List (19). It is evident that Dracula's preparation for his journey to England mirrors Jonathan's own background reading at the British Library. The familiar images reflect his own perception of normality and as a result Jonathan ignores his instincts, which tell him that something is amiss.

As events become mysterious once again, Jonathan's rationalist view of nature demands that he approach his dilemma logically and look for a solution: "So far as I can see, my only plan will be to keep my knowledge and my fears to myself, and my eyes open" (27). The emphasis upon seeing and eyes in this and other passages illustrates Jonathan's dependence upon the empirical grounding of positivist knowledge to understand all that surrounds him. As he witnesses and records events in his diary that increasingly defy his understanding of the laws of nature, he begins to doubt his own vision and sanity rather than accept the inexplicable. When Dracula lunges at Jonathan at the sight of blood from a razor cut, Jonathan notes that Dracula's return to a civilized demeanor was so quick as to make him doubt that the threat had existed (26). When the driver stops the coach to mark the location of the mysterious blue flame, Jonathan remarks that the driver's body did not seem to obstruct the view of the blue flame for he could still see its flicker. His response is to assume that "my eyes deceived me straining through the darkness" (13). Finally, when he witnesses the Count exit the castle by crawling out a window and down the castle walls, Jonathan's first reaction is to doubt his eyes and assume that it is a trick of the moonlight (34). When Jonathan's positivist approach fails to find a suitable explanation for all that he has witnessed, and he can no longer blame it on his vision or a trick of the light, he concludes that Dracula must represent some ancient evil that "mere modernity cannot kill" or define (36).

When confronted with the supernatural in the form of Lucy's illness, Dr. Seward similarly fails to recognize its supernatural origins because he shares Jonathan's need for a visible and rational cause. John L. Greenway argues that the character of Seward is an ironic commentary on normal science as Kuhn might define it.[51] Though Seward believes himself to be an experimental scientist and a physician, as he uses the modern phonograph to keep his diary and speaks of innovative evaluative methods such as unconscious cerebration, he actually embodies normal scientific methods. His study of Renfield yields countless clues as to Renfield's psychic connection to Dracula and Lucy's illness, and yet he is unable to see their relationship, either consciously or unconsciously, as it does not subscribe to his accepted understanding of science.

Furthermore, while the vampire hunters use accepted scientific methods in their search for Dracula, these methods continue to fail them. Stoker's novel is structured around a compilation of letters, diaries, and newspaper articles, and it is due to this fragmented narrative that the individual characters are unable to overview the entirety of events, unlike the reader; the connection between the individual accounts enables the reader to trace Dracula's movements. It is only once Mina and Jonathan construct the archive that the group of vampire hunters are able to recognize the relationship between Jonathan's experiences in Transylvania, Renfield's psychosis, and Lucy's death.

Despite the compiled knowledge and shared understanding of events, the vampire hunters continue to fail to recognize the signs of Dracula's movements and actions. After they have joined forces, the men decide that they must protect Mina and exclude her from their plans. Following this decision, Mina begins to demonstrate the all-too-familiar symptoms of vampirism. She grows pale, quiet, and sleeps a trance-like sleep. Later Jonathan describes the changes in Mina but does not recognize their meaning: "I came tiptoe into our own room, and found Mina asleep, breathing so softly that I had to put my ear down to hear it. She looks paler than usual" (254). Mina's diary entry for the first night she is excluded from the men's confidence clearly suggests a trance, characteristic of mesmerism, as she falls asleep without realizing it and awakes with no memory of proceeding events (257).[52] The parallels with Lucy's illness are evident in Jonathan's description of Mina's pallor and languor, but despite their knowledge and recent experience, the group recognizes neither the similarity between the two cases nor the fact that Mina is the victim of a hypnotic trance. This is because Dracula's hypnotic powers seem to exceed the official scientific understanding of hypnosis as his control over Mina and Renfield suggests a telepathic connection between Dracula and his victims. The link between hypnosis and telepathy was a subject for study in the nineteenth century by the Society for Psychical Research. Roger Luckhurst suggests that Stoker's novel pushes this relationship to the next logical step by creating a remote-controlled person in the forms of both Renfield and Mina—a fact that goes unnoticed by Van Helsing and the others who leave Mina alone in the asylum, completely vulnerable to Dracula's attack.[53] Despite all that they have learned, they continue to hold onto their materialist scientific understanding of the laws of nature. They are unable to make the complete leap to extraordinary science that is necessary to truly perceive the real power of Dracula, that which distinguishes him from his literary predecessors.

Most early nineteenth-century vampire fiction maintains that the vampire is the physical reanimation of a corpse, and emphasizes the narrative of the death of the vampire and its unavoidable rise from the grave. In

Dr. John Polidori's "The Vampyre," Lord Ruthven dies midway through the story and then reappears, alive once more to hunt within English society. What makes him threatening is his mastery over life and death.[54] Similarly, the vampire in William Gilbert's "The Last Lords of Gardenal" (1867) is simply a reanimated corpse whose only transformation is from the beautiful young woman she once was to the decaying corpse she has become, as she pounces upon her victim and drains his blood.[55] This is completely in keeping with traditional vampire folklore and what Paul Barber describes as a "revenant," a corpse that returns from the dead.[56]

The vampire world in Stoker's novel is a ghostly world that exists on the borders of the physical and the ethereal. Stoker's vampires possess very real physical presence and strength, demonstrated by Dracula's handshake that makes Jonathan wince in pain. They also possess an intangible, transitory quality, uncommon in earlier vampire fiction, that enables them to appear and disappear at will. After Jonathan's encounter with the vampire women, they seem to vanish from sight. In his journal he describes how "there was no door near them, and they could not have passed me without my noticing. They simply seemed to fade into the rays of the moonlight and pass out through the window, for I could see outside the dim, shadowy forms for a moment before they entirely faded away" (39). Later in the novel, when Mina describes her encounter with Dracula, she states that it was "as if he had stepped out of the mist—or rather as if the mist had turned into his figure" (287). In his reconception of the modern vampire, Stoker draws upon contemporary developments in electrical sciences that had played a significant role in the changing perception of the natural world in the nineteenth century. He reinvents the vampire through the language and imagery of modern technology and electrical sciences. The ability of the vampires to transform themselves mirrors the shared characteristic of these new technologies, all of which are based upon the conversion of the physical from one form to another. When describing the operation of the telephone, F. J. Garbit stated that "the fact is that it is one of the most beautiful and striking examples which nature affords us of the convertibility of forces from one form to another"[57] and it is these same forces that enable the vampire to transform itself from man to animal to mist as demonstrated in the following two passages from *Dracula*:

We all looked on in horrified amazement as we saw, when he stood back, the woman [Lucy], with a corporeal body as real at the moment as our own, pass in through the interstice where scarce a knife-blade could have gone. (212)

The Count suddenly stopped, just as poor Lucy had done outside the tomb, and cowered back. Further and further back he cowered, as we, lifting our crucifixes, advanced. The moonlight suddenly failed, as a great black cloud sailed across the sky; and when the gaslight sprang up under Quincey's match, we saw nothing but a faint vapour. This, as we looked, trailed under the door. (282)

The manner in which Dracula is perceived by the other characters as both supernatural and natural, for they draw upon both science and religion to pursue and destroy him, appears to be a product of the ambiguity between science and the occult that was prevalent in the late nineteenth century. W. T. Stead, editor of the *Pall Mall Gazette* and the occult review *Borderland*, recognized that the distinction between contemporary developments in electrical science and the supernatural was becoming increasingly ambiguous within popular thought. He recounts an anecdote of an old woman at a séance who is asked to explain the supernatural phenomena she has witnessed. Her first inclination is to blame the devil. When asked what else could be the cause, she answered, "If it is not the devil, it must be electricity."[58] Stead turns this perception to his own purpose by arguing that new discoveries in science, such as x-rays, the telephone, and the kinetoscope, could instruct the modern psychic researcher in the study of the supernatural, for "many of the latest inventions and scientific discoveries make psychic phenomena thinkable, even by those who have had no personal experience of their own to compel conviction."[59]

For Stead and other spiritualists of the period, the establishment of a relationship between the scientific and the spiritual was a means of legitimizing their own spiritual research and beliefs. Edward C. Randall argued that if it is possible to send messages around the world without wires, then it should be equally possible to send messages to the spirit world. Randall saw the attempt to communicate with the dead as the natural next step for science and technology.[60] While these new teletechnologies captured the public fascination, they still retained an air of mystery. The technical manual "Modern Practise of the Electric Telegraph" acknowledged the mysterious quality of electricity by stating, "We do not as yet know, perhaps we never shall know with certainty, what the agent we call electricity really is."[61]

W. T. Stead regularly drew comparisons between psychic powers and recent inventions in communications technology, going so far as to compare his own psychic abilities with a telephone exchange:

> However incredible it may appear, I can, and do constantly, receive messages from my assistant editor, Miss X, as accurately and as constantly

as I receive telegrams from those with whom I do business, without the employment of any wires or any instruments. Whenever I wish to know where she is, whether she can keep an appointment, or how she is progressing with her work, I simply ask the question, and my hand automatically writes outs the answer . . . Nor is this faculty of using my hand as a writing telephone without wires confined to Miss X. I can communicate with many of my friends in the same way.[62]

This relationship between technology and the supernatural was further suggested by supporters of new technological media who, even while explaining how mechanisms like the telephone and the telegraph worked, persisted in emphasizing how easily messages could be transmitted and intercepted from seemingly unknown sources. It was well-documented that when telephone lines ran alongside telegraph wires, the supposedly confidential telegraphic message could often be picked up on the telephone for anyone who understood telegraph signaling to hear, while numerous accounts persisted of music or voices coming through the telephone originating from unknown sources.[63] Many who claimed that they possessed the gifts of telepathy and hypnosis described their skills in electromagnetic terms. Walford Bodie, a stage hypnotist, mesmerist, and healer, described his skill as follows:

A force, an actual influence, a current of magnetism, has passed through the wall, linking my mind to hers, and along this current goes my unspoken will that she should sleep. And more than that—my thoughts can be transmitted along it by wireless telegraphy, so that if I think of a number she will think of it also.[64]

He explained his power by stating that "there seems to be in Nature a subtle, permeating fluid, whose vibrations are more rapid than those of electricity. Then, just as it is possible to change the waves of light into electricity and reproduce them as light at any distance, so it may be possible to convert thought vibrations into subtle permeating fluid and reproduce them as thought vibrations again in a receptive mind far away in space."[65] Similarly, Edward C. Randall describes a conversation with a spirit where the spirit explained that it was electric and magnetic forces that made communication between the living and the dead possible.[66]

For Stoker, the introduction of a vampire into a thoroughly modern setting was a means of exploring these extreme possibilities. In the novel, Dracula possesses this masterly ability to manipulate energy to his will, either to transform himself physically, to throttle Renfield while in gaseous form, or to communicate with the living through hypnosis and telepathy. Van Helsing attempts to use hypnosis but in comparison with the vampire's inherent mastery of these forces, he is a novice. The novel contains countless instances of vampires using hypnosis to overpower their victims: Dracula orchestrates Lucy's somnambulant walks out onto the cliffs of Whitby; Dr. Seward describes how Lucy attempts to enrapture Arthur in the graveyard, seeming to put him under a spell (211-212); Jonathan describes how his driver waved his arms before the howling wolves, which seemed to banish them from sight suggesting the tradition of "mesmeric passes" (13); during Jonathan's second encounter with the vampire brides at Castle Dracula, he feels himself becoming hypnotized as the three women gradually materialize before him.

> They were like the tiniest grains of dust, and they whirled round and gathered in clusters in a nebulous sort of way. I watched them with a sense of soothing, and a sort of calm stole over me. I leaned back in the embrasure in a more comfortable position, so that I could enjoy more fully the aerial gambolling . . . I felt myself struggling to awake to some call of my instincts; nay, my very soul was struggling, and my half-remembered sensibilities were striving to answer the call. I was becoming hypnotised! (44)

The use of hypnosis as a tool of a vampire did not originate with Stoker. Many eastern European vampire legends suggest that the vampire could hypnotize the living in order to overpower their victims.[67] Stoker, like the Society for Psychical Research however, extended the accepted notion of hypnosis to include telepathic communication for, like Bodie, Dracula also uses a "subtle permeating fluid" to act as a conductor, blood. The exchange of blood between Dracula and his victims enables him to transmit his thoughts like an electric current through their bodies. When Mina is vampirized by Dracula, she, Van Helsing, and Dr. Seward all gradually realize that she will come further under Dracula's hypnotic influence but this means more than her becoming susceptible to his hypnotic suggestion. At Mina's urging, Van Helsing hypnotizes her and realizes that by placing her under his own influence, he has established a psychic telegraph wire between himself and Dracula. As a result of her blood connection, which acts as a conductor, Mina can now act as a human telephone exchange, informing the team of vampire hunters of Dracula's whereabouts on his return journey to Transylvania. Stoker reinforces this connection by describing

Mina's thoughts as coming to her in "currents" (312). Dracula uses his telepathic connection with Mina as a means of communicating across the miles between them and she uses the same connection as a tracking device. Their vampirism enables them to defy the parameters and limitations of traditional conceptions of time and space as well as to supersede human understanding and manipulation of energy. Together they suggest the limitless possibilities for humanity should it continue to push science beyond the established paradigms of normal science into the realm of the extraordinary.

In the characters of Mina and Dracula, Stoker's novel draws upon the clash between nineteenth-century materialist culture, defining itself by what it can measure, and developments in technology and electrical science that began to undermine the positivist philosophy. Alongside the bureaucratic standardization of scientific practice, Mina and Dracula convey an explosion of new scientific possibilities in the late-nineteenth century. All of Dracula's characteristics—his ethereal nature, his embodiment of electromagnetism, his ability to transform himself, his use of telepathy and hypnosis—are products of a nineteenth-century reexamination of science and the supernatural, and suggest the entrance of scientific study into a period of extraordinary science where all systems of belief are challenged and anything is possible. The battle between Dracula and the vampire hunters is therefore not a battle between good and evil, but a war between normal and extraordinary science, between the known and the unknown.

The possibilities generated by science are, like Dracula, both wondrous and terrifying as they bring both the suggestion of progress and the potential for destruction. As modernity is defined by the contradictory necessity to destroy and create anew, *Dracula* represents how the modern world's desire for progress in science, business, and technology, sows the seeds to its own destruction, not in favor of the primitive but in favor of modernity itself. It is the up-to-dateness of London that attracts the vampire and it is with his physical embodiment of modernity that he threatens to infect the living. Mina, more than any other character, seeks to modernize her life as a means of grounding herself within the practical and functional world of bureaucracy and business discourses. She surrounds herself with signifiers of modern science and technology and uses them to systematically hunt down and destroy Dracula. She fails, however, to recognize how her own dependence upon these technologies serves to transform her into Dracula's image. This undermines her view that modernity is fixed—the final step on the path of progress. Instead it is in a constant state of flux, and Mina's transformation demonstrates the destruction of the modern, by its own hands, in favor of the even more modern. Modernity in Stoker's *Dracula* is not simply expressed through the novel's setting and technological accoutrements, but in the very conflict it presents between the different stages of modernity itself. Vampirism need not be a representation of the primitive; as Stoker demonstrates, vampirism can not only emerge from within the culture and technologies of modernity, but also be a product of it, encompassing the whirlwind of change and evolution that is intrinsic to the modern world.

CHAPTER TWO

The Cinematic Spectacle of Vampirism: *Nosferatu* in the Light of New Technology [1]

In a pivotal scene in *Shadow of the Vampire* (2000), a fictional film about the making of F. W. Murnau's *Nosferatu* (1922), the real vampire Max Schreck finds a small hand-cranked film projector amongst all of the technological equipment the filmmakers have brought into his castle. Like a child left alone with his toys, he curiously begins to crank the lever, which results in a projected image of a sunrise on the wall. He is transfixed by the sight of the first sunrise he has seen in centuries, but the sequence changes as soon as Schreck instinctively places his hand before the lens to project his own shadow on the screen. (Figure 2.1) On the surface, this sequence seems to suggest the clear-cut opposition of the premodern vampire with modern technology. As the shadow is created through the combination of Schreck's body and the light, however, this sequence actually presents a symbiosis rather than an opposition between the vampire and technology, a symbiosis that is key to the vampire's representation in the cinema.

Made up of still images, ghostly shadows of the dead that are reanimated through technological means, film bears striking parallels with vampirism. To create the illusion of movement and life, a series of consecutive still images are projected in succession at a speed of between sixteen to twenty-four frames per second. As explained by Steve Neale, "You have only to freeze a film image and then set it in motion again to appreciate the difference [between photography and film]. A photograph embalms the ghosts of the past; film brings them back to life." [2] Not life as it was once lived, however, but trapped like the vampire and "forced to repeat the same gestures over and over again . . . condemned to an eternal repetition." [3] Despite the medium's own similarities with vampirism, *Dracula* would not appear on the screen until 1922 with the production of *Nosferatu* in Germany by F. W. Murnau. [4]

Figure 2.1. The vampire transfixed by his shadow in *Shadow of the Vampire*.

As the vampire was absent from the early days of cinema, so was the cinema absent from Stoker's modern study of vampirism. As discussed in the previous chapter, *Dracula* is littered with references to contemporary new technologies. It is therefore fascinating that a form of technology that is not included in the novel was launching just as Stoker was writing it: the cinematograph. The first film show in London took place in early 1896, just over one year before *Dracula* was published. An active member of London's theatre community, Stoker would very likely have been aware of these technological developments. One possible explanation for this curious omission is that, to Stoker, the cinema was not a new technology, but rather the next stage in the development of technologies that had been around throughout the nineteenth century, such as the magic lantern, photography, the x-ray, the phonograph, or even telegraphy and electricity. While these new technologies were treated as modern, they were equally perceived as uncanny. They are all transformative technologies in which something as insubstantial as light, sound, or electrons are transformed into a visual or aural product. The cinema, similarly transformative in that it turns light into images, inherited from many of these technologies a language of tricks and techniques with which to portray the ambiguity between the scientific and the occult. Furthermore, like film, the magic lantern and photography were used to raise the dead through technological means. It is this legacy of technological necromancy that comes together in *Nosferatu* to present the cinema's first entirely cinematic vampire, drawing upon the ambiguity between the living and the dead, the scientific and the fantastic. On the surface, *Nosferatu* seems to be a faithful adaptation of Stoker's novel in plot and action, particularly with respect to Jonathan Harker's journey to the Carpathian Mountains.[5] This film, however, appears to mark a decided break from the novel with respect to its relationship to modernity. Murnau and the screenwriter Henrik Galeen moved away from Stoker's fascination with the modern world by setting the story in the past and in the town of Wisborg, Germany, far away from the "whirl and rush" (20) of modern London, or even Berlin. The vampire, renamed Count Orlok for the film, is explicitly associated with disease and pestilence, as opposed to the modern business practices, transport, and technology described in the novel. Orlok's facial features resemble a rodent, and his claw-like fingers are predatory. The boxes of earth that he transports to Wisborg are filled with vermin, and when he leaves the ship, he is followed by a horde of rats escaping into the town.

Nosferatu, however, has more in common with the novel than is immediately apparent. In *Dracula*, the story is presented as the product of modernity since the very manuscript is produced through a range of modern technologies, including stenography, the phonograph, and the typewriter, all collated by Mina. Dracula is an almost invisible presence in the novel because he does not contribute to the documents, but is glimpsed through the narratives of the others. While the vampire hunters of the novel are presented as modern in their use of technologies to facilitate their hunt for the vampire, Dracula emerges as a product of the technological union of the documents. Count Orlok in Murnau's film is similarly an embodiment of technology, his vampirism emerging through the filmic process itself. In this chapter, I will show that this process was informed by nineteenth-century technologies that bridged the gap between the scientific and the supernatural and were absorbed into the film language of *Nosferatu* to become a defining part of the vampire film's cinematic heritage.

One of the leading precursors to horror cinema was the Phantasmagoria, a form of magic lantern presentation that specialized in raising ghostly specters.[6] It operated by projecting hand-painted images from slides onto a diaphanous screen, accompanied by the sound effects of rain, thunder, and funeral bells to create atmosphere. The slides were projected from behind the screen so that the mechanics of the show were concealed from the audience.[7] The imagery of the Phantasmagoria was decidedly Gothic, often directly inspired by Gothic tales or paintings. Furthermore, the slides were not only calling forth spectral images but were also specifically making the dead rise again; it was popular to present the images of historical figures, long since dead, such as Bonaparte, Shakespeare, and Washington. Laurent Mannoni has further discovered that Paul Philidor, the inventor of the Phantasmagoria, would go so far as to invite audience members to request an apparition of a deceased loved one, with a few days notice, allowing him the opportunity to prepare the slide.[8]

The true spectacle was the manner in which these images were presented to suggest a ghostly apparition. Mannoni distinguishes the Phantasmagoria from other magic lantern shows not simply because of its ghostly content but because its pictures "were animated and mobile, appearing to rush towards a terrified audience who were certainly not used to such an assault of images."[9] Through technical manipulation of the slide equipment, these images would be made to increase and decrease in size, advance and retreat in space, dissolve, vanish, and pass through each other. A great attraction was the illusion of metamorphosis where, through the use of two slides, one image would magically transform into another image.[10]

While the Phantasmagoria was clearly a form of entertainment, the magic lanternists presented their exhibitions to debunk superstitious belief in the supernatural, for their specters were quite openly the product of technological illusion. For instance, Henry Dircks, the inventor and operator of the Dircksian Phantasmagoria, claimed that "natural magicians" like himself make "no pretension to an occult science, but on the contrary tend to dissipate many vulgar errors, by disabusing the public mind, even on matters long considered supernatural."[11] The magic lanternists, however, did not give away the secrets of how they created illusions during their performance. They simply made it clear that these specters were not spirits but rather from the scientific and technological world. However, as Terry Castle suggests, by demystifying the supernatural, the magic lanternists nevertheless mystified their own technology. The Phantasmagoria shows would begin with a speech by the lanternist explaining that what they were about to see was in no way supernatural, but that the performance was designed as a "gothic extravaganza" with "Radcliffian" decor, atmospheric music, and a spectral lightshow.[12] Audiences would know that the specters were not real, but were not informed how the images were produced. A review of the Dircksian Phantasmagoria illustrates this: "Why did not the mediums and spirit rappers get hold of this invention before it was made public? The illusions might fail to convince, but at least they would have left all seekers after spiritual revelations in a sore state of puzzle and uncertainty, as they most certainly do now at the Polytechnic."[13]

The Phantasmagoria went out of fashion in the early 1840s but was followed in the 1870s by a new kind of ghost show entitled Pepper's Ghost. This process projected phantom images that were no longer drawings on slides but rather the reflections of hidden and costumed actors.[14] This was accomplished through the careful positioning of three transparent and colorless mirrors on and beneath the stage in order to capture and project the reflection of the brightly illuminated actor before the audience.[15] The ghost would disappear when the light was brought down on the hidden actor. Pepper's Ghost and the similarly designed Dircksian Phantasmagoria demonstrate a move toward portraying greater realism by projecting images of actual people, for this achieves a more unsettling and uncanny effect when the images disappear, fade away, or are made to appear translucent. Dircks explains,

> The best results are obtained by bringing to bear on the spectral figure all the characteristics of an actual human being, and then causing their disappearance by means of such a well regulated light that its gradually closing screen causes the spectre slowly to dissolve into the appearance of a thin vapour. This part alone, well managed, leaves an audience in breathless astonishment, so striking and so marvellous is the transition from the apparent robustness, vigour, and tangibility of life to intangible air.[16]

The spectral quality of the Phantasmagoria and the realism of Pepper's Ghost are elements that are present in another nineteenth-century optical medium: photography. Even more than the Phantasmagoria, photography was perceived as a scientific and objective process. Jennifer Tucker has shown that "from the time of photography's invention, Victorians identified it as a certain type of human: a 'witness,' a 'detective,' and a 'discoverer.'"[17] While the Victorians did not unconditionally accept the photograph as fact, it was adopted for scientific and policing purposes because of its seeming ability to record events or objects realistically and accurately. André Bazin has argued that photography was viewed as objective because it is a mechanical process unaffected by human interference and/or artistry: "Photography enjoys a certain advantage in virtue of this transference of reality from the thing to its reproduction."[18] This understanding of photography draws upon the perception of photography as an indexical sign—that is, a sign physically produced by the thing it is meant to represent without human interference, in the manner of a fingerprint or shadow (such as Schreck's shadow in *Shadow of the Vampire*).

This perception has contributed to photography's equation with truth and, as a result, it became a key part of a culture of scientific study, surveillance, and classification.[19]

Tom Gunning, however, counters this view by suggesting that although photography appeared to be steeped in scientific authority, it was equally perceived in this period, like the Phantasmagoria before it, as an uncanny process. Its ability to create a spectral double of the object being photographed seemed to undermine the "unique identity of objects and people" and served to create "a parallel world of phantasmatic doubles alongside the concrete world of the senses verified by positivism."[20] So while the Phantasmagoria was used to debunk the supernatural and mystify itself, photography's uncanny nature enabled it to bridge the separation between technology and the supernatural. Spiritualists recognized an affinity between the spirit world and the ghostly apparitions in photographs trapped in the borderland between life and death. As a result, they used the uncanny properties of this new technology to either support their belief system or, at times, mislead others through the presentation of supposed evidence of the afterlife. As previously discussed in relation to *Dracula*, the emergence of new sciences and technologies offered powerful support for the belief in spiritualism that shared a certain intangible quality with these technologies. One of the main arguments used by spiritualists and scientists alike for the belief in the possibility of photographing spirits was the invention of the x-ray (Röntgen Ray) and the ghostly quality of the skeletal image it produced. If an x-ray could photograph that which is invisible to the naked eye—the skeleton concealed beneath layers of tissue—then it could be possible to photograph the spirit world that was similarly invisible.[21] The very properties of photography were utilized to provide proof of the afterlife.[22]

Early cinema constructed a similar relationship between the seemingly scientific authority of the reproduction of reality and the uncanniness of the spectral image, a heritage drawn from these earlier optical technologies and the spiritualist tradition. While it has been common practice to describe early cinema as split between two types of filmmaking—realist and fantasy, as represented by the actualities of the Lumière brothers and the trick films of George Méliès—recent theorists have begun to rethink this concept. The early screenings of the cinematograph and other film systems were deemed scientific in that they showcased the new technology, while the content of the films was perceived as spectral. Whether the film simply recorded the workers leaving a factory or the more magical vanishing lady trick—each the subject of films by the Lumière brothers and Méliès, respectively—the medium was viewed as performing some sort of trickery. Gunning points out that "Méliès himself recognized this at his first viewing of Lumière films, proclaiming the projection, 'an extraordinary trick' ('un truc extraordinaire')."[23] In the eyes of the audience, the motion created, like the Phantasmagoria, was an illusion.

That this illusion appeared spectral to audiences of the time, is supported by the following extract from Maxim Gorky's review of a Lumière film program in 1896.

> Last night I was in the Kingdom of Shadows. If you only knew how strange it is to be there. It is a world without sound, without colour. Everything there—the earth, the trees, the people, the water and the air—is dipped in monotonous grey. Grey rays of the sun across the grey sky, grey eyes in grey faces, and the leaves of the trees are ashen grey. It is not life but its shadow, it is not motion but its soundless spectre . . . When the lights go out in the room in which Lumière's invention is shown, there suddenly appears on the screen a large grey picture, "A Street in Paris"—shadows of a bad engraving. As you gaze at it, you see carriages, buildings and people in various poses, all frozen into immobility . . . But suddenly a strange flicker passes through the screen and the picture stirs to life . . . It is terrifying to see, but it is the movement of shadows, only of shadows. Curses and ghosts, the evil spirits that have cast entire cities into eternal sleep, come to mind and you feel as though Merlin's vicious trick is being enacted before you.[24]

As in his discussions of the telephone and telegraph, W. T. Stead recognized the uncanny quality of the new technology of cinema when he drew upon the Kinetoscope—an early form of film exhibition—in his discussion of the similarities between the spirit world and science. In the article entitled "Kinetiscope [*sic*] of Nature," Stead describes an encounter with a "rehearsal ghost" where the existence of what he calls "a natural kinetiscope [*sic*] which reproduces automatically, as vividly as life, the stirring scenes of long ago" is documented.[25] Stead equates the cinema's ability to endlessly repeat events of long ago with the supernatural. Similarly he describes a case of a "kinetiscope [*sic*] of the mind," whereby a person can visualize and project before himself or herself "living pictures of the past."[26] These examples demonstrate the parallels between spirit visitation and the cinema, for the psychic in his parlor as well as the camera and projector are able to recreate and project, as "vividly as life," moments from the past.

As the cinema moved from recording actual or staged events to multi-shot narratives, it began to develop and establish its own language and conventions for storytelling, many of which drew upon traditions previously established by earlier optical mediums. X. Theodore Barber argues that the "transformations, superimpositions, and rear projection not to mention frequent appearances of ghosts, skeletons, and the like," which all became integral parts of early cinema and specifically the trick film (a type of early film that exploited cinema's ability to manipulate time and space to create the illusion of magic), grew out of the tradition of the Phantasmagoria.[27] Thus the cinema maintained its affinity with the magical and spectral through its technological manipulation of the photographic image.

George Méliès, a stage magician prior to moving into cinema, began to work with film to further develop and explore the technological potential for his magic act. While best remembered for his science fiction film *A Trip to the Moon* (1906), Méliès' early film career was devoted to exploring the "'supernatural' capacities of the moving picture" through a series of "magical, mystical, and trick films."[28] His catalog of films is dominated by titles bearing strong associations with the devilish and the magical: *The Vanishing Lady, The Laboratory of Mephistopheles, A Hypnotist at Work, The Bewitched Inn*, and, of course, *Le manoir du diable*. *Le manoir du diable* both drew upon the imagery of the vampire legend and was presented through the language of spectral technology. The film begins as a bat transforms into a cloaked, satanic figure who proceeds to conjure up a parade of witches, ghosts, and imps from a magic cauldron. Two soldiers enter the castle and are terrorized and tormented by ghostly visions and magical transformations engineered by the satanic figure. The film ends as they destroy the magician by brandishing a crucifix, causing him to vanish in a puff of smoke. While the emphasis upon transformation and disappearance are elements of the Phantasmagoria, the imagery of castles, crucifixes, and bats turning into devilish figures are intrinsic elements of the vampire legend of the nineteenth century. The exploration of the potential for film and the development of more elaborate fantasy narratives went hand in hand as Méliès and other trick filmmakers began to master "double exposures, masks, stop motions, reverse shootings, fast and slow motion, animation, fades, dissolves."[29]

So these early films not only inherited a technological language from photography and magic lanterns but also the preoccupation with the fantastic as a means of showcasing the spectral nature of film. Developments in special effects technology, therefore, facilitated the exploration into the borderland between the known and the unknown, the living and the dead. Thus Murnau brought the most famous nineteenth-century vampire, Count Dracula, into the cinema, presenting him as a product of filmic special effects.

Nosferatu has always stood apart from other expressionist films made in Germany in this period, such as *Cabinet of Dr. Caligari* (1919), because of its use of real locations rather than expressionistically designed sets and lighting. While *Caligari* projects the madness of a tormented mind in its distorted sets, makeup, and costumes, *Nosferatu* showcases photographic realism through its effective use of real locations, long takes, and mise-en-scène. It is precisely for this reason that André Bazin suggested that the attempt to capture reality is the essence of Murnau's work rather than any attempt to manipulate the image through montage and expressionist techniques.

> Murnau is interested not so much in time as in the reality of dramatic space. Montage plays no more of a decisive part in *Nosferatu* than in *Sunrise*. One might be inclined to think that the plastics of his image are expressionistic. But this would be a superficial view. The composition of his image is in no sense pictorial. It adds nothing to the reality, it does not deform it, it forces it to reveal its structural depth, to bring out the preexisting relations which become constitutive of the drama.[30]

While Murnau's work does foreground natural and real locations, it is not at the expense of more expressive filmic techniques but rather in tandem with them. Thomas Elsaesser has argued that Murnau's ability to blend "exquisitely crafted artifice" within an "utterly realistic depiction of a natural environment" was one of the defining features of his style, illustrated in *Nosferatu*'s careful balance between realism and fantasy.[31] In fact, like most contemporary horror films, *Nosferatu* evokes its horror through the eruption of the fantastic from within a realistic setting. Furthermore, Bazin's argument was based upon his belief in the detached objectivity of the camera. Murnau's emphasis on the uncanny properties of film, however, represents the supernatural and the duality of the medium, drawing upon a repertoire of techniques established by the magic lanternists and trick filmmakers in the nineteenth and early twentieth centuries. Murnau creates his vampiric specter through a legacy of spectral technology. As Angela Dalle Vacche suggests, "Nosferatu's bloodsucking, which drains the world of its vital forces, plays on the notion that cinema, the art of movement of life, may also be a form of death at work, with one image exhausting itself into the next."[32] David J. Skal points out that the relationship between the vampire and film was part of the earliest conception of *Nosferatu*. A sketch by the producer and set designer Albin Grau (himself a spiritualist) "almost explicitly evokes film itself as demonic magic. Standing over a woman's bed, the vampire illuminates his intended prey with beams of light projected from his eyes."[33] *Nosferatu* imbues its vampire with the filmic and photographic qualities of the cinema as a means of exploring the inherent vampirism of this new technology.

Early cinema has often been described as the capture and projection of the shadowy images of the living.[34] *Nosferatu* similarly uses the image of the shadow to equate the vampire to a shadow of humanity. When Hutter is left to rendezvous with Orlok's carriage, his driver tells him that he will go no further because the land beyond the mountain pass is haunted. To represent this land of phantoms, film itself is presented as ghostly; Hutter's entrance into the vampire's realm is distinguished by the use of the film's negative image, which creates an artificially shadowy world. Furthermore, the intertitles are filled with references to shadows in relation to Orlok. For instance, the book of vampires warns Hutter not to let the shadow of the vampire "burden [his] dreams with horrible fears," and the vampire's departure at dawn after Hutter's first night at Orlok's castle is heralded with an intertitle: "As the sun started to rise, the shadows of the night left Hutter." The evening of Hutter's second night begins with an intertitle reading, "The ghostly evening light made the shadows of the castle appear to come alive again," followed by a shot of Hutter and Orlok as they go over various business papers. Orlok, in this case, is the shadow that comes alive after dark and recedes with the sunrise.

That Orlok is paralleled with the shadowy nature of the cinema is visually supported by the film's use of expressionistic shadows to suggest the presence of the vampire, particularly in two key sequences in the film that show the vampire attacking his victims: the attack on Hutter at the castle and the attack on Ellen in Wisborg. Once realizing that Orlok is a vampire, Hutter collapses in fear and the vampire enters his room to feed. His attack is filmed in a medium shot of Hutter lying unconscious on the bed as the shadow of the vampire emerges from the bottom of the frame and moves up over Hutter's body until he is almost completely engulfed in its darkness. Later, when Hutter's wife Ellen offers herself to the vampire, Orlok's shadow stalks stealthily up the stairs and the shadows of his elongated fingers are shown stretching out toward the door. The film then cuts to an image of Ellen, like Hutter in the earlier scene, collapsed on the bed as the vampire's shadow once again looms up from

Figure 2.2. The touch of a vampire in *Nosferatu*.

the bottom of the frame, gradually consuming her in its shade. (Figure 2.2) In these sequences, Orlok's shadow is "projected" onto the bright, white surfaces—Hutter's bed and Ellen's nightgown, respectively—like film itself is projected onto a screen.

Gilberto Perez Guillermo describes this seemingly disembodied presence as "a mere phantom disconnected from the physical world, an impotent shadow struggling to possess the young woman's body." [35] But what this sequence actually suggests is that the vampire—like film, which is both a physical strip of celluloid and the illusion of movement when projected—crosses the boundaries between the corporeal and the spectral. As Orlok reaches out to Ellen, the shadow of his arm moves along her outstretched body, pauses just above her heart, and then clasps shut. Ellen writhes in pain in direct response to this gesture. Orlok's shadow has both spectral and physical form. [36]

While the vampire shares film's shadowy properties, he is also associated with its ability to manipulate time. According to Mary Albert, from its earliest days, film had the ability to manipulate time through the over- or under-cranking of the camera. Before the advent of sound, when a standardized camera and sound speed became a necessity, cameras and projectors were hand-cranked. Variations in speed were therefore unavoidable and resulted in either the slowing down or speeding up of movement. Albert argues, "Film audiences must have taken for granted slight oscillations of temporality when unintended, and no doubt fully appreciated full blown spectacles of manipulated time when it was carefully constructed by the film-makers."[37] In *Nosferatu*, when Hutter is met by the carriage that will take him to Orlok's castle, the coach's approach is shot in fast motion, and later Orlok himself is filmed in fast motion as he packs his coffins of earth onto a cart bound for Wisborg. The supernatural quality of the scene culminates when Orlok climbs into one of the boxes and, through stop-motion photography, the lid of the box is magically placed on top to seal him in. According to Albert, the manipulation of camera speed allowed the filmmaker to capture forms of movement made possible exclusively through the intervention of the camera and made visible through projection. This type of photography was used by scientists to thrill audiences with displays of fast motion, showing "plants growing, flowers opening and buildings being constructed before their eyes."[38] Filming the vampire in this way suggests that his supernatural movement can only be captured by the camera and further blurs the boundaries between the supernatural and the scientific. This interpretation is furthered by the fact that the vampire's arrival in Wisborg is intercut with Professor Bulwer's analysis of nature's vampires, the polyp and the Venus flytrap, suggesting that Orlok is a similar product of nature. As Hutter watches Orlok load his cart, is he witnessing an uncanny event or a scientific experiment in motion?

The previous examples draw upon film's cinematographic properties, but *Nosferatu* also equates the vampire with the medium's capacity, through editing, to manipulate the perception of time and space. By 1914, crosscutting between parallel actions was commonly used in American cinema, though it took longer to become standardized in Europe.[39] While some filmmakers began to experiment with crosscutting as a means of suggesting a contrast in action, and Griffith's *Intolerance* (1916) used crosscutting to suggest parallel themes rather than actions, it was most commonly implemented as a "narrational process" in which "two or more lines of action in different locales are woven together."[40]

It is this latter form of crosscutting that Murnau uses to great effect in *Nosferatu* both to create tension and suggest the intrusion of the supernatural. For instance, on the third night of Hutter's stay at the castle, Count Orlok sheds his disguise and reveals himself as a vampire to Hutter, who hides in his room. As Orlok slowly approaches Hutter, the film cuts to a sequence of Ellen waking up with a start and taking a somnambulant journey around the house. This example of crosscutting is, at first glance, quite a conventional use of parallel action. However, as the sequence continues, the use of crosscutting begins to suggest a greater connection between these events than simply their simultaneity. The scene cuts from Ellen to a closeup of Hutter's collapsed body as the vampire's shadow looms over him. The scene then cuts to Ellen who, having been subdued by her friends and returned to her bed, leaps up once again, reaches out towards the left of the screen and calls out to Hutter to beware. This gesture precipitates a cut to Hutter, still unconscious, as the vampire's shadow begins to recede. The film cuts to a medium shot of Orlok backing up and slowly turning towards the right of the screen. The sequence returns to Ellen reaching out towards the left and then cuts to Orlok as he leaves Hutter's room. The editing of this sequence breaks with conventional use of parallel editing for these two lines of action are no longer simply occurring at the same time but seem to be interacting with each other. Through the juxtaposition of the shots of Ellen facing screen left and the vampire turning to face her on the right, space and time are compressed. Not only does his withdrawal from Hutter suggest that he is responding to Ellen's plea, but as they each look out of frame, the juxtaposition of these shots, as well as a clear eye line match, suggests that they are looking at each other. The editing creates a telepathic link between the vampire and Ellen.

Murnau's use of crosscutting in this sequence does more than reinforce the presentation of the vampire as a supernatural monster; it also links the vampire to a modern conception of space and time. According to Stephen Kern, "The ability to experience many distant events at the same time, made possible by the wireless . . . was part of a major change in the experience of the present" in the early part of the twentieth century.[41] The present was no longer being perceived as "a sequence of single local events" but instead was viewed as a "simultaneity of multiple distant events," manifested in the development of new technologies including the wireless, telephone, and the cinema.[42] With the development of crosscutting, the cinema was able to visualize a culture that, through technology, experienced a simultaneous and interconnected present. This is illustrated through Tom Gunning's analysis of the opening sequence of *Dr. Mabuse the Gambler* (1922), which features Mabuse orchestrating an elaborate heist, placing him "at the centre of a terrain of modernity." According to Gunning, in order to address "the way one form of technology interacts with another to create the abstract and fully co-ordinated grid of space and time," director Fritz Lang manipulates the cinema's own technological facility to command time and space through crosscutting. In this sequence, Mabuse is the linchpin in a carefully devised succession of actions that depend upon the synchronicity of modern technologies. The film repeatedly intercuts between Mabuse watching the clock and anticipating each action, and the series of events, all carefully timed with modern precision. As Gunning argues, "This abstract system cannot be visualised in a single shot or image, but rather becomes evident in the way different spaces and time interrelate in a film."[43]

While Lang's command of the juxtaposition of shots is used to mirror Mabuse's own command of technology, Murnau draws upon the supernatural potential of editing to suggest the uncanniness of the modern conception of space and time. The vampire's arrival in Wisborg is presented in an elaborate sequence of crosscutting between Orlok's ship arriving in port, Hutter's journey by land, and Ellen and Knock's psychic realization of Orlok's arrival.

Comprised of forty shots, the sequence begins once the Captain, the last person on Orlok's ship, has been killed and Orlok has taken control. The first few shots establish the simultaneous whereabouts of each of the main characters; while the ship continues on its journey, the film cuts to a shot of Ellen standing on the balcony looking out into the night. This is followed by a shot of Hutter in a coach arriving by land. The race between Orlok and Hutter to reach Wisborg has begun. Meanwhile, the repeated cutaways to shots of Ellen in a trance suggest her anticipation of someone's arrival. Eventually, in a medium closeup, Ellen turns to the camera to announce, "He's coming. I must go to meet him," before running out of frame. Meanwhile, Knock, the fly-eating madman trapped in Orlok's power, also anticipates Orlok's arrival and climbs up to the window of his cell to look out. The film cuts to the ship sailing into the harbor under a form of ghostly power and then cuts back to Knock shouting, "The Master is coming! The Master is here!"

The sequence does not stop once Orlok's ship has arrived in Wisborg but continues as he escapes the ship, with one of his coffins under his arm, and sneaks through town to find his newly purchased, but derelict, house. Meanwhile, Knock, feeling Orlok's influence all the more strongly due to his proximity, attacks the guard of his cell. As Orlok's house is directly opposite Hutter's, Orlok's journey through the town can be seen as a race to reach Ellen first. His creeping through the town is intercut with Hutter rushing to his house to find Ellen. As Hutter enters his home, the film cuts to a medium closeup of Orlok outside the house turning to look in its direction followed by a closeup of Ellen and Hutter falling into each other's arms and kissing. The film then returns to Orlok still outside, and almost as if he is aware of Hutter's success in reaching Ellen first, he turns away from their house and moves on towards his own residence.

Thomas Elsaesser points out that the crosscutting in this sequence is not the kind conventionally used in classical narratives. What "Murnau builds up here is a kind of architecture of secret affinities, too deep or too dreadful for the characters to be aware of, and even for us happening only at the edges of our perception, but none the less lodging in the viewer, too, that pull between horror and fascination which the vampire exerts on the protagonists."[44] This sequence suggests more than "secret affinities" between the protagonists; it indicates a telepathic connection that binds the characters together over vast spaces. The characters' movements suggest an interconnection of purpose and an awareness of each other. While Mabuse is a master criminal manipulating and controlling the technology, Orlok is simply an element of this network of communication. This network mirrors the telepathic communication between Dracula and his victims explored in Stoker's novel, which is characterized as an internal telegraphy system. In *Nosferatu*'s case, the film uses its ability to edit and juxtapose shots together to embody the modern collapse of time, space, and communication, and to suggest the uncanny quality of the culture of simultaneous and interconnected experience brought about by modernity.

As previously discussed, one of the most significant ways that the vampire came to physically embody the modern in Stoker's novel was through his ability to transform himself from one form to another, in the manner of electrical, telephonic, and telegraphic signals. Orlok is similarly modern through his physical embodiment of the photographic. While Orlok in *Nosferatu* is not shown to transform himself, he is presented as an ethereal being through the use of dissolves and superimpositions, techniques traditionally associated with transformation in the Phantasmagoria, magic lantern performances, and early cinema, and that served to merge the magical with the modern. When the first sailor mysteriously falls ill on the ship that is unknowingly transporting Orlok to Wisborg, he is left alone in the hold with Orlok's boxes. As the sailor leaps up in fear of an unknown force, Orlok appears, through a superimposition, seated on top of one of his boxes, staring back at the sailor. He then fades away. The diaphanous quality of his image harks back to spirit photography whereby ghostly images were created through superimposition. Further, when Orlok arrives at his house in Wisborg, he enters the building by dissolving into nothingness. These sequences reinforce the idea that Orlok's ghostly presence brings out the spectral quality of the film technology.

But the most significant use of the dissolve occurs when Ellen lures Orlok to her room and, by sacrificing herself, keeps him at her side until after the sun has risen. In this sequence, Murnau uses a slow dissolve to suggest the vampire's disintegration in the rays of the sun. As he realizes the time, Orlok stands up, becomes trapped in the sunshine coming through the window, and fades away into nothingness for the last time. Murnau's use of the dissolve in this manner is quite significant because it introduced a new convention that would become an integral part of the twentieth-century vampire. In Stoker's novel, the sun simply disempowers the vampire, while in Murnau's film it is the primary method of destroying the vampire. The emergence of this new convention in the first major vampire film is strongly linked to the fact that light is the essence of cinema. It is light that burns an image onto film and then projects that image onto a screen. Orlok, a creature of the night, fades away in the sunlight in the same manner that a photograph or the image on a strip of celluloid fades into nothingness when overexposed. This suggests that the vampire is made up of similar properties as film itself, an interpretation further supported by the ending of *Shadow of the Vampire* (2000). In that film, as Murnau shoots Orlok's death scene, a door is thrown open, bathing the vampire Schreck in real sunlight. To convey his destruction, rather than simply fading into nothingness, the frame of his image is burnt away like a film frame trapped in the gauge of the projector, re-affirming the symbiotic relationship between the vampire and the cinema that began with *Nosferatu*.

The Legacy of *Nosferatu* and the Spectral Vampire

Filmmakers of the horror genre in Hollywood in the 1930s drew upon the stylistic devices and artistic talent of German Expressionism, and continued to use filmic trickery to suggest the supernatural and the spectral. Universal Studios in particular, through the work of photographic effects supervisor John P. Fulton, pushed the boundaries of special effects and established themselves as one of Hollywood's leading producers of Gothic horror. The full potential of these effects were, however, not initially associated with the vampire film. The first of the studio's classic monster movies, *Dracula*, was based upon the successful stage play and therefore presents its narrative in a theatrical manner, setting any transformations or death scenes offscreen. It was only in the 1940s, following the success of Fulton's work on *The Invisible Man* (1933), *The Werewolf of London* (1935), and *Bride of Frankenstein* (1935), that the spectral quality of the vampire established in *Nosferatu* continued with such films as *Son of Dracula* (1943) and *House of Dracula* (1945). It was, however, truncated into recognizable, generic conventions based on the role sunlight plays in the vampire's destruction as well as the vampire's ability to transform. For instance, in *Son of Dracula*, Fulton presents the vampire's transformation from mist into a man through a simple dissolve, while in *House of Dracula*, Dracula transforms from bat into man through animation. Furthermore, when Dracula's coffin is pulled into the light of the rising sun, his disintegration into nothingness is presented through a series of dissolves, as each layer of his body—skin, tissue, and skeleton—painlessly fades away. The image is both reminiscent of Orlok's painless death in *Nosferatu* and the x-ray craze of the late nineteenth century.[45]

Return of the Vampire (1943), however, produced by one of Universal's rival studios, Columbia Pictures, suggests a movement away from a purely spectral presentation of the vampire to a more physical one. When the vampire is pulled out into the sunlight and staked to death, the tissue of his body is burned away leaving behind a rotting corpse. Similarly, in Hammer Studios' *Horror of Dracula* (1958), Dracula's death by sunlight is presented as a painful attack upon the vampire's body. It is less of a confrontation between the light and a creature of the night, and more the burning of the vampire's skin to ash, introducing a new element to the genre that has subsequently become an accepted generic convention to be discussed in Chapter 7. In both cases, however, the effects were not achieved through camera trickery or other spectral effects, but by simply cutting away to a reaction shot to conceal the replacement of the human actor by a dummy. Despite the low-tech quality of the effects, these two films set the standard for the vampire films that followed, enhanced by developments in special makeup effects in the 1970s and 1980s, which will be discussed in Chapters 6 and 7. The physical did eventually replace the spectral, and with it came a new conception of the modern. Yet, the spectral has not disappeared entirely from the vampire film, partly due to the increasing use of computer-generated special effects, which will be discussed in Chapter 11, but also because films such as *Bram Stoker's Dracula* (1992), *Shadow of the Vampire*, and *Dracula: Pages from a Virgin's Diary* (2002), deliberately allude to the heritage of *Nosferatu* through their adoption of a similar spectral representation of the vampire, and the use of photographic effects that once again portray the vampire as technologically embodied. In these films, however, the vampire no longer represents the uncanniness of modern technology but rather old technology, as well as conveying a nostalgia for cinema of the past.

In the symbiotic relationship between cinema and the vampire, *Nosferatu* captured the changing conception and experience of modernity. That its own modern qualities have since been overtaken by newer technologies and effects and therefore have come to represent the past in these later films, reaffirms the notion that modernity operates as a cycle, replacing what was once modern with a more up-to-date incarnation.

CHAPTER THREE

From Hollywood Gothic to Hammer Horror: The Modern Evolution of *Dracula*

We're not blind and we're not fools. We are just plain sensible people that refuse to be fooled by a lot of supernatural nonsense.

FRANK STANLEY IN *SON OF DRACULA* (1943)

The Hollywood of Hollywood Gothic *is less the geographical location than the psychic shadow-land we all inhabit to one extent or another, the private theatre to which we return again and again to watch the midnight movies of our minds. For quite some time now,* Dracula *has been the perennial blockbuster attraction.*

DAVID J. SKAL[1]

From the earliest adaptations of *Dracula*, F. W. Murnau's *Nosferatu* (1922) and Tod Browning's *Dracula* (1931), the cinema has harbored an intense fascination with the vampire and this filmic image has colonized the cultural representation of the vampire. The success of Browning's film launched a new genre in Hollywood retrospectively called "Hollywood Gothic," a phrase coined by David J. Skal because of the genre's debt to Gothic literature and the visual style of German expressionism.[2] This genre established many of the parameters for the vampire film that would be consistently drawn upon until the emergence of the modern horror period in the late 1960s when a rethinking of the vampire occurred, which will be discussed in later chapters. What is distinctive about the vampire films—made predominantly by Universal Studios in the 1930s and 1940s and by Hammer Studios in the 1950s and 1960s—is the manner in which they evoke a nostalgic image of a Gothic nineteenth century, while also demonstrating an increasing preoccupation with modernity that defines the twentieth century. In this manner, the vampire in this period is torn between two centuries and embodies the flux between the premodern and the modern.[3]

Prior to Universal's decision to adapt Stoker's novel, American silent cinema's strongest examples of the horror genre were either haunting mysteries such as *The Cat and the Canary* (1927), or Gothic extravaganzas such as *Phantom of the Opera* (1925): films that suggested the supernatural but always resolved the mystery with a rational explanation. The one American vampire film in this period, Tod Browning's *London after Midnight* (1927) starring Lon Chaney, is an interesting example of this formula. In the film, Chaney plays two roles: a detective investigating a series of apparent vampire murders, and the ghoulish vampire himself, featuring one of Chaney's more unnerving make-ups, with wide-staring eyes and razor sharp teeth. The film contains the accoutrements of the vampire genre—Gothic lighting and set design, grisly murders, and an iconographic image of the vampire—before finally revealing that the vampiric events have been staged in order to force a confession from a murderer. The vampire is unmasked and revealed to be in fact the detective.[4] The rational ending wins out.

Dracula, Tod Browning's second foray into the vampire genre, initiated the move away from this formula of rational explanations to a genre of purely supernatural narratives. In these films, the existence of vampires must be accepted for, as Van Helsing warns in the film, "The strength of the vampire is that people will not believe in him." The success of Browning's film established the popularity of the genre and its formula by setting the film in studiobound versions of Transylvania and London, which were more mythic than realistic or modern, unlike Stoker's *Dracula*, which took great pains to situate the vampire in a recognizably contemporary setting. As Charles Derry argues, the very nature of classic horror is to present the horror symbolically in order to maintain a distance from the audience and the real world, while Robin Wood suggests that this tendency served either to disavow the monstrous or to present a "country of the mind," evoking a psychological horror.[5]

Browning's *Dracula*, for instance, is set in London, but neither the Victorian London of the novel nor the modern city of 1931. Rather it is set in a studio-built facsimile of the city. The first long shot of London shows a busy city street with cars and double-decker buses circulating around its center, the sound of traffic dominating the shot. This setting, however, stands in contrast to Dracula's attack of a lone cockney flower seller who he murders, hidden in the shadows of a Gothic London fog. This image evokes the nineteenth-century murders of Jack the Ripper, an association reinforced by the subsequent shot of Dracula calmly walking away from the attack with the sound of police whistles heard in the distance. Furthermore, following this introduction to London, the film retreats from the city and centers its narrative in the parlor of the film's primary characters, Dr. Seward, his daughter Mina, and her fiancé Jonathan Harker, as well as the bowels of Dracula's new home, the Gothic Carfax Abbey. The geography in the film is also invented, as Dr. Seward's asylum and Carfax Abbey are supposedly based in Whitby, which is described within the film as being an adjunct of London when, in actuality, it is a town on the coast of Yorkshire.

This film not only established the formula of Gothic horror for the other key Universal horror films of the classic period, *Frankenstein* (1931), *The Mummy* (1932), *The Invisible Man* (1933), and *The Wolf Man* (1941), but was also followed by a series of sequels including *Dracula's Daughter* (1936), *Son of Dracula* (1943), and *House of Dracula* (1945). These sequels similarly project ambivalence about the period and setting. While both *Dracula's Daughter* and *Son of Dracula* continue to be situated within a seemingly contemporary setting, it is a constructed setting relying upon Gothic convention to create atmosphere. *Dracula's Daughter* begins where *Dracula* ended, the death of the king vampire, but the opening of the film seems to deliberately set up a more overt contrast between the modern world and the Gothic world of the vampire as two English policemen cautiously descend the Gothic staircase in Carfax Abbey only to find the bodies of Renfield and Dracula. When Van Helsing admits to destroying Dracula, the two police officers place him under arrest and exclaim, "This is a case for Scotland Yard!" Of course it is a case that will confound Scotland Yard as its supernaturalness operates outside of their more conventional point of view.

The film, however, does feel more contemporary than its predecessor, not because it draws upon familiar locations or iconography of the modern city, but rather because the film is populated by characters who are more recognizably modern. For instance, police commissioner Sir Basil Humphrey and Dr. Garth demonstrate how modern law and science must come to terms with the existence of vampirism. More significantly, the characters of Garth and his assistant Janet, through their comic repartee, call to mind the modern screwball couples of such films as *The Thin Man* (1934) and *My Man Godfrey* (1936).[6] Also, the cockney flower seller from *Dracula* is here replaced by a down-and-out American named Lily who seems to be a modern victim of the Depression, alone, hungry, and vulnerable, and as such, she falls prey to the vampire Countess Zaleska.

The film, however, like *Dracula*, rarely escapes the confines of the upper-class drawing room until the vampire, followed by Garth and Scotland Yard, returns to its native Transylvania. As a result, the film seems timeless and distant from the real world. The characters may be familiar, but the world that they inhabit is a constructed vision of contemporary London.

Son of Dracula raises further interesting questions of location and time. While most examples of Hollywood Gothic locate their narratives outside of the United States in a somewhat fictional representation of Europe, this film is set in the United States in the 1940s. It therefore represents the infiltration of an old-world, foreign monster into modern America, which is established at the beginning of the film as a train arrives to deliver Count Alucard (Dracula spelled backward) into the town. The fear of what danger the vampire represents to the New World is addressed later in the film when Dr. Brewster and Professor Lazlo discuss Alucard's reasons for the move to America.

> LAZLO. My own homeland in the Carpathian Hills where Count Dracula lived is sad testimony to its truth. What was once a happy, productive region is today barren waste. Villages depopulated . . . the land abandoned.

> BREWSTER. Maybe that is why he left there and came here to a younger country. Stronger and more virile.

> LAZLO. Of course. And he will fasten on it and drain it dry just as he did his homeland.

Having said this, while the film is seemingly set in contemporary United States, it uses a number of Gothic conventions to distance itself from the real world in favor of a constructed reality in which one can accept the existence of vampires. This conforms to Chris Baldick's argument that the Gothic text must confine the story within the past or, if set in the present, within a confined and timeless location in which "the past's destructive cruelty" prevails.[7] The majority of the film takes place in just such a timeless location, the plantation of Dark Oaks, an isolated old manor house surrounded by swampland, a graveyard, and a mausoleum. The house even lacks the modern convenience of a telephone for, as the film's main character Katherine (Kay) points out to her sister Claire, "There are other means of communication," referring to telepathy. Other Gothic conventions include an old gypsy fortune teller, who informs Kay that evil things await her and that she is destined to marry a corpse, and Dr. Lazlo, the vampire expert. Kay herself appears as a classic Gothic heroine, with pale skin, shining black hair, and often wearing flowing white gowns, quite unlike the modern dresses worn by her sister. Described by Dr. Brewster as "morbid," it is no surprise that Kay is destined to become a vampire and, in fact, it is she who meets Alucard in Budapest and invites the evil into her town.

In addition to their ambivalent representation of time and place, each of these films contain signifiers of the modern while continuing to present the vampire as existing outside of the modern, in much the same way that the films seem to be both set in the present and the past. Both *Dracula* and *Dracula's Daughter* espouse the argument, often spoken by Van Helsing, that the belief in vampires need not be anachronistic with the modern world for the superstition of today is the science of tomorrow. This is consistent with the arguments in Stoker's novel. However, science is presented to be as Gothic and ritualized as vampire folklore and religious mysticism. The two key science scenes in *Dracula* feature an autopsy and a sequence in which Van Helsing tests Renfield's blood. The autopsy scene begins as an extreme, high-angle, long shot of the operating theater in which a crowd of doctors overlook Van Helsing as he makes his final observations about Lucy's death. The bright white lab coats worn by all of the doctors and the white covering on the autopsy table contrast strongly with the dark shadows that fill the rest of frame. (Figure 3.1) The scale and chiaroscuro of this shot mirrors the overtly Gothic shots of the interior of Dracula's castle and the looming staircase in Carfax Abbey. Each location is, by their nature, preoccupied with the spectacle of death and decay. As such, the film creates, through its expressionist mise-en-scène, a link between the scientific and the Gothic. Similarly, the sequence when Van Helsing tests Renfield's blood presents science as being as ritualized as religion. (Figure 3.2) Beginning in a medium close-up of Van Helsing as he pours liquid into a test tube, the camera tracks back to reveal that Van Helsing is surrounded by a group of attentive men. He asks a colleague to read a passage of Latin text from a book and this is followed by Van Helsing's pronouncement, "Gentlemen, we are dealing with the undead." While the implication is that the test upon Renfield's blood proves the existence of the undead, there is no explanation for the basis of his conclusion. Van Helsing simply pronounces his judgement and the reading of the Latin text gives the sequence the air of religious ritual. It is worth noting how in both sequences science is presented as being the subject of reverential observation. In these films, science is the religion of the modern man.

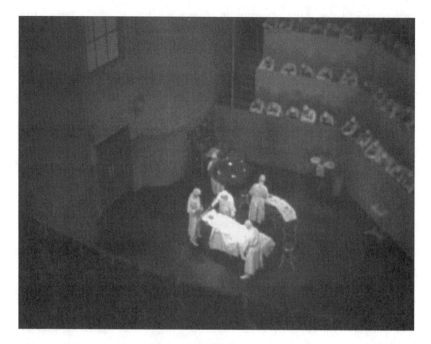

Figure 3.1. Gothic science in Browning's *Dracula.*

In *Dracula's Daughter,* a tension is established between the dark powers of vampirism and the powers of science. Learning that Dracula has been destroyed, Countess Zaleska steals his body to perform a ritual of dark magic that will sever her link with the king vampire and restore her humanity. When this attempt to find release fails and she once again gives in to her bloodlust, she turns to psychiatrist Dr. Garth for a cure. As she explains to Garth, the "strength of a human mind against the powers of darkness . . . your strength against his" establishes Garth's science as a force of opposition against the powers of the vampire. This too fails when she succumbs to her desire for the young girl Lily. What is revealed in this scene is that Zaleska's vampirism is too strong a force to be broken either by superstition or science. Additionally, Zaleska's own power of hypnosis, which she uses to overpower her victims, is paralleled in Garth's scientific machine used to induce a similar hypnotic state. Again, however, Zaleska's power is stronger than Garth's science. His attempt to counteract her posthypnotic suggestion that Lily forget everything that happened results in Lily's death. Zaleska represents an old dark magic that his science cannot fight.

Figure 3.2. The science of vampire hunting in Browning's *Dracula.*

Science plays a particularly important role in *House of Dracula* despite the fact that it contains the most fantastic narrative within the series. Located in an unspecified time and in a coastal castle that serves as both home and laboratory, the story brings together the collection of Universal Studios' monsters—Dracula, the Wolf Man, and Frankenstein's monster—all to be the subject of the scientific scrutiny of Dr. Eidleman. The film is, however, the only one of the Universal Dracula series to use a transfusion, addressed in Stoker's novel, to counteract the powers of vampirism, but it does this in a very unusual way. In *House of Dracula,* Dracula feigns remorse for his existence as a vampire and turns to Dr. Eidleman for a cure. The doctor tests Dracula's blood and discovers an unknown parasite within his blood cells, foreshadowing many contemporary films and television series that have turned to science to explain and find a cure for vampirism including *Dark Shadows* (1966–1971), *Ultraviolet* (1998), *Blade* (1998), and *Underworld* (2003). In an inversion of sequences in Stoker's novel, the doctor decides that the recommended cure is a series of blood transfusions in which he will transfuse his own blood *into* Dracula. During the final session, Dracula reverses the procedure and infuses the doctor with his blood. This results in the doctor repeatedly transforming, along the lines of Dr. Jekyll and Mr. Hyde, into a monstrous killer who goes on a murderous rampage within the village. While this film initially suggests that science can unlock the mysteries of vampirism, the rules of the supernatural and the fantastic win out in the end as Dracula's blood proves more powerful than Eidleman's cure.

While *Son of Dracula* does not feature science as a major component—both Dr. Brewster and Professor Lazlo operate purely in the form of vampire experts seeking to stop the vampire along folkloric lines—it does introduce a key signifier of the modern, most notably the femme fatale. As it was directed by Robert Siodmak, who would go on to be one of the leading directors within film noir, there are strong associations within this film with that most modern and American of genres and most focus on the character of Kay Caldwell. What is significant about this film is the character Kay, who courts Alucard to orchestrate her own induction into the undead. She is not seduced into her life as a vampire but chooses it. As James B. Twitchell explains, "She has wanted what she should not want, done what she should not have done, and so is done for."[8] Furthermore, her plans are revealed to be more calculated than her initial arrangement with Alucard. She agrees to marry him so he can acquire her plantation, a modern American equivalent of his own castle in Transylvania, in exchange for her own immortality. But her plans extend to transforming her lover Frank into a vampire so they can be together forever. Once made immortal, she double-crosses Alucard by convincing Frank that he must destroy the vampire. As such, she not only puts his life and sanity into jeopardy—for Frank barely escapes a confrontation with Alucard, is blamed for her apparent death, and is later made hysterical by all that he has witnessed including a visitation by Kay in his jail cell—but she also threatens his very soul. Unlike Mina Seward in the film *Dracula*, Kay is not in the thrall of Dracula, nor does she share the reluctance of Countess Zaleska, but instead embraces vampirism as an acceptable price for immortality. In this manner, this film prefigures the move toward the modern and the familiar that defines the post-1968 vampire films while continuing to contain the vampire himself within the safety of the Gothic and the premodern.

The tension between the modern and the premodern that is evident in these Universal films dominated the genre from the first wave of Gothic horror films in the 1930s and 1940s through the next major cycle at the British Hammer Studios in the 1950s and 1960s. In 1958, Hammer followed the success of their entry into Gothic horror, *The Curse of Fran-*

kenstein (1957), with their own adaptation of Stoker's novel, *The Horror of Dracula*.[9] Entirely shot at Bray Studios in Windsor, this version distances the monstrosity of vampirism from contemporary experience by relocating the narrative to a constructed representation of nineteenth-century Germany and yet, through the performance of Christopher Lee as Dracula and the set design of the castle, the film presents us with a vampire who is seemingly modern in every way. Unlike the Gothic ruins of Dracula's castle in Browning's film, this castle is intact, well-decorated, and while ornate and clearly the home of gentry, appears homely. When Jonathan Harker arrives at the empty castle, he finds a note from Dracula written on rather official letterhead marked by the Dracula family crest, instructing him to make himself at home until the Count returns. He does this, and with none of the discomfort or fear clearly expressed by Renfield upon his arrival at the castle in Browning's film. Similarly, Dracula's first appearance is designed to undermine generic expectations of the vampire. The first glimpse of Dracula comes as Harker turns toward the staircase to see a tall, cloaked figure in silhouette looming at the top of the stairs as the James Bernard music score bursts in with loud Gothic overtones. Suddenly the figure briskly walks down the stairs and toward Harker, coming into the light as he steps into a close-up, and introduces himself as Count Dracula. In this single shot, the figure transforms from a Gothic monster to a polite businessman. He carries Harker's bags to his room, discusses their work plans for the library, and plays the ideal host. As Nina Auerbach points out, "In this inaugural appearance he is brisk and entrepreneurial, more up-to-date than the little men who scurry around to protect their strapping, sexy women," and he possesses none of the "willed difference of accent, costume, and rhythm" that defined Lugosi's performance.[10]

If Dracula is modern in appearance in this version of Stoker's story, Van Helsing is modern in action. Like Dracula, Van Helsing is no longer the eccentric foreigner of Browning's film who speaks in broken English; he has been reimagined through the performance of Peter Cushing as an articulate Englishman. More significantly, he is presented as someone who, more than merely advocating a belief in vampires, has actually studied the superstition and ascertained the distinction between fact and fiction. The character is introduced in the film as he enters a local inn that is bedecked in garlic flowers. He does not dismiss the local beliefs but instead tells the innkeeper that he knows their beliefs are more than superstition and that his investigations have shown a real threat within this community. His words demonstrate that he is neither doubting nor blindly superstitious.

He speaks with the authority of one who "knows" rather than "believes." Even when discussing metaphysical concepts such as peace, the soul, and evil, he does so in scientific terms. While Van Helsing's characteristics are a nod to modernity, they also represent, according to David Pirie, echoes of the past, for Van Helsing "takes up the familiar stance of the Renaissance mastermind, and represents for a fleeting and nostalgic moment the union of scientific exploration with religion."[11]

Van Helsing's authority is further reinforced through his uses of modern technology in the form of the blood transfusion—which he uses to save Mina's life after her second encounter with Dracula—and the phonograph. Van Helsing uses the phonograph to record his research notes, much like Dr. Seward in Stoker's novel. He is shown reviewing his notes as he plays back his recording of basic facts about vampirism before being interrupted by his butler who, having heard voices in the room, is surprised to find Van Helsing alone. The technology is unfamiliar to the butler and therefore signals the doctor at the forefront of modernity. It of course must be noted that this sequence also suggests the class distinction between Van Helsing and his butler. Van Helsing's class privilege provides him with this technological knowledge in much the same way that his encounter with the peasants, as pointed out by Peter Hutchings, suggests that he possesses the "enlightened knowledge of a middle-class expert."[12] Furthermore, this representation of modernity is tinged with nostalgia, for as Hutchings reminds us, "In Stoker's novel, a machine of this kind features as one of the numerous signifiers of modernity associated with the vampire hunters. In Hammer's film the machine becomes instead a rather quaint part of the period setting."[13]

Having established that *The Horror of Dracula* demonstrates a rather conflicted attempt to modernize the Dracula story, it is important to note that as the films in the Hammer Dracula series progress, this interest in the modern seems to wane, particularly in relation to Lee's performance. With each subsequent film, Lee's modern demeanor gradually disappears in favor of snarls and close-ups of his bloodshot, lusting eyes, and as such he becomes associated with animal hungers rather than modern aspirations. Similarly, in *Dracula: Prince of Darkness* (1965), Van Helsing is replaced by a monk, which serves to overtly resituate the series in the context of traditional religious ritual over modern science. Furthermore the seemingly modern *Horror of Dracula* eschews the threat to the modern world that so defined the novel and subtly underscores the Universal *Dracula* films; there is no journey to a modern city and the distance between Castle Dracula and the villages he attacks seems to have been collapsed. As

Gregory Waller points out, "This Dracula does not so much invade the modern world searching for brides or converts to a new order of being as he makes forays into surrounding villages, towns, and monasteries, then retreats back to his castle."[14] While the Hammer films of the 1970s seem to represent a renewed attempt to situate Dracula within the modern by setting them in 1970s London, and as such engaging with the theme of invasion, this is a restricted entry into the contemporary and will be discussed in Chapter 4.

With regard to the 1950s, however, it is worth noting that in contrast to Hammer, Paul Landres' film *The Return of Dracula* (1957) does maintain and develop the theme of invasion of the modern that exists within the original novel as demonstrated by the opening voice-over:

> Though human in appearance and cultured in manner, [Count Dracula] was in truth a thing undead. A force of evil. A vampire. Feeding on the blood of the innocent, he turned them into his own kind thus spreading his evil dominion ever wider. The attempts to find and destroy this evil were never proven completely successful and so the search continues until this very day.

This voice-over is followed by a sequence in which a group of modern-day vampire hunters enter a cemetery and open a coffin only to find it empty. Where could Dracula have gone? The sequence then cuts to a train station where it is gradually revealed that Dracula has escaped Romania to journey to California. His entrance into America is presented through a montage of a boat arriving in New York with the Statue of Liberty to welcome it, followed by a shot of a train crossing the American landscape before arriving in California. The image of the Statue of Liberty is important here as it is a symbol of immigration into the United States and thus seems to be equating the vampire with America's growing immigrant communities. It, however, also calls to mind the promise of liberty in contrast to the oppressive regime of communist Romania that Dracula is escaping. In this manner, the film not only sets the Dracula story in modern America but also includes the backdrop of the Cold War, for which the threat of invasion was of paramount concern.

Here Dracula can be read as not only representing the threat of vampirism but the perceived threat of communism as he infiltrates this small Californian town, a foreigner to the community both in accent and behavior, and begins to transform its citizens from within. However, the film is more complicated than this; Dracula is himself escaping communist Romania, and it is the Romanian authorities that pursue him in association with American immigration officers and the church. Furthermore, when Rachel, a teenage girl clearly drawn to the rather exotic and artistic stranger, encourages him to come to the Halloween party and integrate with the community, he responds by asking her if the "price of your acceptance is for me to conform?" In this manner, the film uses the vampire narrative to offer a complicated representation of 1950s America in which the threat of communism is mirrored by the need to assimilate. This parallel is brief, however, for the vampire is still presented as monstrous and therefore must be contained. Andrew Tudor argues that invasion narratives often "embrace" characteristics of both "secure and paranoid horror."[15] In this case, the film undermines the distinction between good and evil by blurring the boundaries between the vampire and the small town community through the character of Rachel, who shares certain similarities and affinities with Dracula, while at the same time the film offers a clear cut resolution. In *The Return of Dracula* it is left to the young all-American couple, Rachel and her boyfriend Timmy, to destroy the vampire, save the town, and protect American values. "Normality," a major attribute of assimilation, is therefore restored.

In these films from the 1930s through to the 1960s, while there was a move to modernize the vampire for contemporary audiences, the monstrous continued to emerge from a fantasy representation of Europe and as such evoked an atmosphere of dreams and nightmares rather than a real and recognizable landscape. It was a genre of the fantastic and the Gothic, creatively exploring issues of sexuality, religion, miscegenation, and later, fears of communism, through the premodern figure of the vampire. As Skal suggests in the quotation that opens this chapter, this "psychic shadow-land" was dominated by the image of Dracula.[16] It was only in the 1970s that the genre began to break away from the dominance of Dracula, although Stoker's novel and king vampire continue to play a significant role, and as a result, both the genre and the vampire began to be reformulated and reinvented. These new vampires who began to emerge in film, television, and literature demonstrate a direct engagement with the contemporary and, due to the rather tumultuous changes occurring in the Western world within this period, the violent experience of modernity.

PART TWO

THE BIRTH OF THE MODERN
AMERICAN VAMPIRE

CHAPTER FOUR

The Seventies: The Vampire Decade

Bram Stoker's nineteenth-century novel *Dracula* featured a significant metamorphosis in the traditional representation of the vampire that captured a cultural anxiety over the changing perception of the modern world. While Dracula embodied the ambiguity between the occult and the scientific, he also emphasized the transitory nature of modernity itself. Dracula's very nature undermined the definition of the modern as understood by the vampire hunters and his death paved the way for his replacement by the next wave of modernity. Stoker's work illustrated how the vampire as a mythical creature could be a construct of the modern age, a position that, while alluded to in the films of the classic Hollywood period as discussed in the previous chapter, was more overtly revived in vampire films of the 1970s and resulted in yet another transformation of the vampire genre.

In this chapter, I will focus on the 1970s when the representation of the vampire became directly engaged with the reinvention of modernity. Filmmakers accomplished this by embroiling the vampire in the transition from industrialism to postindustrialism, a shift that had a profound effect upon the definition and iconography of American modernity. I will demonstrate that, just as Marshall Berman describes modernity as "a maelstrom of perpetual disintegration and renewal," all that had represented modernity in the 1890s was in a period of disintegration in the 1970s.[1] What the novel *Dracula* had come to embody was being undermined and overthrown by a structural reinvention of modernity in the late twentieth century. This period of radical change removed the vampire from its mythic representation, reinvented it as a modern vampire, and relocated it to America.

In the 1970s, America transitioned from an affluent and modern postwar nation to a postindustrial nation. This transition, however, did not begin in the 1970s but rather in the political, social, and cultural events of the 1960s that marked a significant attempt to break from or transform the social conventions of previous generations. As Stephen Paul Miller points out, "'The sixties' conveys a sense of total cultural rupture that most Americans perceived at the time or have later come to sense."[2] Tod Gitlin, one-time president of Students for a Democratic Society (SDS) and an organizer of the first national demonstration against the Vietnam War, described the early days of the student movement as a postwar generation's response to the aspirations and failures of their parents. He points out that

> this generation was haunted by history. They had been taught that political failure or apathy can have the direst consequences, they had extracted the lesson that the fate of the world is not something to be left to the authorities ... All wanted to redeem their parents' ideals in the face of their parents' failures. All breathed the intellectual air of existentialism: action might not avail, but one is responsible for choosing. And so, from under the dead hand of history, they leaped to a paradoxical conclusion: that history was alive and open.[3]

The result, he argues, was that the "SDS compressed a lifetime of politics into a handful of years—or rather, it was compressed into us. We were force-fed with history. The pace of change was dizzying—still feels that way, even at two decades remove."[4] Youth in this period sought to challenge authority and change the world by attacking the status quo from every angle. As the fight became more difficult and the authorities' resistance to change more violent, the movement became increasingly fragmented. In this period of social and cultural revolution, a climate of intimidation and violence dominated American culture. This included an increasing awareness of the atrocities taking place in Vietnam, committed by and against American soldiers, as well as backlashes on the part of the authorities against civil rights activists, antiwar protestors, and student demonstrators, all reported upon openly by the media. There was also an increasing awareness of less politically motivated acts of violence taking place in the United States. For instance, Charles Derry partially attributes the rise of the "horror of personality" film to the violent crimes and meaningless murders of the Boston Strangler, Richard Speck, and Charles Whitman.[5] Gregory A. Waller points out that the birth of the modern horror film in 1968 coincides with the first National Commission on the Causes and Prevention of Violence and the launch of the Motion Picture Association of America's new rating system, which replaced the Production Code.[6] According to Tod Gitlin,

> It was as if the assassinations, the riots, and the war distilled all the barely suppressed violence seething through American life. Palpably, just as Rap Brown said, "Violence was as American as apple pie." The eruption of public violence fused murder with madness, tore the heart out of rational faith, felt like some kind of historical repressed returning with a vengeance.[7]

While the end of the decade saw a restoration of social order and authority, this did not necessarily mean a return to the climate and structures of the world before the 1960s. The emergence of new social forces, such as ethnic and minority groups, and student's and women's movements, could not be ignored nor controlled by the methods of previous decades.[8] As Stephen Paul Miller suggests, the 1960s had succeeded in "discrediting official, government-sponsored reality." As a result, the assumptions upon which society was previously based had been far too compromised for society to feel comfortable with them again.[9] This served to reinforce the prevalence and independence of the aforementioned distinct social movements.

While individuals and social groups gained strength from the fragmentation of society, this fragmentation also contributed to a climate of self-doubt. While the events of the 1960s were generated by the belief in the possibility for change, the 1970s were characterized by a feeling that little was possible. As Miller argues, "America's view of itself was arrested, its sense of social progress upended."[10] America began to accept its own limitations; limitations reinforced by events such as the Vietnam War, Watergate, the Jonestown massacre, the hostage crisis in Iran, the fuel crisis, and the collapse of industrialism. The United States was no longer identified with progress and change but was increasingly uncertain about the value of the label, "Made in the USA."

In addition to social and political changes, this period also witnessed a massive transformation in Taylorized industrialism, developed in the early twentieth century and previously one of the most notable emblems of American modernization.[11] Based upon the reorganization of human labor to simulate mechanization, this system revolutionized the American work ethic in the 1920s and became a symbol of modernization both in the United States and abroad. Henry Ford's adoption and implementation of Taylor's methods in his automobile factories were incredibly influential and sparked huge debate about the positive and negative characteristics of modernity. After reaching a peak in the 1920s, however, Ford's productivity began to decline as it became increasingly difficult to improve upon the assembly line method. The system was far too regimented to reorganize and was still greatly dependent upon mechanized unskilled labor. While American industrialization achieved a second boom of activity in the 1950s due to the increasing demand around the world for American consumer products such as automobiles and household appliances, the financial crisis of the 1970s brought this boom period to an end. Competition with other postindustrial methods proved that Taylorized industrialism was becoming increasingly obsolete, and while other industries began to turn to more fully automated methods of production, the car industry could not and would not abandon its established methods.[12]

Even the Hollywood studios were affected. The old system, renowned in its heyday for a factory-style approach to film production, was gradually dismantled and replaced by a new system of production.[13] Once the studios were forced to abandon their vertically integrated monopoly over production, distribution, and exhibition they "gradually fired their contract personnel and phased out active production, and began leasing their facilities for independent projects, generally providing co-financing and distribution as well."[14] This transition between classical and postclassical American cinema production created anxiety for an industry in crisis about the potential for the fall of Hollywood, as expressed in regular articles in the *New York Times* throughout the late 1960s and early 1970s. In November 1969, Vincent Canby of the *New York Times* asked the question "Is Hollywood in Hot Water?" and in the months that followed, a series of unrelated articles attempted to answer that question.[15] In mid-November, concern was reported about financial problems at Paramount while in January 1970, Leonard Sloane reported that "M-G-M is Hopeful on Earnings." By 27 May 1970, however, Mel Gussow reported that "Movies Leaving Hollywood Behind: Studio System Passé—Film Forges Ahead."[16]

As these headlines suggest, this was a period of uncertainty whereby the studios were constantly reshuffling management, experimenting with the types of films being produced, and like American culture itself, the industry was becoming fragmented. As a result, independent filmmakers were increasingly free to experiment with established genres. The vampire film was one such genre that became the subject of generic reformulation linked to the social change of the period. So while America sought to reinvent itself in the face of a national identity crisis, the wealth of vampire films, television programs, and novels produced in the 1970s demonstrate a decided attempt to redefine and modernize the genre.

In 1954, American author Richard Matheson presented a dark vision of the future in his novel *I Am Legend*. A disease, mistakenly developed as the by-product of Cold War germ warfare, transforms everyone into vampires except for one man.[17] Set in suburban America in the 1970s, this vampire novel was quite prophetic in its vision. In the 1970s, the United States, as well as the world beyond its borders, was taken over by vampires repeatedly in literature, film, and television. In this period, there was a renewed and significant interest in *Dracula*. In 1972, Raymond Mc-Nally and Radu Florescu traced the origins of Stoker's novel to eastern European folklore, history, and the real-life fifteenth-century Romanian prince, Vlad the Impaler, in their publication *In Search of Dracula*. According to the authors, these facts contributed to a "revival of interest in the subject of Dracula and vampires" as well as developed the trend towards rethinking the vampire conventions traditionally associated with Dracula.[18] At the same time, there was an increase in the academic interest in Stoker's novel, such as Judith Weissman's "Women and Vampires: *Dracula* as a Victorian Novel"[19] and Phyllis A. Roth's "Suddenly Sexual Women in Bram Stoker's *Dracula*," both of which reconsider the novel in the light of the feminist movement.[20]

Hammer Studios continued its series of Dracula films with its two modern day interpretations: *Dracula A.D. 1972* (1972) and *The Satanic Rites of Dracula* (1973). There were three television adaptations of *Dracula*, starring Norman Welsch (Canada, 1973), Jack Palance (US, 1974), and Louis Jordan (UK, 1977) as the Count. The Jack Palance version, produced by Dan Curtis, demonstrates a specific debt to McNally and Florescu by directly linking Dracula with Vlad the Impaler. John Badham turned to the Balderston and Deane stage play of *Dracula*, which had recently been a major success on Broadway with Frank Langella in the title role. Langella reprised the role for Badham's film (1979). Finally, the decade's fascination with Dracula was parodied in the comic spoof, *Love at First Bite* (1979).

The interest in vampires extended beyond *Dracula*. Significant and influential vampire novels were written in the 1970s including such notable works as *The Dracula Tape*, *Salem's Lot*, and *Interview with the Vampire*.[21] Vampire films were produced across the globe. Hammer launched its lesbian vampire series with *The Vampire Lovers* (1970), which was followed by *Lust for a Vampire* (1970) and *Twins of Evil* (1971). Harry Kumel directed

Daughters of Darkness (1971), a Belgian, German, Italian, and French co-production, based upon Elizabeth Bathory, a sixteenth-century aristocrat who used to bathe in the blood of virgins in order to maintain her youthful appearance. Jean Rollin produced a series of art house vampire films in France such as *Requiem for a Vampire* (1971). Canada's David Cronenberg adapted the vampire genre to his own fascination with body horror in *Rabid* (1976). Werner Herzog produced a remake of Murnau's *Nosferatu* (1979) in Germany. In the United States, the vampire embodied marginal cultures in *Blacula* (1972) and *Scream Blacula Scream* (1973), two entries into the Blaxploitation movement, while Stephanie Rothman's *Velvet Vampire* (1971) featured a lesbian vampire. The years 1966–1971 produced the first American daytime soap opera, *Dark Shadows*, to feature not only a Gothic atmosphere but also a vampire antihero, and was followed by a number of vampire-related made-for-TV movies and pilots for television series including *The Night Stalker* (1971), *Salem's Lot* (1979), *Vampire* (1979), and *I, Desire* (1982).

In these films, novels, and television programs, the horror genre began to turn inward, both in the choices of setting and the sources of horror. The mythic European villages and cities of Hollywood Gothic were gradually replaced by familiar American settings and locations, both urban and suburban. The year 1968 has been credited with marking the beginning of modern horror with the relocation of the genre to contemporary America, specifically in George Romero's *Night of the Living Dead* and Roman Polanski's *Rosemary's Baby*.[22] The vampires that emerged into this new world discovered that the world did not project its horrors beyond its borders but rather turned to the domestic space to find its monsters. The genre also began focusing upon the breakdown of the human mind rather than upon the supernatural; in this period, the monster was often all too human.[23] The horrific no longer infiltrates from an anonymous outside source, easily divorced from the real world. The truly monstrous exists within the interior landscapes of humanity and America itself.

It was because of this transition, Robin Wood argued, that the horror genre became the most important of the American genres in the 1970s, as it was best able to explore radical alternatives to contemporary society and express the "cultural crisis and disintegration" that defined the decade.[24] According to Wood, the monstrous in the horror genre is a product of sexual, political, and/or social repression. In the classic period of the genre, the monstrous is released in order to satisfy the fantasy of destroying repressive and oppressive forces before safely killing the monster and restoring normality. In the 1970s, a decade of intense change in American history—marked by Vietnam, Watergate, the Kent State massacre, and the assassinations of Martin Luther King Jr., Malcolm X, and both John and Robert Kennedy—normality could no longer be restored: normality itself was deemed monstrous.[25] Nina Auerbach has suggested that "perhaps, in twentieth-century America, monsters are shadows, not symbols, of crises; or perhaps we live in a continuing crisis—fanned by rabid journalism and seemingly incessant change—that sometimes takes the shape of vampires."[26] Therefore, the redefinition of the vampire in horror films of the 1970s is a part of this transformation of the horror genre.

When Dan Curtis decided to introduce the character of Barnabus Collins to his daytime soap opera *Dark Shadows* he was admittedly merely trying to maintain the ratings that he had gained by introducing a taste of the supernatural to what was originally a rather mainstream soap opera with a Gothic atmosphere.

> Unless you count the ratings, there was nothing particularly horrific about the old *Dark Shadows* during its first year. The series was heading nowhere except for cancellation. Executive producer Curtis had sold ABC on his idea for a gothic soap opera, but viewers weren't flocking to Collinsport, Maine . . . "So I [Dan Curtis] put a ghost on, and when the ghost appeared, the ratings jumped. And that's when I started experimenting . . . Barnabus was brought in because I wanted to see exactly how much I could get away with, never intending that he would be anything more than a vampire that I could drive a stake into," Curtis recalled. "I wanted to see how far I could go on the show into the supernatural, and I figured there was nothing more bizarre than a vampire."[27]

The popularity of a nineteenth-century vampire emerging into twentieth-century America was not expected by the show's producers and that, along with the presentation of Collins as a suffering, reluctant vampire, was clearly the main reason the show evaded cancellation and became a cult classic.[28] What therefore began as a trick to boost the ratings of a dying TV soap opera was the beginning of quite a significant change for the vampire film, although it did not push the boundaries of the genre too far. The program writers kept their vampire hero confined in timeless old manors of New England with occasional visits, through flashback, to a Victorian past. Jonathan Frid, the star of *Dark Shadows*, described the show as "Brigadoonish and charmingly naive. Collinsport was in Maine, but that was as close as you ever got to a specific geography. Once in a while somebody would mention Boston, but that is about it."[29] This approach allowed the program to introduce new elements to the genre without overturning the conventions completely. But the show's success demonstrated that the manipulation of genre conventions could capture audience's interest in an overfamiliar genre.

Many films of the period made similar attempts to revitalize the genre through slight variations to its conventions. Some films, like *Love at First Bite*, parody the vampire genre by playing on the humor of having an old-world vampire lost in the modern world, or, like *Count Yorga, Vampire* (1970), confine the vampire in a church or manor house so that he never makes contact with the modern world, except through a few well-chosen victims. Hammer Studios' foray into the modern world barely allowed Count Dracula to escape the nineteenth century. In *Dracula A.D. 1972*, Dracula never escapes the ruined Victorian church in which the young hippies enact the black mass that resurrects him. In *The Satanic Rites of Dracula*, a much bolder attempt to modernize the Dracula legend, Dracula returns as a corporate executive, a move that positions the vampire as a metaphor for global commodity culture and prefigures other contemporary corporate vampires discussed in Chapter 12 such as in *Ultraviolet* (1998), *Kindred: The Embraced* (1996), the *Blade* trilogy (1998/2002/2004), and *Underworld* (2003). Despite this innovation, however, Dracula is barely seen in the film and never really escapes his past incarnation. His offices are built upon the site of the church where he died in the last film, and he seems trapped in a timeless loop of resurrection and destruction that he himself tries to end through his apocalyptic plans to destroy humanity. Despite the corporate setting of this film, he is eventually revealed to be the same monstrous vampire, directly contrasted with the forces of modernity that seek to thwart his scheme.

These films and television programs preserve a traditional generic structure by containing the supernatural within seemingly timeless Gothic boundaries, divorced from the real world.[30] A new vampire narrative began to emerge in the 1970s, however, that suggested a transitional flux between the past and present, and a release from confined timeless settings into the boundless expanse of the urban landscape. These films increasingly integrated the vampire within recognizable locations and reworked the vampire conventions or narrative through the very timely cultural contexts of the period.

William Crain's *Blacula* tells the story of an African prince turned into a vampire by Dracula, imprisoned in his coffin for centuries, and relocated to contemporary Los Angeles when two interior decorators purchase the contents of Dracula's castle. This backstory reinterprets the vampire myth through the discourses of racial oppression and slavery, relevant to the 1970s civil rights movement, as the prince is effectively enslaved by Count Dracula through his transformation into a vampire.[31] Furthermore, much of the film is shot on location in Los Angeles, specifi-cally in the Watts community, which serves to place the vampire in the context of civil rights and racial violence. In 1965, the city was engulfed in race riots that began in Watts with an altercation between the police and a twenty-one-year-old African-American and his family, who had been stopped for a traffic violation. While this event was the spark, a legacy of racism, police brutality, unemployment, poverty, and neglect was the cause of the ensuing violence.[32] As a result, the memory of the Watts race riots circulates throughout the film through references to police corrup-tion, institutional racism, and the eventual invasion of Watts by the white police force in search of the black vampire. Leerom Medovi suggests that as the black vampire runs amok within the black community, the film embodies both the perception of the riots as an outburst of rage against "a history of white oppression" and as further violent victimization of "the victims of that history" as Blacula's own enslavement by Dracula is sub-sequently imposed upon the citizens of Watts.[33] While the film is critical of the self-destructiveness of this violence within the black community, it also sides with Blacula as he defends himself from the white Los Angeles police officers. The modern vampire in this film comes to embody a very specific modern reality.

Similarly, Bob Clark's *Deathdream* (1974) places the vampire genre within the context of the Vietnam War. This film begins in Vietnam as an American soldier, Andy Brooks, is killed in battle. As the image of his face is held in freeze-frame over the film's credit sequence, the sounds of the prayers of his overbearing mother are heard, insisting that he cannot die. As a result, Andy's death is frozen in time as he returns to his family and hometown, but now as a vampire who must drink blood to keep his body from decomposing. Locating the cause of his vampirism both within the family and the war, this film quite overtly uses the vampire as a metaphor for the returning soldier, traumatized and changed by the events he has experienced, and unable to live up to family and social expectations. No longer the innocent teenage boy who left home to defend his country, he literally returns as a monster, dispassionate and detached from the living, revealed to be a killer capable of horrific atrocities. This metaphor continues even in Andy's method of drinking blood; he injects himself with the blood of his murder victims as if he were a drug addict. In *Deathdream*, an American home, a syringe, and a military uniform replace the castles, fangs, and costumes of traditional vampire films.

On television, Dan Curtis' follow-up to *Dark Shadows*, *The Night Stalker* (1971), escapes the sanctity of a Gothic setting by releasing the vampire into the modern urban setting of Las Vegas and transforming the vampire narrative through its representation of the vampire hunter.[34] In the film, Las Vegas is being tormented by a series of mysterious murders. Reporter Carl Kolchak follows the trail of a madman who he comes to realize is a true, mythic vampire. While he tries to convince the authorities that the killer they have on their hands is really a vampire, they maintain their bureaucratic line and ignore his advice. Even when they agree to follow Kolchak's suggestion to arm the police with crosses and wooden stakes, they betray him by threatening arrest after he murders the vampire, Skorzeny. The authorities' resistance to Kolchak seems to grow from the fact that he is as much an anachronism in 1970s America as Skorzeny. Steven Connor argues that part of the modern experience is the need to unify and synchronize different temporalities, which means that there is a resistance to anything that suggests temporal disjunctions or anachronisms.[35] The idea that modernization is a linear progression conceals the fact that past, present, and future coexist within modern life. The representation of Kolchak and, by association, Skorzeny, in *The Night Stalker* captures this coexistence, as they both seem to embody the past and the present simultaneously and both seem at home and out of place in the modern city. This simultaneity is achieved largely by mixing the vampire narrative with conventions of the detective and newspaperman archetypes.

Kolchak's entire demeanor is reminiscent of a hard-boiled Hollywood detective or newspaperman, both of whom, like the professionals in *Dracula*, represent the modern professional, working within the circulatory system of the urban environment. As the detective, Kolchak is allowed to investigate alongside the police and has a plethora of informants who work within the system. However, he, like the hard-boiled detective, also exists on the margins of society and throughout the course of his investigation he regularly comes into

> conflict with representatives of the official machinery, though he may also have friends who are police officers. His position on the edge of the law is very important, because one of the central themes of the hard-boiled myth is the ambiguity between institutionalized law enforcement and true justice. The story shows us that the police and the courts are incapable of effectively protecting the innocent and bringing the guilty

to appropriate justice. Only the individual of integrity who exists on the margins of society can solve the crime and bring about true justice.[36]

Similarly, as a reporter, Kolchak seeks to expose the corruption of the authorities and reveal the truth.

Furthermore, like the detective and the newspaperman, Kolchak seems at home in the city, which is highlighted in the sequences that focus upon his investigation. He is incredibly proficient in securing information through informants or listening to the police radio in his car, enabling him to reach the scene of the crime directly on the heels of the police. He constructs his own routes through the city by creating short cuts and detours rather than passively following the flow of traffic. When he hears over his police radio that Skorzeny has been spotted, he instinctively turns his car around and speeds to the location of the sighting, cutting across the grain of the traffic. The fluidity of his motion and the speed with which the movement is executed suggests an instinctual familiarity with the landscape, the roads, and his own control over the city space. In his car, Kolchak is constantly framed against a backdrop of bright lights and urban imagery as he maneuvers his way across the city by taking both established routes and personal short cuts. This attitude informs his approach to the investigation following both official and unofficial lines of inquiry. The bureaucrats, however, attempt to impede his movement by imposing channels through which he must move. This is conveyed through his encounters with the authorities that directly follow the investigation sequences that demonstrate Kolchak's command of the urban environment. This juxtaposition reveals that Kolchak's embodiment of the professional newspaperman is now out of step with the modern bureaucratic and political methods of investigation. His personality, appearance, and methods connote an air of nostalgia rather than modernity. The reporter is no longer a hard-hitting investigator but an anachronistic dinosaur from an industrial era, trapped within a city designed as a center for consumption rather than production. Kolchak, in his crumpled suit and with his old typewriter seems out of place surrounded by neon signs, glamorous settings, and showgirls.

Kolchak is aware of his increasing obsolescence as he describes himself as growing extinct in his own lifetime and thinks he should light a candle in memory of Ben Hecht, newspaper reporter, playwright, and Hollywood screenwriter. Hecht had already memorialized himself and his breed by writing in 1959 that even in the early days of Hollywood the writer was a dying breed, transformed from "the fanciest scribblers of the world" into a "moody, pallid, stuttering, droopy lot of ineffectual human beings" by incompetent film producers with "little but fog" in their heads.[37] By 1971, Kolchak is similarly downtrodden by the authorities who, like Hecht's producers, use Kolchak as their errand boy to destroy the vampire and then, in the fashion of the Hollywood producer, rewrite his story to suit their taste. He is a threat to the order that they want to maintain because he undermines their perception of the present by reinfusing the present with the sensibilities of the past.

In this manner, Kolchak is the mirror image of Skorzeny who equally embodies the past and the present. Skorzeny is by some standards quite a conventional vampire. He has an Eastern European heritage, supernatural strength, drinks blood through his fangs, and can be destroyed with a stake through the heart. He however also appears as a modern serial killer, stalking the city at night, attacking young women on the street, and leaving them for dead without the Gothic romance of *Dracula*. His victims do not turn into vampires but simply die. He also adapts in order to benefit from modern conveniences and to avoid capture. Realizing that a string of bodies will lead the police to his door, he steals blood from a hospital and transfuses it into a woman he has abducted in order to maintain a regular blood supply. Furthermore, he shares Kolchak's confidence in navigating the complexities of the city. While he may for the most part be, like Dracula, an invisible presence in the film, Kolchak's movements mirror the vampire's as he follows the trail of crimes, demonstrating that it is the vampire who paves the way through the city.

The connection between Kolchak and the vampire is reinforced in a sequence where there is a transition in point of view from Kolchak to Skorzeny. When the FBI offer to show Kolchak the face of the killer, the film cuts to a close up of an artist's sketch, presumably from Kolchak's point of view. The image is subsequently revealed to be on the cover of a newspaper purchased by Skorzeny. The shot of the sketch offers a transition in subjectivity between Kolchak and the vampire, demonstrating that in many ways they are interchangeable. Their similarities, however, do not end there. One of the reasons that Kolchak is in Las Vegas is because he has been run out of New York, Chicago, and Boston due to his journalistic style and method of alienating newspaper editors and government officials. Similarly, Skorzeny leaves a trail of cities, urban violence, and crime in his wake, moving from London during the Blitz, the German aerial attacks on Britain during World War II, to the cities along the Canadian American border before finally arriving in Las Vegas. They both demonstrate a modern sensibility by disembedding themselves from tradition and community, allowing free movement from urban center to urban center. It is also their alienation from the modern world, however, that forces them to keep moving and avoiding entrapment by the authorities. They both exist in the heart of the city but on the periphery of society, anachronisms that cannot be acknowledged by the evolving modern world.

Together Kolchak and Skorzeny embody the simultaneous existence of the past and the present and demonstrate how the vampire narrative has adapted to signal this period of transition between what was once modern and its new evolving definition. *The Night Stalker* suggests, in its representation of vampire and vampire hunter, that the vampire narrative is struggling to escape ghettoization in the past and is evolving yet again into a narrative focused upon the changing nature of modernity. From within this whirlwind of social, political, cultural, technological, and economic change begins to emerge a modern vampire, like Dracula in Stoker's novel, not only drawn to the whirl and rush of modernity in transition but also a product of it. While this is suggested by the narrative relationship between vampire and vampire hunter in *The Night Stalker*, it is absolutely central to the representation of the vampire in George Romero's vampire film, *Martin*, which will be the subject of discussion in the next chapter. While all of the vampire films of the 1970s demonstrate a degree of revision and reinvention of the vampire mythology to suit modern tastes and modern times, *Martin* offers a completely new image of the vampire capturing the changing perception of the self and the transition from industrialism and postindustrialism that defined 1970s America.

CHAPTER FIVE

George Romero's *Martin:*
An American Vampire

*If such a character, a vampire, existed from the beginning of time, he'd
really have a tough time today because he'd have to get a new ID every
twenty years or so. I mean, a vampire today would really have some
sweats.*

GEORGE ROMERO ON *MARTIN* [1]

While most of the vampire films and television programs of the 1970s
play with generic conventions, George Romero's *Martin* takes a more
overt revisionist approach to the genre. One of the film's chief methods of
doing this is to present the vampire as American. While *The Night Stalker*
demonstrates how, in the evolution of the modern world, the past is fundamentally embedded in the present, the vampire is still an external force
infiltrating, by accident or design, the modern Western world. Furthermore, films such as *Count Yorga, Vampire* and *Blacula* also feature American vampires, but they were vampirized by European and African vampires who invaded American cities. Romero's vampire in *Martin* is distinct
because, like Andy in *Deathdream*, it is an American teenager. As a result,
America is not vampirized, but rather the vampire is Americanized.

The film's revisionist approach to the vampire is conveyed in its trailer,
which advertises the film as "Another Kind of Terror," and features the
title character talking to the camera, explaining that he is a vampire but
not like the ones from old movies. Martin describes how careful he must
be, how he struggles against superstitions, and how he suffers from an illness that requires him to drink blood. His statements are juxtaposed over
a montage of clips of Martin meticulously planning, instigating, and concealing each murder in grainy, faded images that undermine generic expectations of studio-produced Gothic horror films. According to Romero,
he and his cinematographer Mike Gornick consciously manipulated the

film stock in order to create a gritty aesthetic. "[Gornick] used reversal stock instead of negatives, so he was able to get saturation and wash it down. We wanted it to be seedier and there's no great difference between some of the color sequences . . . and the black-and-white. In fact, we had to push the black and white sequences further to make them grainier and grittier than the color ones."[2] The film's visual style is just one of the ways in which *Martin* distinguishes itself from classic vampire films. A further generic difference is that unlike traditional vampires, Martin does not have fangs but uses hypodermic needles to sedate his victims and slits their wrists with a razor blade, drinking the blood as it spurts out from the vein.

The original poster design for the film draws upon this generic innovation by featuring an image of a blood soaked razor blade with vampire fangs protruding from either end. Inscribed on the top of the blade are the words "Made In USA." These two campaigns, the poster and the trailer, seem to emphasize that Martin *is another kind of terror*, not only because of his unique methods and his realistic representation, but precisely because he was *Made in USA*. Although there is a suggestion that he has come to the United States from Europe to live with his cousin Tata Cuda, a traditional vampire hunter whose aim is to either save Martin's soul or destroy him, Martin has actually only traveled from Indianapolis to come to Pittsburgh and actually appears more American than his cousin. Unlike Cuda—whose accent, style of dress, and demeanor suggest that he comes from Europe, despite the claims that he has been in the town a long time—Martin is identified, from his accent to his T-shirts, combat trousers, and sneakers, as an American youth of the 1970s. (Figure 5.1)

Martin's youth is a key signifier in his embodiment of the modern and is emphasized by the oppositional relationship he holds with his elders in the town. When he arrives, the patrons of Cuda's store comment that they can't remember when a young man moved into Braddock. One of the customers vocalizes her disapproval of his living in the same house with Cuda's granddaughter Christina, which suggests a distrust of the young despite Cuda's assurances that "his family know how to behave." Later, Martin is lambasted by the same woman for being lazy, as she claims, "*We* work in this town." The "we" in her statement can only refer to the older generation as all images of the young in the film do not show them working. In fact Christina's boyfriend Arthur is constantly complaining, to Cuda's disapproval, that there is no work in the town. Young people are shown hanging out on the street outside Cuda's house, riding motorcycles in gangs, selling drugs, and harassing women outside of grocery stores. The presence of these images, however, does not neces-

Figure 5.1. Vampire as 1970s teenager in *Martin*.

sarily support the woman's view of the laziness of the young but rather demonstrates the alienation of the two generations and their response to the decline of industry in the town.

Martin and Cuda's relationship as vampire and vampire hunter has therefore been reinterpreted to signify this opposition between young and old, as well as new- and old-world. Cuda believes in the old superstitions and religious fervor while Martin claims that "there is no magic," demonstrating the agnostic cynicism of contemporary youth and their desire to tear down the structures that confine them. Further, Martin's cousin Christina similarly dismisses Cuda's superstitions, and the young community priest (portrayed by George Romero) does not share the older generation's belief in the supernatural history of Catholicism. He barely contains his laughter and mocks an older priest's criticism of the accuracy of the religious rites performed in the film *The Exorcist* (1973). Reinterpreting the vampire and vampire-hunter relationship as an expression of the tension between generations positions youth itself as the primary threat to tradition and therefore the object of horror. As Robin Wood points out, "Since *Rosemary's Baby*, children have figured prominently in horror films as the monster or its medium," and the increasing association between horror and the family is reflected in the genre's "steady geographical progress toward America."[3]

Martin is not the first vampire narrative to draw upon the horror of children. The concept of vampire children is suggested in Stoker's *Dracula* through Lucy's attacks on young children, although this is never fully explored (177–178). Similarly, Richard Matheson's *I Am Legend* implies the existence of vampire children, as the entire population has been infected by a blood disease that transforms its victims into vampires, including the protagonist's daughter.[4] Hammer Studios' *Dracula A.D. 1972* suggests that the evil that regenerates Dracula emanates from the rebellious youth who terrorize their seniors and whose unrestrained desire for sensual, libidinal experiences causes them to recklessly bring Dracula back to life. It was George Romero's *Night of the Living Dead* (1968), an unofficial adaptation of Matheson's book, that fully exploited the horror of an undead child when a little girl who was attacked by zombies is transformed into one and subsequently murders and consumes her parents.[5] Stephen King's novel and the subsequent television miniseries, *Salem's Lot,* take the next logical step in this tradition of vampire children; the young Glick boys are transformed into vampires and instill terror in the adults they feed upon. This is demonstrated by the character Matt Burke's description of the unearthly sounds coming from the guest room of his house:

> He could not have risen even if the brass knobs on his own door had begun to turn. He was paralysed with fear and wished crazily that he had never gone out to Dell's that night. *I am afraid.* And in the awful heavy silence of the house, as he sat impotently on his bed with his face in his hands, he heard the high, sweet, evil laugh of a child—and then the sucking sounds.[6]

As Gregory A. Waller points out, "The evil laughter of the undead schoolchildren in *Salem's Lot* has its echo in *The Omen* (1976) and the many other 'demon-child' stories, and also the opening sequence of *Halloween* (1978). In these stories children do indeed become objects of extreme 'fear and loathing,' murderous creatures who cannot be reasoned with or disciplined, only destroyed."[7]

The scene in which Martin follows Cuda into the playground to frighten him suggests a fear of the young and the threat that is seemingly inherent to adults in their rebellion. In this sequence, Martin attempts to terrorize Cuda by appearing in full Dracula costume, with cape, makeup, and plastic fangs. As Cuda looks around the space, cane in hand to protect

Figure 5.2. "It's only a costume" in *Martin.*

himself, the sudden movement of a playground swing startles him. The film cuts to a close-up of Martin exposing vampire fangs and bloodless face. (Figure 5.2) This is followed by a long shot as he stands up straight and spreads his cape like great bat wings, invoking a classic filmic vampire image. The next shot is of Martin spinning around Cuda, forcing him into a corner. The shot ends in a high angle close-up with Cuda cowering on the ground, clasping his rosary in fear of Martin. Martin's movement through the frame serves to invert the dominance of each character. Cuda, usually the strong patriarch, is forced by Martin to take on an emotionally and graphically subservient role. This is reinforced by Martin's riotous laughter at Cuda's expense. Still pictured in a high-angle close-up, Cuda looks up at Martin and states "Devil . . . you are the devil." His attempt to reassert his control by hitting Martin with his cane as Martin turns away is thwarted; Martin swiftly turns and grasps Cuda's cane as he begins to swing again. Martin slowly lowers the cane, spits out his fangs stating, "It's just a costume . . . It's only a costume," and then wipes the makeup off his face before exiting the scene. In this sequence it is not Martin's vampirism that is threatening but his youthful aggression toward the older generation and his defiance of Cuda's will. The use of low-key lighting, glowing fog, and eerie music, invokes an atmosphere of Gothic horror that is subsequently undercut by Martin's mocking laughter. This scene indicates the implied threat in the young's lack of respect for authority and their perceived ability to overpower the older generation through fear and intimidation, as well as the self-conscious undermining of the generic conventions of vampire films. This act of physical intimidation serves both to terrorize Cuda and to tear down the foundations of his beliefs. In this film, however, the danger that youth represents is portrayed as a product of the postindustrial world that surrounds them. Youth have nothing to do but loiter, complain, and harass their elders because they have been raised in a dying industrial landscape with no prospects. Even Martin cannot escape the heritage imposed upon him by Cuda's superstitions about vampirism, as his memories seem to be informed by a history of vampire films rather than the reality within which he lives. Like the other youths in the film, Martin is trapped in a seemingly hopeless world created by the adults who surround him.

Martin's character, torn between his secular beliefs and the superstitions that are imposed upon him, becomes increasingly fractured as the film continues. Stephen Paul Miller argues that the 1970s, a period scarred by scandal and conspiracy in America, were marked by a transition from a culture of surveillance into a culture of self-surveillance, a characteristic of the nation's growing identity crisis.[8] Martin captures this transition in his own identity crisis. It is a common characteristic of the vampire to stalk his or her victims, as demonstrated by the sequence in Stoker's novel wherein Mina and Jonathan witness Dracula following the young woman in Piccadilly Circus, his eyes fixed upon her every move. In this sequence, Stoker evokes a broader nineteenth-century understanding of the power of the gaze. In his discussion of superstitions about the evil eye and their relationship to George Du Maurier's *Trilby*, Daniel Pick points out that fear of the evil eye was still prevalent in the nineteenth century. The eyes were believed to have a physical effect upon the observed, possessing the power to paralyze, damage, or bring about bad luck. This belief became increasingly represented in literature through narratives of trances and hypnosis.[9] While Pick discusses the "penetrative effect of a hostile gaze"[10] as evoked through Du Maurier's master villain Svengali, this gaze is equally present within Stoker's *Dracula* and is visually presented in the filmic vampire genre. The close-up upon the face or eyes of vampires as they stare at their victims has become a staple convention of most vampire films, used to emphasize both their power over their victims and their desire for blood. Count Orlok in *Nosferatu* regularly watches Ellen from his house and awaits her invitation into her room. In Browning's *Dracula*, Bela Lugosi's hypnotic stare is presented through a special fill light that highlights his eyes throughout the film. When Renfield cuts his hand on a staple, the film cuts from a close-up of the blood on his finger to a medium shot of Dracula, his eyes fixed on Renfield as he slowly approaches. Gloria Holden in *Dracula's Daughter* demonstrates a particularly hypnotic gaze as she locks eyes with a young girl who has agreed to model for her, putting the girl into a trance. The Hammer Studios' Dracula films regularly feature an extreme close-up of Christopher Lee's bloodshot eyes as he is overcome by blood lust and rage, while the only glimpse of the vampire prior to his death in *The Night Stalker* is an extreme close-up of his eyes, highlighted by the same spotlight as Lugosi, as he selects his next victim. A similar blood lust is conveyed through his gaze.

While these sequences emphasize the importance of the gaze in vampire films, Romero's *Martin* takes the notion of watching beyond the expression of desire to a systematic mode of surveillance. In the trailer to the film, Martin tells us that he does not have a lot of women but that he does "watch them. I watch them a lot. All the time. I have to, to be sure that nothing goes wrong." What sounds at first like an admission toward voyeurism and desire, ends as a declaration for the need for surveillance as a means of protection. The film introduces Martin watching his victim in a similar way to the aforementioned films. He boards the train and turns to watch a woman talking to the conductor. He overhears her say that she will be continuing on to New York, and a cut to a close-up of a cabin number indicates that Martin has made note of the location of her room. In that instant Martin has made his choice and planned his attack. As the film progresses, however, it becomes clear that Martin does more than stalk and select his victims, since the need for caution and care in the modern world has caused him to survey every situation. In the quotation that opens this chapter, Romero explains that one of the motivations for making *Martin* was to explore the problems facing a vampire in the modern world; a vampire in the 1970s must work hard to conceal his existence from modern surveillance and he does it by becoming the surveyor.

John Amplas' understated performance emphasizes the automated quality of his surveillance, as his gaze demonstrates none of the bloodlust of his vampire predecessors. His stare is neutral and everything around him is given equal attention. When Martin first meets Cuda, Christina, and Mrs. Santini, he refuses to speak to them, but stands silently and stares at them and their surroundings, listening to their every word and absorbing every detail like a human surveillance camera. When Martin goes to

Pittsburgh on his own, he stares out of the window of the train. The film then cuts to a montage sequence of him walking through the red light district at night, looking in all of the windows and flipping through the books in the sex shops. These shots are directly followed by an image of a woman exiting a grocery store while being harassed by a group of young men. Martin stands in the background of the image observing the situation. This transition segues into a series of shots of Martin following and watching this woman. He watches her from the sidewalk, from the woods that surround her house, and even climbs up on the roof and watches her and her husband through their bedroom skylight. The structure of this montage sequence clearly juxtaposes the images of Martin casually observing the world around him with those of him stalking his next victim, suggesting that there is no difference. He watches and absorbs everything: this defines his vampirism. Even his casual observation of the members of the community who come to the store and to whom he delivers meat, is revealed to have ominous overtones when Martin informs a radio talk show host that he has been deliberately watching them, considering their potential as victims.

Martin's surveillance turns to self-surveillance when, despite his meticulous preparation, he unexpectedly finds the Pittsburgh housewife, who is to be his next victim, with a lover. This failing clearly shakes his confidence and once he has subdued both the man and the woman, he changes his plan. He tells the woman, as she begins to succumb to the sedative he has given her, that he doesn't have to hurt her anymore "because of him," the lover. He then drags the lover out into the woods, punctures his throat with a branch from a tree and drinks his blood, almost failing to remember to remove his shirt to avoid covering it in blood. This unexpected failure in Martin's research threatens his belief in his methods and creates a need to reassess himself.

As he runs from the scene of this crime, Martin's voice-over, broadcast on a radio talk show, is introduced for the first time. He confesses that "for a long time I didn't care if they'd kill me. People spend their lives worrying about dying. For a long time I wished I would die. I wished somebody would kill me. It's been a long time for me. A long time full of crazy people." As his voice-over begins, the film cuts to black-and-white images of Martin running from the scene of a similar murder, washing the blood off his face with the water from a well while being pursued by angry villagers. This sequence is intercut with color footage of him showering and meticulously concealing any evidence of his presence in the house of his most recent victims. The juxtaposition of these two sequences and his voice-over, begins to suggest that Martin is starting to sift through and compare past experiences, attempting to understand and explain how and why he lives the way he does. This sequence indicates that Martin is undergoing a transition from surveillance to self-surveillance that in turn leads to greater introspection.

This self-surveillance, however, leads to greater insecurity and self-questioning. Richard Lippe has suggested that because Martin separates sex from blood drinking—for example, when he caresses the nude body of the unconscious Pittsburgh housewife without killing her, as well as when he initiates a sexual relationship with Mrs. Santini—he loses the taste for blood.[11] Robin Wood has further suggested that Martin's subsequent hesitation to pick a victim is an indication of Romero's own hesitation to make a horror film in the first place. Wood argues that Martin is not really a vampire but simply a victim of the family superstitions imposed upon him by Cuda and the other elders in the family, suggesting that Martin's condition is an illness that can best be cured by the love of a good woman. "The later stages of the narrative actually suggest that, by learning to have sexual intercourse instead of sucking blood, Martin can be 'saved' for normality."[12] The sudden introduction of Martin's voice-over confessions and his initiation into sex without blood drinking, however, suggest that his subsequent indecision is a result of his self-exploration. He complains that he continues to survey his surroundings but cannot choose a victim. His relationship with Mrs. Santini does not cure Martin of his bloodlust but fragments his desires; his sexual desires are satisfied but his thirst for blood remains unquenched and this paralyzes him. He begins to question his motives and his relationships with Mrs. Santini and his cousin Christina, both of whom are undergoing their own self-exploration and use Martin as a channel for their unhappiness. Mrs. Santini engages in a sexual relationship to escape her unhappy marriage, while Christina uses Martin as a reason to rebel against Tata Cuda and the family heritage. Martin wants blood, but can no longer decide upon what to base his decision.

It is his self-surveillance that generically allows the film to shed any remaining vampire mythology. He constantly reiterates to Cuda, Christina, and his radio listeners that there is no magic, that the vampire mythology is not true. For Wood, the reduction of Martin's vampirism to "a cloak, makeup, and imitation fangs" empties the mythology of its potency, leaving empty fantasies "with no positive connotations."[13] The reduction of Martin to a fragmented, paralyzed figure questioning his very being and seeking to find definition for himself, however, embodies the paralysis and identity crisis that characterized America in the 1970s. Vampirism itself was undergoing an identity crisis.

One of the results of the fragmentation of Martin's identity is the suggestion of a coexistence of the past with the present. Throughout the film, scenes of Martin's activities are intercut with images of what appear to be his memories of the past, including Martin pursuing a potential victim through an old manor house and being hunted through cobbled streets by angry villagers. The images are shot in black-and-white, and the location, mise-en-scène, and the costumes suggest that it is set in the past, possibly in an old European village. However, the film features an additional flashback that undermines this interpretation. At the beginning of the film as Martin is on a train from Indianapolis to Pittsburgh, the film cuts to a black-and-white image of Martin entering a cabin to be met by a woman in a long flowing nightgown who welcomes his entrance. The image suggests a cinematic relationship with previous vampire films such as *Horror of Dracula* (1958) when Lucy opens her bedroom window and lays on the bed waiting for Dracula's arrival. The black-and-white fantasy scene in *Martin* is contrasted with the actual event, presented in a less romantic style. The room is empty when he enters and, as he scans around in disbelief, the sound of a flushing toilet is heard, and the door to the bathroom opens to reveal a woman in a green terry cloth bathrobe, hair pinned up, with a mud-pack on her face, blowing her nose. These two sequences suggest that, rather than being Martin's memories, these black-and-white images are "remembrances from fictional films Martin has seen into which he now projects himself," linking Martin to a history of vampire films rather than to a personal history.[14]

The manner in which these sequences are structured and inserted within the film, however, defies the classical method of continuity editing for inserting fantasies and flashbacks. The editing structure suggests a sense of simultaneous experience across different times and spaces. Where the first flashback on the train suggests a difference between fantasy and reality, the later sequences suggest a type of fragmentation, allowing Martin to be in two places at the same time. When Martin arrives in Braddock and Cuda takes him to the house, Cuda turns to Martin and calls him "Nosferatu." The film cuts to a black-and-white image of Martin turning, seemingly in response to the accusation. The film then cuts to a medium shot of a priest performing an exorcism. The use of eye-line matches in this sequence suggests a continuity of time and space that defies the reality of the situation. Similarly, the sequence where Cuda and Father Zulemas enter the living room to perform an exorcism is intercut with black-and-white footage of a similar exorcism. Again the sequences are intercut to suggest continuity of time and space, and furthermore the sound of both the black-and-white and color footage is overlapped to suggest a simultaneous experience. For Martin, the past and present seem to coexist.

The manipulation of iconography of nineteenth-century modernity in *Martin* further suggests an overlap of past and present in the transition between the modernity of the past with a modernity of the present. This transition was suggested in *The Night Stalker* as professional reporter Kolchak uses twentieth-century variations of the technology used by Mina in *Dracula* to track and keep record of the vampire and vampire hunters' movements. In Kolchak's case, however, these technologies do not transform him into a modern organizational machine as they do Mina, but, like his rumpled suit and straw hat, they are used to identify him with the past. As a result, they do not effectively assist his mission for they are technologically outmoded and obsolete. His photos are confiscated or ignored, his stories go unpublished, and his tapes are played only for himself. Andrew and Gina Macdonald have argued that Kolchak, the city reporter, is portrayed as an aging dinosaur in a modern city,[15] while Stuart M. Kamisky suggests that Kolchak's tools are key signifiers for his alienation from the modern governmental system for, like him, they are products of an earlier period.[16]

The Night Stalker ends with Kolchak's recorded voice explaining that no other evidence exists to support his account as all the evidence has been destroyed, and the witnesses are either silent, dead, or have been run out of town. The last shot of the film, a close-up of Kolchak's tape recorder and the typewritten text of the story, recalls Jonathan's final words in *Dracula*: "There is hardly one authentic document! Nothing but a mass of type-writing" (378). In this case, however, the mass of typewriting does not signify the transformation of the vampire narrative into a textual embodiment of modernity, but rather marks his story as an obsolete form that cannot be heard in the modern world.

In *Martin*, the title character's embodiment of the transitional icons of the past and present is manifested in the manner in which he has come to signify the evolutionary flux between what once was modern and what is now modern. Like Dracula, Martin is associated with nineteenth-century signifiers of modernity such as technology, the railroad, and the urban landscape, but the manner in which he interacts with these things suggest the transitory nature of modernity. Martin is visually and narratively associated with the railroad. The film begins as Martin boards a train to

Pittsburgh and the film's title appears on screen over an image of a train at night, moving slowly towards the camera as it blows its whistle. Furthermore, the train becomes an integral element of Martin's hunting techniques and he is often filmed walking through Braddock by the railroad tracks and traveling into Pittsburgh by train. The railroad is significant in this film because of its place in American history. It was an intrinsic element of the civilizing and modernizing of the American frontier and the creation of the American nation. By the 1960s, however, the situation had quite reversed itself as decaying passenger coaches were not able to compete with the "airlines' sleek and shiny new jets" nor the fluid motion of the modern highway.[17]

Martin's use of the train as a part of his hunting technique suggests both an affinity with the Americanness it represents, and the transformation of the railroad from an image of modernization into an image of death and decay. The train whistle over the opening credits is a lonely and alienated sound, while the railroad stations are virtually deserted, populated only by the homeless. That the railroad is no longer the central symbol of urban circulation is demonstrated by a number of shots of Martin or Cuda statically waiting for a train with a parade of cars speeding by in the background. (Figure 5.3) The motion circulates around but not within Braddock. While Martin utilizes the train to travel from Braddock to Pittsburgh's city center, this movement suggests a circular motion that leads nowhere, while the highway and the automobile offer freedom and escape. When Martin's cousin Christina and her boyfriend Arthur leave Braddock, they do so in Arthur's car and Christina admits that she is only going with Arthur because he is her way to escape the insular circle that seems to encase Martin, Tata Cuda, and the others within Braddock.

Martin is linked to other modern technologies such as the telephone and the radio. The radio does not play a role in Stoker's *Dracula*, but as a method of communicating across space and time, it is a natural extension of the telegraph and the phonograph. Martin's cousin Christina struggles against Cuda's prejudices against the telephone and has one installed despite Cuda's disapproval. Cuda is so antediluvian that even in 1977 he considers this modern instrument to be a danger in the home. Like the railway, the representation of these technologies reflects Martin's relationship with outmoded modernity and their decline as tools of communication. Christina wants a phone to feel more connected to the world, but her first conversation on it, as the installers are walking down the stairs, is a violent argument with Arthur. Martin's use of the phone is a similarly

Figure 5.3. Going nowhere in Braddock in *Martin*.

weak attempt to communicate. He calls a late-night talk show to talk about his vampirism, but the shallow response of the DJ and the callers to Martin's plight suggests that they do not truly hear what Martin is saying. They simply respond to what they think is a good but superficial gimmick.

When Martin breaks into the house of the lonely Pittsburgh housewife and unexpectedly finds her with her lover, he manipulates the clumsy nature of telephone communication in order to thwart her attempts to call for help. Martin finds a phone in the game room and uses its keypad to interfere with her dialing the number of the hospital. The tension of the situation is exacerbated by the woman's screaming to her lover, thinking it is he who is interfering with her call, to hang up the phone. Not listening to her request, the man attempts to call the hospital himself which leads to them both crossing wires, while Martin listens silently on the third phone and interferes in both of their calls. The technology in this situation is seen to be easily thwarted, and showcases the lack of communication between people as they undermine each other's attempts to make the call. Martin controls the telephone but as this sequence shows, this is a technology that frustrates communication rather than facilitates it.

While Dracula and Mina's vampirism enabled them to physically absorb the immediacy of modern communication through their telepathic connection, Martin's vampirism shows the emptiness of modern communication and its technologies. The use of technology in both *The Night Stalker* and *Martin* illustrates what Martin constantly reminds Tata Cuda and his radio listeners: "There is no magic." The magic that defined nineteenth-century modernity has been replaced by the death and decay of an aging technology awaiting its replacement. In neither Las Vegas nor Pittsburgh is there magic. The bureaucracy that facilitated the vampire hunters' pursuit in *Dracula* has now placed a stranglehold on Kolchak the vampire hunter, while the industrial, Taylorized world of the American factory city in *Martin* no longer bears the marks of a productive and efficient form of mechanization.

Martin, both the film and the vampire, is a product of a transition in American modernization from industrialism to postindustrialism. The film itself is an independent feature made possible by the breakdown of the Hollywood studio monopoly over film production. As the poster states, Martin is *Made in USA*. This statement can imply, as I've already suggested, the relocation of horror to the United States, but it also serves to link vampirism to the concept of industrialization. The expression "Made in USA" connotes an industrialized consumer product, something that is made and marketed as American. The decision to set the film in Braddock, an industrial satellite city of Pittsburgh, suggests that Martin is not just American, but that he is himself a product of this dying, industrial setting. The value of American products was being questioned in the 1970s, making the choice of Braddock as a setting for the film all the more significant. At the time of the film's production, Braddock was a city in an industrial crisis. Once a prosperous steel town whose motto was "What Braddock Makes, the World Takes" and with a population of twenty thousand people, Braddock has since been reduced to approximately five and a half thousand with the decline of industry and the closing of the mills.[18] Tony Buba, soundman on Romero's early films including *Martin*, as well as a documentary filmmaker who has chronicled the decline of Braddock, describes the town as "a microcosm for all the problems and the whole decline of the industrial Northeast."[19] Romero acknowledges the significance of Braddock as the setting and the impact it has on his narrative.

> The setting to me signifies that, for a traditional vampire, the old days are gone: the industrial pride is gone, the jobs are gone, the church is collapsing. Everyone is just surviving. The disintegration is so evident

around Pittsburgh. The little mill towns that used to be thriving, proud communities are gone with the wind. It made one of those towns, Braddock, the perfect setting for this kind of situation.[20]

Romero consciously wanted to tap into the industrial landscape of the town and draw upon the history of industrial urban disintegration in the creation of his vampire tale.

Born in the Bronx, Romero moved to Pittsburgh in 1957 to study at the Carnegie Institute of Technology and stayed in the city to launch his own filmmaking company. Working independently of mainstream filmmaking, he began to accumulate a team of native talent both on- and off-screen. *Martin*, therefore, has a stronger link to Pittsburgh and Braddock than simply as a backdrop. The cast were all Pittsburgh natives, most notably John Amplas, the actor who portrayed Martin and continues to work there. The cinematographer, Mike Gornick, was a second-generation native of Braddock, and Tony Buba offered up his family home to be the primary setting of the film. He also allowed Romero to use his family history and photos, as the heritage that spawned both Cuda and Martin. The film is completely grounded within Braddock.

Martin also taps into the heritage of industry in Pittsburgh. In 1964, the former mayor of Pittsburgh, David L. Lawrence, praised the city for its attempt to rejuvenate itself and look to the future. Lawrence felt that the city was entering a period of renaissance, cleaning up its pollution and changing

> as fast as it can from the environment of the old nineteenth century technology into the sleek new forms of the future. The city is racing time . . . The city welcomes tomorrow, because yesterday was hard and unlovely. Pittsburgh likes buildings that glisten with stainless steel and aluminum, and it has little time for the niceties of architectural criticism when it compares what it gained with what it lost. The town has no worship of landmarks. Instead, it takes its pleasure in the swing of the headache ball and the crash of falling brick.[21]

This statement captures both the hope of the 1960s and the impending doom of the 1970s, for it expresses the desire to shed the past but offers only suggestions for destruction not growth or development. No indication is given of what the "sleek new forms of the future" will be. *Martin* is plagued with similar images of a dying steel industry and although there are no images of a headache ball and falling brick, the repeated shots of cranes lifting cars into compacters which subsequently pummel them into anonymous blocks of steel—the only images of functioning industry in Braddock—reflect the harsh reality of Lawrence's words. Romero's film shows a town incapable of surviving the industrial evolution towards increased automation. Braddock was a town that once manufactured resources for production but these images imply only automation and commodification of waste material. Arthur bemoans that there is no real work in Braddock and complains that he is a good mechanic and should be fixing cars. It is, however, clear that Braddock is no longer set up to directly produce tangible goods; it is simply a merchant in arbitrary destruction of the goods it once helped to produce. Mirrored in the decline of the auto industry, these images reflect the fall of industrialism as an icon of modernity.[22]

One of the final scenes in Tony Buba's pseudodocumentary *Lightning Over Braddock: A Rustbowl Fantasy* (1988), features one of Buba's regular characters, would-be entrepreneur Jimmy Roy. He stands in an empty lot, dressed in a tuxedo with a full orchestra accompanying him as he sings, "Braddock, city of magic, Braddock, city of life, Braddock, where have you gone?" Buba argues that the point of this particular moment in the film is to convey that this film is a fantasy. "What I thought, as soon as I had that song playing, 'Braddock, City of Magic,' is this is not reality. Right there, that one line would tell the audience that what they were seeing is not real."[23] These lyrics, therefore, suggest that if Tony Buba's documentary is a fantasy then *Martin* is the reality, for Romero's film evokes quite the opposite. In *Martin* there is no magic and the city is dying.

While Stoker's novel *Dracula* uses the vampire as a means of portraying the experience of the changing world as supernatural, Romero's film introduces a vampire that sheds any identification with the supernatural or the occult and grounds his existence in the superindustrialized reality of 1970s America. As Martin regularly points out, all the traditional folklore no longer applies. Churches, crosses, garlic, and religious exorcism have no effect on him. He does not possess the hypnotic powers of Dracula nor the ability to transform himself. Rather he implies that he has developed an almost mechanized approach to his vampirism as demonstrated by his painstaking stalking and preparation for the attack on the Pittsburgh housewife. His failure with the housewife, however, suggests that even his methods are becoming obsolete. The shedding of the icons of modernity by stating that there is no magic, actually serves to lay the groundwork for the future. Martin is a modern vampire on the cusp of new foundations for modernity. Modernity is a whirlwind of change, and *Martin* exists at its epicenter, dramatizing the disintegration and renewal processes that are intrinsic to the experience of the modern world. Martin's death and disappearance from the airwaves enables his listeners to reinvent him for themselves by conjecturing upon where he is and what he might be doing, and even writing a song about him. The last caller ushers in the potential for a new vampire by suggesting that he has a friend who he thinks is "the Count." Martin lives on in his audience's imagination.

CHAPTER SIX

Walking Corpses and Independent Filmmaking Techniques

In 1980, James Monaco wrote an article outlining the changes to the modern horror films that had emerged in the 1970s. He argued that contemporary cinema had become more violent and horrific. While not condemning the genre as a whole, he did critique the manner in which the films were made, their "technique," and suggested that modern Hollywood had been taken over by *"technicians."*[1] Of course, during the 1970s, Hollywood was in the throes of being taken over by a group of new filmmakers who, building upon the collapse of the studio system, were seeking to redefine the industry. Similarly, the horror genre in this period saw the emergence of a group of young, independent filmmakers including George Romero, Wes Craven, David Cronenberg, Tobe Hooper, and John Carpenter, described retrospectively as "the class of '79," who turned to the horror genre to establish themselves within the film industry as well as to express their own anxieties about modern America.[2] They achieved both notoriety and acclaim by focusing upon the horror of reality through an explosion of violence and realistic gore, and as a result the horror genre "produced films more gruesome, more violent, more disgusting, and perhaps more confused, than ever before in history."[3] Tobe Hooper, the director of *The Texas Chainsaw Massacre* (1974), explains how the films they were making were focused upon "reflecting man's inhumanity toward man, and realizing that the ultimate monster is man."[4] This fundamental change to the genre, accompanied by an almost guerrilla form of independent, low-budget filmmaking, would have a widespread influence upon horror and the vampire film in particular.

In his critique of contemporary horror Monaco claimed that,

> historically, horror films were set in human, humane contexts. They
> always provided a catharsis of sorts. Now we have learned to make them

more *effective*. They work *mechanically* as thrill machines, like the rack, and provide as little psychological release as possible since, after all, the human context would detract from the "*visceral*" *clout* of the movie.[5]

My emphasis in this passage demonstrates how Monaco's choice of words suggests a physical quality to the effect of these films. The films seem to ignore spiritual or psychological themes explored in classic horror films, which is, according to Monaco, a result of their being made by technicians rather than artists. These films are effective, mechanical, and have "visceral clout," and their effects are achieved through the use of bladders, animatronics, and hydraulics; the words themselves evoke physicality and industrialisation. Monaco's comments are, however, symptomatic of much criticism of the genre in the 1970s and 1980s that saw contemporary horror as being overreliant on state-of-the-art special effects, a dependence that seemed to, in their eyes, rob the genre of any substance or meaning. For instance, Morris Dickstein described "the new wave of horror film" as "hard core pornography of violence made possible by the virtual elimination of censorship."[6] Monaco, however, saw the spate of Dracula films that came out of the 1970s as an opposition to the graphic horror films of this period, offering a glimmer of hope for the future of horror. He suggests that the political integrity and allegorical potential of the vampire myth could rescue the genre from the grips of graphic body horror.[7] What this type of response does not recognize is that perhaps rather than simply being empty and mechanical, this new wave of horror films is a product of a culture confronted by very real horrors and violence on a day-to-day basis.

For instance, special makeup effects artist Tom Savini, known throughout the 1980s as the Splatter King, began working in the 1970s with such films as *Deathdream, Martin,* and *Dawn of the Dead,* and claims that one of the reasons for his commitment to realism in makeup and monstrous body horror effects was his experience in Vietnam. In Vietnam, as a photographer documenting wartime atrocities, he was able to see firsthand violence and destruction of flesh and bone. He was confronted daily with the inner workings of the body, which he subsequently recreated for the cinema. As he explains,

I was actually able to look at bone, blood, placement, geography. When I was a kid watching *Frankenstein* and *The Wolf Man,* I would go home and try to recreate those guys, so I would study them. The shape of the brow. Where the nose started. What the colors were. So here I was looking at what I was thinking of as special effects, real gore, and actually studying them and so if I wanted to recreate them what would I have to do. Foam latex here, some chunks off here, some bone marrow and that is what carries into my work. I think that is what Vietnam did. It gave me the desire and the sense that if it is going to be horrible, it will be horrible the way I saw it.[8]

While in Vietnam, Savini confronted inexplicable horror and violence in an inhumane context, as did the audiences who would later respond to his movies, whether they had been to Vietnam themselves, or had watched the violence on the news. The news not only reported the violence in Vietnam but also violence at home, such as the high-profile assassinations of John F. Kennedy, Martin Luther King Jr., Malcom X, and Robert Kennedy, civil rights demonstrations, and student protests culminating in the violent attack by the police at Kent State University. The nation was traumatized by the accounts of the Tate and LaBianca murders by the Manson Family in 1969. The violence of the case, as well as the location of Sharon Tate's murder within Hollywood, created an appetite for the increasingly gruesome details reported extensively in the press. There was the best-selling account of the crimes and the hunt for the killers, *The Manson Murders*, written by the prosecuting attorney Vincent Bugliosi, as well as a two-part television movie *Helter Skelter* (1976).[9]

The growing familiarity and fascination with violence and brutality, made visible through the media, was increasingly manifested through the proliferation of violence and gore in the cinema, not only in the horror genre, but also in the western with *The Wild Bunch* (1969), and the outlaw movie with *Bonnie and Clyde* (1967). The sudden proliferation of public violence in America mixed with a national identity crisis caused primarily by economic decline, made this period the ideal time for the renewed engagement with body trauma. Therefore it is not surprising that rather than rescue the genre from the grips of graphic realism, the vampire became completely defined by it. This change is less of an emptying of the genre of its allegorical meaning, but more of a shift in the meaning of the allegory and an emphasis upon the vampire as a site for the negotiation of the politics of the body. This chapter will explore how the vampire in 1970s cinema, particularly influenced by George Romero's *Night of the Living Dead* (1968), was stripped of its spectral nature and fully transformed into a physical being, defined by the boundaries and discourses of the body, made possible by changing approaches to horror filmmaking and special effects.

The tensions between the horror of suggestion and graphic depiction, expressed in Monaco's criticism, are part of a much broader debate about the opposition between the genres of terror and horror. Although the terms are often used interchangeably today, in the history of Gothic literature they have possessed radically opposing meanings. While terror leaves the monstrous to the imagination, horror describes it in graphic detail. There is a similar opposition in cinema between psychological horror and graphic body horror. These critical distinctions, however, do not begin with literature or film but are part of a historical perception of the body as subordinate to the mind or soul. While the soul was perceived as pure, the body was perceived as animalistic and therefore in need of control and discipline.[10] Denying the body, by avoiding graphic descriptions of horror as well as the physical responses to horror, parallels this desire for control. As a result, writing tales of terror was perceived to be a more worthwhile ambition because it was a genre of the intellect while horror stories were a genre of the body, resulting not in catharsis but rather a physical effect upon its reader. In 1826, Ann Radcliffe wrote, "Terror and horror are so far opposite, that the first expands the soul, and awakens the faculties to a high degree of life; the other contracts, freezes, and nearly annihilates them."[11] The very language used locates the effects of horror in the body much like Monaco's description of the modern horror genre or Dickstein's equation of the genre with pornography.

The opposition between mind and body is a debate that emerges in critical studies by contrasting the works of Noël Carroll and Julia Kristeva, which attempt to define the nature of horror as the confrontation with impurity, defined as that which crosses established natural or societal boundaries. Both theorists draw upon the work of anthropologist Mary Douglas who argues that concepts of boundaries, around society or the human body, are there to construct order out of disorder by establishing clear-cut binaries such as "within and without, above and below, male and female, with and against."[12] When faced with something that challenges or defies these binaries, the individual or society must either rethink these categories in order to find a place for the anomaly or condemn it as unnatural.

Noël Carroll uses Douglas' ideas to argue that monsters in horror films by their very nature break boundaries, whether conceptually or physically. He claims that they are impure because they are "categorically interstitial, categorically contradictory, incomplete, or formless."[13] For instance, many monsters in the horror genre, such as vampires, mummies, and zombies, blur the boundary between life and death because they are both alive and dead. By his argument, the revulsion caused by these forms of impurity is a cognitive, rather than visceral, response to their physical ambiguity. As he suggests, "They are unnatural relative to a culture's conceptual scheme of nature. They do not fit the scheme; they violate it. Thus, monsters are not only physically threatening; they are cognitively threatening."[14] By being both living and dead, vampires confound our sense of a natural order and are therefore impure. This impurity is captured in the spectral representation of the vampire in *Nosferatu* as it is both solid and ethereal, undermining the boundaries between the real world and the spirit world.

Carroll does not suggest that the audience knowingly recognizes the vampire's interstitial qualities but rather that the vampire is categorically interstitial, causing "a sense of impurity in us without our necessarily being aware of precisely what causes that sense."[15] As a result, the cause of the audience's revulsion is more conceptual than physical. In the novel *Dracula*, when Dracula leans over Harker and touches his hand, Harker's response is an involuntary shudder accompanied by an unexplainable bout of nausea. Although he explains that it may be a response to the rankness of Dracula's breath, his hesitancy suggests that it is something more abstract than physical. It is not that Dracula is obviously, physically impure (18).

While Carroll's recognition of impurity lies primarily in the mind, Kristeva recasts impurity as abjection and locates it in the body. Both argue that the response to the impure is physical, with such natural responses as gagging, spasms, and recoiling. Yet in Kristeva's case the object of our horror is physical as well. Drawing upon Douglas' anthropological work, Kristeva equally locates the impure within objects that do "not respect borders, positions, rules," and break through cultural categories imposed upon the world to create order. But unlike Carroll, she emphasizes the body as the location of these forms of impurity.[16] Douglas argues that "the body is a model which can stand for any bounded system," and that while all boundaries are sites of vulnerability to transgression and alteration, "we should expect the orifices of the body to symbolize its specifically vulnerable points. Spittle, blood, milk, urine, faeces or tears by simply issuing forth have traversed the boundary of the body."[17] Barbara Creed, applying Kristeva's concepts to the horror film, argues that the genre abounds in such graphic images of abjection and that the crossing and blurring of borders is "central to the construction of the monstrous."[18] According to Kristeva and Creed, the most abject thing of all is the corpse, "the body without a soul," for the corpse represents the reduction of the self to waste.[19] Robbed of its spectral qualities, the vampire is just that, a corpse without a soul.

The growing fascination with a realistic representation of violence and body horror in the 1970s led to a reworking of the vampire genre conventions and a new representation of the vampire as a physical, rather than spectral, being. As a result, the genre engaged in these discourses around the impurity of the body. By making the vampire physical, the genre transforms the object of horror from a conceptual terror to a very real confrontation with the abject body. While Dracula is an object of horror because he is the living dead invading the land of the living, the vampires in films from the 1970s and 1980s are not only conceptually abject but physically abject as well, and the boundaries between the worlds of the living and the dead collapse. Through the influence of George Romero's *Night of the Living Dead*, the vampire was robbed of its spectral nature and became trapped within the boundaries of a mundane body made of easily destructible flesh.

While *Night of the Living Dead* is a zombie film rather than a vampire film, it does have more in common with the vampire tradition than many of the zombie films that came before it. Films like *White Zombie* (1932) and *I Walked with a Zombie* (1943) focus upon plots of voodoo rituals, reanimated corpses, and powerful witch doctors manipulating the zombies for their own evil purposes. Like vampires, however, Romero's zombies are living dead, not controlled by voodoo ritual or a witch doctor, but rather compelled to action by their need to consume human blood and flesh. Julia Kristeva claims that "the corpse, seen without God and outside of science, is the utmost of abjection. It is death infecting life."[20] This description directly applies to the vampire myth for vampires are corpses that infiltrate and infect the living. The pseudoscientific explanation for the reanimation of the dead in Romero's film—the appearance of a satellite recently returned from Venus entering earth's atmosphere and contaminated with strange radiation—does not make sense of the dead's resurrection so much as demonstrate that the explanation for this phenomenon is incidental. Nor can their existence be explained by Christian superstition, for while Romero's zombies are reminiscent of the hapless vampires of European folklore, their rise from the dead cannot be attributed to damnation, excommunication, birth on holy days, or conversion to a non-Christian religion.[21] Their presence has no explanation and is an infection upon humanity as their victims become zombies when they die.

This particular form of generic revamping is not new, for Richard Matheson's novel *I Am Legend*, which inspired *Night of the Living Dead*, equally divorces the return of the dead from scientific and religious explanations. In Matheson's novel, Neville, the sole survivor of a worldwide plague that transformed all of humanity into vampires, attempts to use scientific method to understand the cause of the plague and to find a cure. Although his research helps him understand the bacterial origin of the plague, it leads to endless further questions until he finally realizes that ultimately there are no answers. He must simply accept his new place in the order of things. When asked why they have been punished in this way by the vampire-spy posing as a survivor, he answers, "There's no answer, no reason. It just is."[22] Like Matheson's hero Neville, the protagonists of Romero's film must simply focus upon the real existence of the living dead rather than look for explanations or an authority figure to intervene.

David Pirie has argued that by conforming to the most basic definitions of the vampire, being dead and sucking blood, Romero's film presents the only "truly modernist reading of the vampire myth, and for this reason its theme and technique have been subject to constant imitation."[23] The mix of zombie and vampire imagery resulted in more than imitation but rather a significant rethinking of the vampire genre, for these zombies have had all supernatural qualities stripped away, making them simply flesh, bone, and physical desire. The vampire is no longer a singular threat like Dracula, but a leaderless mob of monsters that are dangerous simply because of their sheer numbers. They are not infused with any magical power nor preternatural cunning, they are simply walking corpses, possessing an endless hunger and the force of ever-increasing numbers as their own victims join their ranks. The film's emphasis upon realism through its use of a form of guerrilla film technology detaches the vampire myth from the supernatural and psychological horror film in favor of the horror of the abject body.

Night of the Living Dead was made by a group of young filmmakers, who were working in the commercial advertising sector but looking to make their first feature film. They decided that with the decline in the film industry and the breakdown of the traditional studio system this was the ideal time to push their way forward and try to make a film. As Romero explains,

In 1968, the film industry was beginning to lose breath under the stranglehold of television growth. The precious ticket-buying dollar was no longer supporting Bergman or Fellini or even Doris Day. It was recognized that films had to be produced less expensively and promoted more carefully if they were to make money at the box office. The independent film

distributor was becoming as significant a force as the major studio . . .
While escapism pap was being dished to the public in great, heaping,
twenty-four hours-a-day bowlfuls on the tube, the exploiters of the big
screen turned to violence, horror and sex.[24]

Wes Craven describes the period that followed the release of *Night of the
Living Dead* as "a time when there were a lot of underground/guerrilla
movements going on," and he argues that this is reflected in the raw qualities of the films.[25] *Night of the Living Dead* was made for $114,000 and was,
according to Romero, a collaborative production in the truest sense of the
word. Every member of the crew took turns "loading magazines, gaffing,
gathering and making props, shooting, recording, editing."[26] Only two of
the actors were professionals; most of the cast were friends of the producers, who also play major roles. The film was shot in black-and-white as
the film stock was less expensive to use, but this also lent the film an aura
of authenticity. As George Romero explains, in the late 1960s the news on
television was in black-and-white, while fiction films, with a few excep-
tions, were made in spectacular Cinemascope and Technicolor.[27] While
realism was clearly not the purpose of the black-and-white film stock, it is
the result, particularly when juxtaposed with the television news coverage
of the events taking place in the farmhouse.

Furthermore, the use of black-and-white facilitated the filmmakers'
desire to show the horrors of the zombies rather than leaving them to
the imagination. According to John Russo, black-and-white stock served
to conceal the limitations of the low-budget special effects being used to
create the often grotesque makeup for the zombies, as well as the moments involving the splattering and dripping of blood.[28] For instance, in
some sequences they used ink or chocolate syrup for blood, depending
upon whether they wanted it to streak or splatter, and these effects appear
quite graphic and realistic. The use of black-and-white stock facilitated
these choices by not showing the artificiality of the effect while allowing
the gore to be shown in detail.

The desire to show horror in realistic and graphic detail was one of the
defining characteristics of these underground movies of the 1970s, and it
is largely due to the success of *Night of the Living Dead* that this was possible. Romero's film shows horror in two ways: the special makeup effects
of the zombies, and the explicit portrayal of the zombies feeding upon the
living and being killed.

The filmmakers desired to make the zombies appear as the regeneration of the recently deceased. This meant that in some cases their bodies

Figure 6.1. Homemade special effects in *Night of the Living Dead.*

showed the manner in which they had died, or demonstrated a certain level of decomposition. The look of the zombies was influenced not only by the desires of the filmmakers but the economics of the film production. To save money, the filmmakers did the makeup themselves rather than have a professional makeup artist. John Russo explains that George Romero himself made the prop of the partially consumed corpse in the farmhouse by applying false hair, clay, ping-pong-ball eyes, and paint to a plastic educational toy called "The Living Skull." (Figure 6.1) Similarly the film's producer, Karl Hardman, constructed the makeup for Russo's zombie cameo appearance by applying Dermawax to his skull and scooping out a hole in the forehead where the zombie received a blow from a tire iron. It was designed so that a dollop of blood would run out of his head as he hit the ground.[29] These and many more special effects were simple and homemade, and they successfully emphasize that the monstrosity of the zombies lay in their bodies. They are walking corpses, reanimated flesh, and the simple makeup techniques emphasize their physical decay.

While the appearance of the zombies is disturbing at times, their consumption of the flesh is the second and most effective example of Romero's emphasis upon realism and horror. This is particularly evoked in the sequence after Tom and Judy, the film's young lovers, have been blown up in their truck as they organize an escape attempt. After the explosion, the zombies crowd around the truck searching for food, followed by a montage sequence of close-ups of the zombies chewing on human limbs and organs, ripping bits of flesh from the bones and, most memorably, scooping up a long trail of intestines. Romero points out that in this film he

> directed for naturalism and saw no reason to cut away for reaction shots when the ghouls began devouring the flesh of their victims. In fact I was delighted when one of our investors, who happened to be in the meat-packing business, turned up on the set with a sackful of animal innards which made the sequences seem so real, never realizing the extent of taboo-breaking the scenes would achieve.[30]

These sequences in particular proved to be hugely influential to the vampire genre. After this film, drinking blood could no longer be presented purely as an act of sexual desire, but rather as an act of hunger and physical craving. Up until the 1960s and early 1970s, Dracula was still presented drinking blood through the clean puncturing of the jugular vein, suggesting an act of sexual penetration with little actual violence. His victims, while under his mesmeric influence, were usually portrayed as willing. With *Night of the Living Dead* and its images of zombies ripping flesh and bone, the vampire was suddenly transformed into a carnivorous creature feeding an insatiable hunger that defied romanticism or sexual desire. This graphic realism would transform the vampire in film from the 1970s through to the present. Equally influential in this regard was Anne Rice's novel, *Interview with the Vampire*, with its equation of drinking blood with an insatiable thirst. When Louis encounters the child Claudia for the first time and is tempted to feed off her, he explains, "You must understand that by now I was burning with physical need to drink. I could not have made it through another day without feeding."[31] Subsequently, most vampire films from the 1980s and 1990s treat blood drinking as feeding and this is largely due to the treatment of drinking blood in Rice's work as well as the evocative images of zombies feeding in *Night of the Living Dead.*[32]

The vampire films that followed *Night of the Living Dead* shared the film's removal of the vampire's spectral qualities in favor of presenting them as walking corpses modeled on Romero's zombies. While films such as *Count Yorga, Vampire* (1970), *The Return of Count Yorga* (1971), *Blacula* (1972), and John Badham's adaptation of *Dracula* (1979), all feature an aristocratic, European or African vampire at their centers, the vampires they sire are depicted as mindless, hunger-driven, moblike, and in some cases, they appear more like resuscitated corpses than transformed vampires. Furthermore, they are all driven by their thirst for blood and, like the zombies, this thirst manifests itself as a physical need and craving rather than sexual desire. For instance in *Count Yorga, Vampire* when the vampire's first victim Erica begins to transform as a result of his attack on her, she initially shows the traditional signs made familiar by Lucy in Stoker's novel: she is pale, distant, and seems to be suffering the effects of a hypnotic trance. When her boyfriend calls her to check on her condition, however, the film cuts to a close-up of her feet as she drops the phone and stumbles through her living room, clumsily knocking objects onto the floor. This is the first sign that all is not well with Erica, even by vampire standards. When her boyfriend arrives home, he walks into the kitchen and, to his horror, finds Erica feeding upon the now bloody and lifeless body of a kitten. The film cuts from his shocked exclamation to a medium close-up of Erica with blood and bits of flesh dripping from her mouth as she screams at his interruption.

Both *Count Yorga, Vampire* and its sequel *The Return of Count Yorga* end on decidedly nihilistic notes that are reminiscent of the hopeless ending of Romero's film. Both films are about Yorga's abduction of the lead female character and the hero's attempts to rescue her before she is transformed into a vampire. In *Count Yorga, Vampire*, the hero is too late; although he kills Yorga, the film ends with the hero locking all of the vampire women into the cellar only to realize that his girlfriend has been changed. The final shot of the film, taken from the hero's point of view, is a close-up of his girlfriend, now made-up with pale skin, dark, hollow eyes, and monstrous teeth, lunging at the camera. The film freezes and ends on this image. The sequel has a similar ending: Count Yorga attacks the hero, the heroine awakens from her trance and kills the count. As she rushes to her boyfriend to embrace him, her expression changes from relief to one of increasing horror as she pulls herself away and realizes that her boyfriend has changed into a vampire. This time he is not only pale and holloweyed, but still possesses the scars and bites from his fight with Yorga and looks the very image of a corpse as he lunges at the girl and plunges his teeth into her neck. Again this sequence is protracted by a series of freeze-frames of the stages of his attack. Not only do the appearance of the vampires and the hopelessness of the films' endings seem reminiscent of *Night of the Living Dead*, but the use of freeze-frames calls to mind the montage of still images of Romero's hero's body, after he was mistaken for a zombie and brutally shot by the posse, being picked up and dropped onto the fire with the other zombies.

In *Blacula*, a group of police officers follow a known vampire into a warehouse hoping to find Blacula's coffin. Instead they find a group of zombielike vampires waiting to ambush them. In this film the influence of Romero's work is twofold. First it shows how, like the zombies, these vampires are easily dispatched individually but are an incredible threat in groups as they are driven by their hunger.[33] Second, the film focuses upon the use of fire as a weapon against the vampires. While guns have no affect on them because they are already dead, they can be destroyed by fire. In this sequence, two of the police officers throw kerosene lanterns at the vampires, resembling the scene in *Night of the Living Dead* where the survivors throw Molotov cocktails at the zombies. Fire, like sunlight, becomes a very real and tangible threat to the vampires not because of any magical element but because of the laws of nature: dead flesh burns.

Even John Badham's adaptation of John Balderston and Hamilton Dean's stage production of *Dracula* owes a debt to *Night of the Living Dead*. While Frank Langella's performance as Dracula embodies the romantic aristocratic hero of previous Dracula films, Badham's presentation of the vampiric Mina is a startling break from the film conventions. Suspecting that Mina has been transformed into a vampire, Van Helsing, portrayed as Mina's father in this adaptation, digs up her grave and finds it empty. Notably, Mina's burial site has been changed from a family tomb to an earthen grave. This is more reminiscent of vampire folklore as is Van Helsing's attempt to get a white horse to walk over her grave as a test of her vampirism. Upon opening her coffin, he finds that a hole has been dug between the bottom of the grave and a mine that runs directly below. Mina's escape therefore is no longer a result of the ability to transmute into mist; instead she uses a practical escape tunnel. When he enters the tunnel, Van Helsing comes face to face with his deceased daughter. She first appears in a reflection in a small pool of water that Van Helsing is examining. As he slowly looks up, there is a tilt up to show her approaching feet, surrounded by rats, and her burial clothes, now torn and dirty from the grave. The camera continues to tilt up until it finally reveals her pale face, sunken dark eyes, decaying skin, and mouth dripping with blood from a recent victim. (Figure 6.2) She has become the image of a decaying corpse and as she slowly walks towards her father, reaching for him in hunger and need, she is reminiscent of Romero's child zombie who eats her father and kills her mother.

Figure 6.2. Zombie-Mina in Badham's *Dracula*.

While Romero's own vampire film *Martin* does not present the vampire as a zombielike monster, it does build upon *Night of the Living Dead*'s nihilism and despiritualized emphasis upon the physicality of the vampire. As previously discussed, Martin strongly argues throughout the film that there is no magic to his vampirism. In the confrontation with his uncle in the playground, he mocks the traditional representation of the vampire by dressing up as a dark, ghoulish figure in a cape and fangs and then spitting out those fangs and wiping off the grease paint covering his face. While the film reveals the constructedness of the traditional vampire image by pointing out that "it's just a costume," the film also introduces innovative makeup special effects by fledgling makeup artist Tom Savini, to show the real violence that is inherent within any act of vampirism.

In the opening scene when Martin attacks a young woman in her train compartment, he uses a razor blade to penetrate her vein and drink her blood. To achieve this effect on camera, Savini came up with a simple technique that would enable Romero to show, in one take, the razor blade cutting a slit down the woman's wrist and the blood pouring out. The actor playing Martin simply held a syringe of fake blood concealed in the palm of his hand, which he squeezed out as he ran a dummy blade down the woman's wrist. The first time he tried it, the syringe did not work and they were forced to try again while the camera continued to roll. Both attempts are used in the film, which serves to emphasize the realism of this process.[34] While the first attempt does not penetrate the skin, the second results in blood spurting out of her wrist in gushes and all over Martin's body as he tries to drink it. This simple makeup effect demonstrates the precision of the cut to her wrist by seeming to show the penetration of the blade into her flesh.

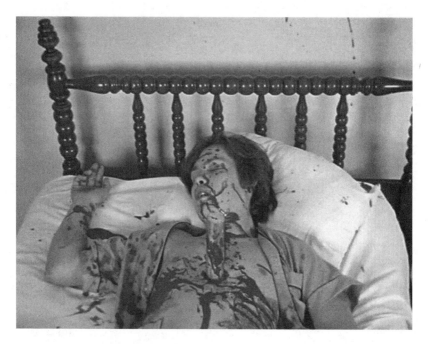

Figure 6.3. Brutal death for *Martin*.

Martin's own demise at the hands of his cousin Tata Cuda is portrayed as an empty triumph for Cuda's old-world rituals. Believing that Martin has murdered one of the citizens of Braddock, Cuda kills Martin by hammering a wooden stake through his chest in a manner familiar within the vampire genre. (Figure 6.3) The way in which this murder is portrayed, however, breaks substantially from the genre conventions of previous films. While classic vampire films such as *Dracula* or *Dracula's Daughter* stage the staking off-camera, and later vampire films like Hammer's *The Horror of Dracula* feature the vampire magically burning to ash when trapped in the sun's rays, Romero's film portrays Martin's death as a murder as violent as those that he himself commits.[35] It takes place on-camera and is achieved by creating the illusion of Cuda hammering the stake into Martin's chest through the manipulation of perspective and camera angle. The effects of this staking were achieved by Tom Savini hiding under the bed and spraying a torrent of blood up and over Martin's body with each blow to the stake, followed by a zoom out from Martin's blood-soaked body with a stake lodged in his abdomen.[36] This sequence serves to remove the vampire himself from the realm of the supernatural and shows that while Cuda appears to have won, his method of killing the vampire did not grant spiritual redemption or salvation. Rather it shows that, like his victims, Martin's death is limited to the destruction of his body.

From *Night of the Living Dead* to *Martin*, the vampire genre underwent a period of reinvention originating from its absorption into an underground film aesthetic that highlights graphic realism in its technological depiction of violence, death, and the destruction of the body. As a result, the vampire has been transformed into a despiritualized being, defined by the abjectness of its corpselike body and its hunger for human flesh and blood. This transformation was due in no small part to the physical presentation of the vampire through the techniques of independent filmmaking as well as the development of special makeup effects that grounded the vampire within the boundaries of its corporeal body.

CHAPTER SEVEN

Special Makeup Effects and Exploding Vampires

When a vampire buys it, it is never a pretty sight. No two blood-suckers go out the same way. Some yell and scream, some go quietly, some explode, some implode. But all will try and take you with them.

EDGAR FROG IN *THE LOST BOYS* (1987)

While the vampire films of the 1970s were primarily located in an underground film movement, the success of this new wave of American horror films led to the legitimization of a graphic and realistic style of filmmaking in mainstream cinema in the New Hollywood of the late 70s and early 80s. This served to professionalize the special makeup effects artists, rescuing them from their home workshops and garages, and recognizing them within the industry. The launch of the horror fan magazine *Fangoria* in 1979 was a response to the success of the genre and contributed to the popularity and celebrity of special makeup effects artists including Dick Smith, Tom Savini, Rick Baker, Rob Bottin, and Stan Winston. With their more visible and recognized presence within the industry, the genre increasingly began to foreground their effects in graphic detail, sacrificing realism for a spectacle of gore; the body became the site upon which the special effects artists experimented and showcased their skill.

Philip Brophy describes this new trend in modern horror as "horrality," a hybrid term drawing upon the concepts of horror, textuality, morality, and hilarity, all of which are defining features of modern horror.[1] The vampire genre became increasingly embroiled in this transition between graphic realism and horrality. The vampire in the 1980s was still defined by its body but, through the evolution and standardization of special makeup effects, the body was continuously undergoing transformation, stretching, redefining its boundaries, and often disintegrating or exploding those boundaries in the process. This chapter will explore how the vampire body became the site upon which our concerns and anxieties about the body in the 1980s were projected. They become physical, de-spiritualized, out of control, and when they die, they explode in an excess of all that we expel.

The legitimization of the special effects artist, according to John McCarty, began with the success of Douglas Trumbull's special effects work on the science-fiction film *2001: A Space Odyssey* (1968) and Dick Smith's makeup effects in the horror film *The Exorcist* (1973). In *The Exorcist*, Smith and his assistant Rick Baker were called upon to develop a series of unprecedented special effects that would transform Linda Blair from an innocent thirteen-year-old girl into a monstrous devil. While Romero's graphic horror films were made within the underground sector and their emphasis upon realism was inextricably linked to budget limitations as well as aesthetic design, *The Exorcist* was a much bigger-budget film made within the mainstream Hollywood system. Its production and success therefore foreshadowed and partially contributed to the legitimization of graphic realism in the horror genre of the 1980s.

The Exorcist is significant specifically because it pushed the boundaries of makeup special effects to physically showcase the possession of the young girl Regan by a demon. Like *Night of the Living Dead*, *The Exorcist* uses its focus upon the body to rethink the supernatural in terms of the physical. The future of Regan's soul is at risk but it is through the damage to her body—the tearing of her skin, the contusions on her face, the spinning head, the spider walk, the vomiting of green bile, the spelling of "help" on her stomach, and the graphic sequence of her masturbating with a crucifix—that the possession manifests itself. In this film, the body becomes the site for the confrontation between good and evil as well as science and religion.

This emphasis upon the body as a site for horror would continue throughout the 1970s and 1980s and would be further legitimized by the success of John Landis' *An American Werewolf in London* (1981). Like *The Exorcist*, Landis' film achieved a great deal of crossover success, largely as a result of the humorous presentation of quite startlingly graphic special effects. The film follows two American college boys who are attacked by a werewolf on the Yorkshire Moors. The survivor, David, as he recovers from the attack, finds out that his best friend, Jack, is dead and that he is doomed to transform into a werewolf himself at the next full moon. While famous for its transformation sequences (which will be discussed more later), the film also features graphic depictions of the destruction and decay of Jack's body, presented with an ironic and emotionally detached sense of humor. David learns of his fate when Jack, his body still bloody and torn from the attack, visits him. With each subsequent visit, Jack appears in an increasingly decomposed state. During one of their final meetings, he forces David to confront the bloody corpses of his victims who, like Jack, are condemned to walk the earth until the werewolf is dead. As Jack's personality and behavior remain the same in death as they were in life, the emphasis in these sequences is not upon his death but upon forcing David and the audience to confront the destruction and decomposition of his body. When David meets his own victims, he doesn't simply have to face his guilt at having murdered them, but must also face in graphic detail exactly what he did *to* them.

In addition to being a major crossover success with mainstream audiences, *An American Werewolf in London* won the first annual Academy Award for Best Makeup in 1981, an achievement that many saw as the final step in the legitimization of the horror genre and graphic makeup special effects in the eyes of the industry. Robert Kurtzman of KNB Effects points out that the early 1980s were a boom time for makeup special effects, for audiences and producers alike were becoming increasingly aware of this type of work and wanted more.[2] Steve Johnson, assistant to Rick Baker on Landis' film and now a special makeup effects artist in his own right, credits Rick Baker for this boom, for the film "was one of the most influential films in this business. It spawned a lot of this stuff. In fact, everything to this day is based on the American Werewolf stuff; it amazes me. Movies have been around since the turn of the century, and it took more than eighty years for people to figure out that you could duplicate a human head and screw with it or stretch it."[3] The film therefore not only set the tone for horror films of the 1980s and created a demand for these types of effects but it also created the technological blueprint upon which other artists would build. While vampire films of the 1970s used special makeup effects to foreground a now transformed vampire, they did not feature the act of transformation itself. This would become a part of the genre in the 1980s, drawing upon the now existing technologies to effect metamorphosis.

The 1980s saw the meeting of the capabilities of technology to present the processes of physical transformation with an increase in the public's obsession with the body. Bryan S. Turner explains that, when he wrote his book *The Body and Society* in 1984, there was little interest in the study of the sociology of the body. But subsequently there has been a flood of publications looking at issues of embodiment in contemporary society, responding to the cultural fascination with the body that took hold of society in the 1980s. This obsession can be seen by the increasing focus upon fitness expressed through an emphasis on dieting, and the rising popularity of aerobics, fitness videotapes, and television exercise programs. The media also acknowledged and capitalized on this new fitness obsession through Olivia Newton John's music video and hit single, "Physical," the thriller *Perfect* (1985), set in an aerobics center, and in the training montages staged in such films as *Flashdance* (1983) and the *Rocky* series (1976, 1982, 1985, 1990). Hollywood also produced a new style of action film that emphasized the muscular bodies of stars Arnold Schwarzenegger (then an internationally prizewinning bodybuilder), Sylvester Stallone, and Bruce Willis. Yvonne Tasker suggests that this new form of action cinema provided "a showcase for the display of the muscular male body" sculpted through bodybuilding.[4]

In addition to these processes of sculpting and beautifying the body, the decade also saw a rise in body modification, largely through tattooing and body piercing. Bryan S. Turner argues that this obsession with the body and its construction allows individuals to express their own personal emotional needs through constructing their own bodies.[5] Rather than defining the self by the soul and/or the spirit, it became defined by the status of the body, the physical extension of the materialist culture of the 1980s. The body was treated as a product upon which a newly constructed sense of self would be projected. John Sweetman claims that many body modifiers view their modifications as a means of asserting their own control over their bodies and their sense of self by directing the physical changes to its shape and image.[6] Both Sandra Tomc and Anthony Giddens have made similar claims for dieters and sufferers of anorexia nervosa, as well as compulsive overeating.[7]

Contrasted with this obsession with bodily control were the images of bodies out of control that became increasingly represented in the media. The most prevalent was the rise of AIDS, first gaining notice as healthy young men began to waste away and die of diseases that should normally not be fatal. These deaths were eventually attributed to a virus that caused the immune system to breakdown, leaving the body vulnerable to disease and infection.[8] As the world became increasingly aware of this disease, the media began to confront the public with images of emaciated men dying. This was briefly matched by the images of the famine in Ethiopia that hit the television screens in 1984 and 1985. Additionally, the decade saw the obsession with controlling the body through dieting and exercise lead to an increase in eating disorders such as bulimia and anorexia that wrought havoc upon the bodies of young women. While the decade tried to locate its self-image in the body, these images of bodies run amok served to undermine that control.

While John Sweetman views the mainstream appropriation of piercing and tattooing as a part of this cultural body project, he argues that these underground forms of body modification also defy the hegemony of the unmarked body beautiful at the heart of consumer culture. They blur the boundaries that define what is perceived as natural and organic by "mixing ink with skin" or "metal and tissue," and bring into question certain natural oppositions, such as body and technology, natural and artificial, and inside and outside.[9] Steven Connor argues that the skin is the natural boundary of the body, serving to protect the body and separate the individual from all that surrounds it.[10] Piercing and tattooing therefore undermine the skin's role as boundary by suggesting the possibility for rupture and infiltration. As such, they embody the abject and their visibility force a cultural confrontation with a body that refuses to be contained or controlled.

This image of the abject body out of control became the central icon of the modern horror film of the 1980s. Pete Boss suggests that the horror film in this period transformed its "gothic legacy" of Frankenstein and other films about creation and destruction of the body into a "matter of fact" treatment of "physical helplessness." The body and not the spirit, he argues, now defined the self.[11] If the body defines the self, then the skin serves to define boundaries of the self. The horror genre therefore confronts the vulnerability of the self by threatening to puncture the skin. As Steven Connor argues,

> The skin is the vulnerable, unreliable boundary between inner and outer conditions and the proof of their frightening, fascinating intimate contiguity. Thus, the threat of "pathogenic impingement" from the outside is matched, as some have noticed, by a new fear and fascination regarding the interior body, as expressed in fantasies of various kinds of eruption through or perforation of the skin from the inside. The skin has become intensely vulnerable and thoroughly unreliable in its combined incapacity to resist external threats and its tendency to harbour (but then to release) internal threats.[12]

As makeup special effects artists successfully managed to penetrate mainstream cinema, they returned to traditional movie monsters such as werewolves and vampires in order to reinterpret their classic mythology through their reconception of the monstrous body. This new interpretation resulted in the merging of Noël Carroll's cognitive approach with Julia Kristeva's arguments about the physically abject body: monsters defy categorization by breaking boundaries through bodily penetration and physical metamorphosis.

This new emphasis on bodily penetration within the horror genre captures the significance of redefining the shape, appearance, and boundaries of the body through body modification. It is not simply the surface appearance that matters but the act of changing the body and breaking those physical boundaries. Sweetman claims that "tattooing and piercing do not simply and magically transform the appearance of the 'outer body'; they are invasive procedures involving pain, blood and the penetration of the skin in a non-medicalized setting."[13] Similarly, vampirism, the act of drinking human blood, is an invasive procedure involving blood, pain, and a penetration of the surface of the skin. While Romero's zombies rapaciously eat flesh and Rice's vampires drink blood with an alcoholic's thirst, the vampires in *Near Dark* (1987), *The Lost Boys* (1987), *Innocent Blood* (1992), *Interview with the Vampire* (1994), and *Blade* (1998) break through the boundaries of the skin to reach the blood with an unprecedented level of precision. In *Near Dark*, Mae tears open the skin on her own wrist in order to feed Caleb, while in the film *Interview with the Vampire*, when Claudia's seamstress accidentally pricks her finger, the child-vampire offers to kiss it better only to painfully bite into the finger with a precision heightened by the sound of the puncture. Both *Innocent Blood* and *Blade* feature sequences in which the vampires graphically rip through the skin and muscle of their victims' necks in order to lap up the blood that issues forth in profusion. In all of these cases, as Philip Brophy explains with respect to the close-up of a razor blade slicing through a thumb in *The Thing* (1982), "One's body is queasily affected not by fear or horror, but by the precision that the photographic image is able to exact upon us."[14] These sequences of blood drinking emphasize the invasiveness of vampirism. It penetrates boundaries between inside and out, breaking and sometimes ripping through the skin.

Anxieties about the vulnerability of the skin and bodily boundaries are not only enacted upon the victims in vampire films but also upon the vampires themselves. Steven Connor points out that in the 1980s, the growing realization that the destruction of the ozone layer could cause cancer through prolonged exposure to the sun resulted in a "fear of a violation of the skin by the light that had previously been believed to nourish and sustain it."[15] This growing fear of the sun is reproduced in vampire films by the increasingly important role it plays as an agent of destruction. While it was his exposure to the sun that made Count Orlok dissolve into nothingness in *Nosferatu*, in more recent films the vampire is less at risk of fading away and more at risk of having its skin burnt away layer by layer, presented in graphic and painful detail, like Dracula in Hammer's *Horror of Dracula*. In *The Lost Boys* when the vampire David reaches after one of the adolescent vampire-killers, his hand is pulled into the light and catches fire. In *Near Dark*, the only thing that threatens the nomadic vampires is the sunlight and as such it is presented as a physical force and a weapon. Throughout the film, the vampires are depicted racing along the highway in search of shelter with the sun rising on the horizon, chasing them from town to town and from sunset to sunrise. The police surround the vampires in a motel where they intend to rest for the day, and the subsequent shoot-out showcases the violent and violating nature of the sun. As Severin prepares to shoot his way out of the motel, a shotgun blast through the door results in a powerful shaft of sunlight bursting into the dark room and knocking Severin on to the ground with real physical force. Each shot at the police is met with a shot of sunlight at the vampires. When the leader Jesse asks how Severin is doing, Severin responds, "I'm down to my last inch of skin." In fact, as their nomadic lifestyle results in their narrowly escaping the sun on numerous occasions, the vampires are usually covered in charred skin that acts as a reminder of their vulnerability. In *Blade*, the vampires' use of high SPF sunblock to protect themselves from the sun further supports the analogy between the increasingly significant role of the sun in vampire films and contemporary concerns for skin damage.

While the above instances evoke the fear for the body at the hands of outside forces and invaders, concern for the boundaries of the body is also evoked from the inside out as is demonstrated by processes of metamorphosis. In what James B. Twitchell calls the "Year of the Wolf," *An American Werewolf in London* and Joe Dante's *The Howling* (1981) gained fame for their innovative new special effects, created by Rick Baker and Rob Bottin respectively, that made it possible to show the transformation of the werewolf before the audience's very eyes.[16] Both films were structured around a major scene wherein the full body transformation of a man into a werewolf was shown in graphic detail and without the camera trickery that defined Lon Chaney Jr.'s wolf man. In the Universal film series, Chaney's transformations were done through the painstaking combination of character makeup and optical dissolves. To achieve this magical transformation, Jack Pierce, the Universal makeup artist who created makeup for *Dracula* (1931), *Frankenstein* (1931), and *The Mummy* (1932), applied twenty-one stages of makeup all while Chaney's hands were held down with pins and his head positioned in a brace as each stage was filmed using dissolves to bridge each transition.[17] Baker and Bottin's techniques involved a whole new form of trickery.

What both Baker and Bottin's creations share is an emphasis upon the physical effects and processes of the transformation from man into werewolf rather than the end result. The optical techniques used in Lon Chaney Jr.'s werewolf films as well as the bat-into-vampire transformations of *The House of Dracula* (1945) emphasize a smooth, spectral transformation in line with magic lanterns and the Phantasmagoria. The before-camera transformations achieved in the 1980s distance the effect from the magical and emphasize real physical change. As Pete Boss argues, it became the role of the special makeup effects artist to present "human tissue in torment . . . the body in profuse disarray."[18] Like body modification, the transformations in *An American Werewolf in London* and *The Howling* are invasive procedures that emphasize pain and physical penetration of the skin, this time, however, from the inside. In both cases, the transformation of the werewolf takes place about two-thirds of the way through the film. In *An American Werewolf in London*, the audience, along with David, the hero, has been anticipating the arrival of the full moon to see whether he will change or not. David's boredom and nervousness as he shuffles around his girlfriend's living room, mirror the audience's own anticipation as Landis draws out the final moments before the rise of the moon. Similarly, although it is clear in *The Howling* that werewolves populate the tranquil community of The Colony, audiences must sit through two-thirds of the film before actually seeing a werewolf in plain view. In both cases the changes that occur are show-stopping spectacles of bone-crunching, skin-stretching metamorphosis.

In *The Howling*, as Eddie changes from man to beast, his face and body pulsate as if something is about to burst forth from beneath his skin. Gradually hair grows through his skin to create a layer of fur, while long fingernails bloodily push through the skin on his fingertips to form elongated claws. His mouth widens, curling up into a hideous smile, while his nose and mouth protrude forward. To heighten this effect, the film cuts to a side view of the face extending into an animal's snout. While Bottin's effects in *The Howling* particularly showcase miraculous facial transformation, Baker's work in *American Werewolf* painstakingly creates a full body transformation. David's body, like Eddie's, grows hair, claws, and a wolf's snout, but David's hands also stretch into extended paws, his wrists swell in size and his ankles contort. The vertebrae in his back relocate themselves to create a curved spine, while his legs stretch and the bones and joints shift into the crouched haunches of an animal. Sound is key to the perception and appreciation of both sequences: the stretching of skin, breaking of tissue, and crunching of bones as each element of their bodies is forced to shift into its new place. The emphasis is not only on our seeing the transformation, but our understanding the physical effect that their bodies are undergoing through the sounds of the body changing. Both sequences last approximately three minutes causing the narrative to stop while the audience observes these phenomenal special effects.

The emphasis upon our experiencing the spectacle of this type of sequence is supported by the presence of the film's heroine in *The Howling* as the audience member for whom Eddie is changing. The film constantly cuts to her watching Eddie change, not to conceal the change, as in *The Return of the Vampire* (1943) and *Horror of Dracula*, but rather to highlight her terror, shock, and disgust at what she is seeing. This is noticeably different from Landis' film where the hero is alone while he undergoes this change, although in many ways David is the audience for his own transformation. The sequence emphasizes, through the use of direct and indirect point of view shots, not only his agony but also his abject terror at witnessing the changes to his own body. While Landis' sequence makes explicit the subjective horror of undergoing transformation, Dante's more self-reflexive approach acknowledges both the horror and the spectacle of watching such transformations.

The self-reflexivity of Dante's film is demonstrated at the end of the film when the heroine, now a werewolf, allows herself to transform on a television news broadcast as a means of warning the world about the existence of werewolves. The transformation is followed by a montage sequence of a variety of people watching the news and responding with shock, horror, disbelief, or bemusement at what they are seeing. The montage ends in a bar where one of the patrons remarks with wonder, "Things they can do with special effects these days." This remark is precisely aimed at the film's audience and is what Steve Neale would call "a 'textual' and an 'institutional' event: a remark addressed to the spectator by the film, and by the cinematic apparatus, about the nature of its special effects."[19] Talking specifically about the famous line in *The Thing*—"You've got to be fucking kidding!" uttered at the sight of a particularly ridiculous embodiment of the alien—but also clearly relevant to this moment in *The Howling*, Neale argues that this type of remark is a sign that the film is self-aware: it is aware that the monster is a product of sophisticated special effects pushed to their limits; that the spectator is aware that the monster is a "collocation of special effects; and the spectator now knows that the film knows too."[20] The spectacle of these sequences serves to horrify its audience because of the graphicness of the bodily transformation, as well as astound them by the sophistication of the special effects.

The significance of these two werewolf movies for the vampire genre is that they successfully integrate a conventional horror monster into the modern horror genre by reinterpreting the genre through the use of special effects and intertextual narrative structures. The vampire films of this period similarly demonstrate a return to a more generically conventional narrative structure, drawing upon much of the iconography previously abandoned by Romero in *Night of the Living Dead* and *Martin*. But as a result, the genre is better able to explore the allegorical potential of the vampire by heightening and manipulating the audience's familiarity with the genre's conventions. As Brophy argues, "The contemporary horror film rarely denies its clichés, but instead accepts them, often causing an undercurrent by overplaying them."[21]

This is demonstrated in *Fright Night* (1985) when the fledgling vampire, Evil Ed, in the tradition of Dracula, transforms himself into a wolf to attack the vampire-killer, Peter Vincent. Although this transformation takes place offscreen, the filmmakers showcase his return transformation from wolf into human after Peter has put a stake through his heart and he is undergoing his final death throes. Peter Johnson, Rick Baker's assistant on *An American Werewolf in London*, undertook the special effects of this sequence and he desired to use the technological effects made possible by Baker's work to create an altogether different type of transformation.[22] While David's transformation emphasizes the physicality of the metamorphosis, it remains systematic and symmetrical in the manner of Lon Chaney Jr.'s metamorphosis. Each stage is one step further along a natural progression to becoming a wolf. In the case of Evil Ed, Johnson's work emphasizes the interstitial quality of this transformation; different parts of the body change in different ways and at different rates so that, for much of the sequence, Ed is a horrifying mix of animal and boy.

Again, sound is absolutely key in this sequence as the mixture of animal howls and human cries evokes a pathos that moves the terrified vampire-killer to tears by the horror of what Ed's body is undergoing. At the same time, however, Peter is revolted by the image of this body in transformation. As Ed changes, he reaches out to Peter who leans forward to take his hand but then pulls away with horror and revulsion. (Figure 7.1) While he cries for Ed, he cannot bring himself to make physical contact. The re-

Figure 7.1. The abject werewolf boy in *Fright Night.*

introduction of a conventional element of the genre—the transformation of vampire into animal—is reinterpreted, confounding the perception of the vampire as being in control of its body and foregrounding the horror of witnessing a body defy that control.

Even in films that do not foreground their use of special effects, vampirism in this period is equated with the body out of control; the act of becoming a vampire is increasingly portrayed as physical change to the body as opposed to resurrection from the dead. For instance, *Near Dark* and *The Lost Boys* each follow a young man struggling against his own transformation into a vampire as his body begins to rebel. In *Near Dark*, Caleb possesses the desire and thirst for blood once he is "turned," but finds his sense of morality at odds with the desires of his body. Michael's body, in *The Lost Boys*, begins to act of its own accord as he wakes up to find that he is floating against the ceiling and is unable to force himself back down to earth. The vampire is presented as an allegory for the bodily changes of adolescence by the manner in which both films focus upon bodies in rebellion. Similarly, in *Fright Night*, a film that does draw upon the techniques of special effects, the vampire Jerry Dandridge loses control of his body when Charlie stabs him in the hand with a pencil as a means of protecting himself. Dandridge, usually in complete control, transforms into a monstrous batlike creature, as if the sudden pain and anger allowed his body to be released from his control long enough to reveal the monstrous body, part-man part-animal, beneath the veneer of sophistication and charm. It is only once he regains his composure that his more handsome visage returns. Through the special makeup effects the true abjectness of the vampire body is allowed to surface.

The Hunger (1983) uses the bodily transformations of vampirism to explore anxieties about the aging process and the desire for immortality. The film follows vampire Mirium Blaylock in her search for eternal companionship. Her current lover John, once human but now a transformed vampire, lives and hunts with Mirium for what he thinks will be eternity. Gradually however he notices subtle changes that lead him to believe that Mirium's promise of immortality was disingenuous. He can no longer sleep and as a result begins to age at an accelerated rate. In one significant scene, while waiting patiently to see Dr. Sarah Roberts, an expert in cryogenics, John ages fifty years in a few hours. As he leaves the hospital, he is virtually unrecognizable as the man who entered, mainly as a result of the sophisticated makeup transitions created by Dick Smith. In this film, vampirism is equated with youth and beauty as all the characters—Mirium, John, and Sarah—seek to find ways of circumventing the natural process of aging.

The horror of the aging process is showcased by the juxtaposition of John's transformation, achieved through gentle dissolves between stages of makeup effect, with the doctors' analysis of graphic videotaped footage of a chimpanzee whose biological clock has been altered to initiate an accelerated aging process, which leads to the complete disintegration of its body before the camera. This process is presented as a violent attack upon the body, whether inflicted by nature or science. In the eyes of this film, with its glamorous and beautiful stars—David Bowie, Catherine Deneuve, and Susan Sarandon—matched by director Tony Scott's characteristically slick visual style, aging is viewed as a disease that can be cured by neither vampirism nor science. This perception is reinforced when the ancient-looking John asks Mirium to kiss him once more, presenting it not as an act of intimacy but horror, and inciting physical recoil.

This attack upon the youthful body by the aging process culminates in the destruction of Mirium at the hands of her still aging ex-lovers who are stowed alive in coffins in her attic. In the climax of the film, each of these emaciated corpses rises up against her. They surround Mirium who, in a paroxysm of abject horror at their presence and touch, backs away and falls over the banister. Falling to the ground incites a monstrous transformation in Mirium's own body as she thrashes and screams in agony while aging into an emaciated skeleton at an accelerated rate. Aging, this film suggests, is a painful and physically violent process that denies any semblance of control over the body.

The image of a body out of control is further conveyed through the clinical appropriation of vampirism in *The Hunger* as well as in Tobe

Hooper's *Lifeforce* (1985), as the process of becoming a vampire is conveyed through a language of medicine. Ed Guerrero argues that films that trace the spread of a disease, either throughout the population or in the body, evoke the 1980s fear of the pandemic spread of disease, particularly acquired immunodeficiency syndrome (AIDS).[23] Both *The Hunger* and *Lifeforce* seem to particularly convey fears about AIDS, as they showcase the transference of the disease of vampirism through same-sex contact, which, in the early 80s, was deemed to be the primary way of acquiring the virus. It should be pointed out that these films were not necessarily consciously made as AIDS allegories; they were made at very early stages in the outbreak, before AIDS was a nationally recognized concern. But they do represent a reinterpretation of the nineteenth-century equation of vampirism with sexually transmitted disease through the language of science rather than simply sex.

In *The Hunger*, when Mirium decides that Sarah is the ideal substitute for John, now safely stowed in the attic, she begins Sarah's transformation into a vampire through the transfusion of her own blood into Sarah's system. Sarah's change into a vampire is therefore clinically explained as the gradual substitution of her own blood cells for diseased blood cells and as this happens she physically undergoes a change in her body. This is not manifested through special makeup effects but rather through the intense physicalization of her pain as her human cells lose against this alien invader. The symptoms begin with a loss of appetite followed by vomiting, dizziness, and a loss of color to the face. Finally, Sarah can no longer move but must lie on the bed in a seizure of pain and muscle contractions until she finally gives in and drinks the blood that her body now demands.[24] Her body has been taken over by the contaminated blood of a vampire.

While only one individual is under threat in *The Hunger*, the vampires in the science-fiction horror film *Lifeforce* present a threat on a more global scale. The film uses special makeup effects as a means of equating vampirism with the ravages of contagious disease. The vampiric narrative of *Lifeforce* chronicles the spread of vampirism across both the body and the population in much the same way that Stoker's novel *Dracula* invokes the concern for the spread of sexually transmitted diseases. Rather than drinking blood, these space vampires suck the lifeforce from their victims, leaving their bodies a desiccated husk until they rise again to suck the lifeforce from their own victims, spreading the disease further. The narrative traces the panic over the spread of disease by following the military as it hunts for the lead vampire who could contaminate the entire country.

The special makeup effects, however, portray the actual mutation of a healthy body into an emaciated corpse, screeching and crying in pain, and then exploding into dust when it is denied a further lifeforce to replenish itself.

The effect of vampirism in both *The Hunger* and *Lifeforce* is to dry out the body of its liquids and energies. This means that death for these turned vampires is manifested in their bodies crumbling into dust. John, as well as each of Mirium's previous lovers, crumbles into a pile of dust and body parts in her attic after she dies; the vampires in *Lifeforce* seem to spontaneously combust into dust as they thrash and throw themselves around their cells in desperate need. While *The Hunger* and *Lifeforce* represent a tradition that began with *The Horror of Dracula* that showcases the breakdown of bodily boundaries by having the vampire bodies crumble inward, there is a second tradition that emphasizes their outward explosions. As Edgar Frog explains to his fellow teen vampire-killers in *The Lost Boys*, vampires in the 80s horror film never "go out the same way" but they do often share an excess of spectacular gore. As the representations of vampires have been made increasingly physical by special makeup effects, they have come to be defined as the sum of their bodily parts. As a result, their destruction has been portrayed as an explosion of those body parts in a bloodbath of abject bodily liquids, all the noxious liquids we seek to expel from ourselves: blood, ooze, pus, and feces. No two films do it quite the same way. In Robert Rodriguez' *From Dusk till Dawn* (1996), when one of the lead characters stabs a vampire in the chest, the knife is shown to be covered in a slimy green liquid rather than blood. Later, as one of the vampire-killers stakes the dead vampire bodies to prevent them from rising again, he walks along a row of bodies, plunging a wooden stake into each of their chests as streams of black and green liquid spurt up around him.

In *Fright Night*, when Charlie stakes Dandridge's henchman Billy in the heart, Billy's body melts into a heap of unrecognizable bodily liquids before Peter and Charlie's eyes. This effect was achieved through a range of special effects techniques. The skin on his hands appears to peel away before the muscles and bones melt into a bright green gelatin that pours onto the floor. This is followed by a similar process that shows Billy's face melting away, leaving nothing but a rotting skeleton that falls to the ground and breaks into tiny pieces. In *The Lost Boys*, when Sam and the Frog brothers find the vampires hanging from the ceiling in the underground cave, they hammer a stake through the heart of one of the creatures and are shocked when his body explodes in a torrent of unrecognizable liquid that covers the young vampire-slayers in slime. Later, when one of the vampires is pushed into a bathtub full of holy water and garlic, not only does the skin on his body slowly melt away leaving only a fleshless skeleton, but the reaction between his flesh and the holy water causes the water to bubble and his flesh and blood to seep into the house's entire plumbing system, as every sink, pipe and toilet explodes in a purple shower of blood, flesh, and other bodily liquids.

While the revival of the vampire genre in the 1970s saw an attempt to strip the vampire of its supernatural qualities and reduce it to a de-spiritualized body through guerrilla film techniques, the horror genre of the 1980s sought to reinterpret the traditional conventions of the genre through graphic makeup effects. By building upon the capabilities of the effects artists to create hyperreal graphic body effects, the destruction of the vampire forced a confrontation with the abject. As a result, the vampire film captures the anguish of embodiment as well as the inability to control the body and to maintain its boundaries.

The proliferation of books, television programs, and films about vampirism in the 1970s was a response to the intensive cultural and political changes that were taking place in America at this time. Facing the decline of its position as the world leader in modernization, America was forced to undergo a period of reinvention, transforming itself from a modern industrial nation to a postindustrial one. This transformation was captured in the vampire genre's own reinvention as it explored a range of new configurations and generic conventions while self-consciously challenging the audience to rethink the nature of vampirism in the contemporary world. While *Dracula* embodies modernity at its peak, *Martin* captures the decay and decline of the icons of modernity as they pass into antiquity. The film's deconstruction of the vampire mythology closes the door on conventional representations of the vampire while paving the way for the next wave of modern vampires to take his place.

By the end of the decade many of the accepted conventions of the vampire genre had been abandoned, but new ones had taken hold. The vampire in film was firmly accepted as American, modern, secular, and disembeded from the spatial and conventional restrictions imposed by premodern tradition. The next section will explore how, as a result of these changes, in the 1980s and 1990s, the vampire was unleashed on the expanse of the American landscape, fragmenting into a series of subgroups based around a range of urban settings, each time reinventing itself to suit its new location. Through this fragmentation, the vampire film charts the reconstitution of the American urban landscape and the rise of the postindustrial city following the economic and social crises of the 1970s. The tensions between the vampire subgroups—most notably the New York vampire, the Los Angeles vampire, and the vampire road movie— evoke the conflicting representations and indecipherable experience of the city undergoing a transition from the modern to the postmodern.

PART THREE

RECONFIGURING THE URBAN VAMPIRE

CHAPTER EIGHT

New York and the Vampire Flâneuse

[New York] was to become in literature what one native son, Herman Melville, described as the city of darkness, of orphanage, of crushing anonymity.

ALFRED KAZAN [1]

Vampirism in Habit *is that part of humanity that is hungry, and insatiable, and New York is the hub of an insatiable culture.*

LARRY FESSENDEN ON *HABIT* [2]

By relocating the vampire to a modern urban setting, *Dracula* and *Martin* are the first steps toward the release of the vampire from superstition and tradition, facilitating a reconfiguration of the vampire from a premodern monster to an urban flâneur, increasingly at home in the city. *Martin* in particular self-consciously demythologizes the vampire in film by stripping away all of the familiar conventions. While films of the 1980s tend to return to these conventions as discussed in the previous chapter, they are not bound by a recognized vampire tradition. Instead the films are individually fashioned from a broad spectrum of old and new vampire conventions, based upon the needs of the narrative and the filmmaker's own interpretation of the vampire legend. The manner in which these films are fashioned, however, is not random. The one consistency in the vampire film of this period is that the vampire is primarily an urban creature. Vampires in contemporary cinema and television are presented as comfortably inhabiting a wide variety of cities including Pittsburgh (*Innocent Blood*), London (*Tale of a Vampire, Wisdom of Crocodiles*), New Orleans (*Interview with the Vampire, Dracula 2000*), Mexico City (*Cronos*), Toronto (*Nick Knight*), and Moscow (*Night Watch*). The ways in which the conventions are reconfigured, manipulated, undermined, or abandoned, therefore, draw upon existing and emerging discourses and representations of particular urban identities. As a result, the range of identities exhibited in these films charts the fragmented urban landscape that characterizes the shifting terrain of modern American culture.

As a means of illustrating how the vampire has come to embody this fragmentation, I will, over the next three chapters, address three urban subgenres of the vampire film, moving from east to west. I will begin with the modern metropolis of New York, followed by the vampire road movie located upon the highways crossing the American landscape, and will end in the postmodern urban sprawl of Los Angeles.[3] William Sharpe and Leonard Wallock suggest that the evolution of the city has involved a westward shift—from the Paris and London of the nineteenth century, to New York at the beginning of the twentieth century, to Los Angeles and Tokyo of today—and with this westward shift the city has become increasingly indecipherable.[4] While this argument suggests a linear progression from the industrial to the postindustrial, the continued presence of these cities and their urban legacies well into the twenty-first century negates the idea of linearity in favor of coexistence and mutual reinvention. This is supported by the simultaneous emergence of these urban vampire films throughout the 1980s and 1990s, as well as the development of the vampire road movie, which merges both the modern and the postmodern.

New York City is a nineteenth-century city that grew out of the rise of industrialism in the United States to become the country's first modern metropolis. As a result, it embodies the move toward modernity that took place in the late nineteenth and early twentieth centuries. It was heavily influenced by European culture as it was the primary entrance into the United States from Europe, welcoming over 2,000,000 immigrants largely from Ireland, Germany, and Italy between 1885–1895 alone.[5] Furthermore, in the first decades of the twentieth century, the city was marked by a series of feats of engineering: the construction of increasingly tall skyscrapers, new bridges and tunnels linking Manhattan to the ever-expanding suburbs, subways and elevated railways that facilitated transport throughout the growing city, and highways that linked New York to the other parts of the state.[6] These developments of modern technologies, engineering, and art shaped the city's cultural identity and architectural design, making the city such an icon of modernity that the sight of it from New York Harbor inspired Fritz Lang's vision of a futuristic city in his film *Metropolis* (1927). This chapter will begin by looking at how this modernist perception of New York is embodied in the lone female vampire in films such as *The Hunger* (1988), *Vampire's Kiss* (1988), *Nadja* (1994), *The Addiction* (1995), *Vampire in Brooklyn* (1997), and *Habit* (1997). I will examine how the perception and discourses around modernity are reinterpreted by the female vampire's command of the urban landscape and her appropriation of the traditionally male role of urban flâneur.

In *Love at First Bite* (1979), Dracula is forced to abandon his ancestral home of Romania, which has come under communist rule, and must follow the tradition of many European immigrants by leaving the Old World to settle in contemporary New York. After this, Dracula's first arrival in New York, a small subgenre of New York vampire films emerged and developed through the 1980s and 1990s. Starting with Cindy Sondheim's acceptance of Dracula's bite in *Love at First Bite*, most of the subsequent New York vampires have been women. Tony Scott's *The Hunger*—adapted from Whitley Strieber's novel and presented as an American reworking of the Belgian film *Daughters of Darkness* (1971)—transports the timeless European narrative to a particular period and locale in New York. The vampire Mirium seems untouched by time. Her secluded apartment, encapsulating the range of periods through which she has lived, distances her from a sense of the present, while her choice of lovers connects her to the modern. *Vampire's Kiss* is similarly a product of its time as it follows the gradual decline of a 1980s New York yuppie, Peter Loew, as his superficial grip on reality and the excesses of his lifestyle cause him to descend into madness. His madness manifests itself in his delusion that the exotic woman he meets in a nightclub and takes home for a one-night stand has transformed him into a vampire.[7]

The Hunger and *Vampire's Kiss* are intermediary films between the mainstream and the independent sector. Neither was shot on a shoestring budget nor were they big-budget blockbusters. Furthermore, both share a certain cross-fertilization of mainstream film and independent art film. While *The Hunger* is very slickly produced and is at times shot like a modern music video, it also borrows from the style of the European art film through its relationship with *Daughters of Darkness*. Similarly, *Vampire's Kiss* is a black comedy, but its emphasis upon the subjective experience of madness, Nicolas Cage's self-conscious pastiche of Max Schreck in *Nosferatu*, and his overall excessive performance style, are clearly influenced by German Expressionism.

By the 1990s, however, the New York vampire film had become increasingly associated with New York independent cinema, a tradition of experimental and art cinema dating back to the 1930s city symphonies

such as *A Bronx Morning* (1931) and *City of Contrasts* (1931), through the
New American Cinema movement of the 1960s led by film critic and independent filmmaker Jonas Mekas, and the personal filmmaking practices
of such New York raconteurs as Martin Scorsese, Woody Allen, and Spike
Lee.[8] Films such as *Undying Love* (1991), *Red Lips* (1995), *Nadja, The Addiction*, and *Habit* are low-budget vampire films that reinterpret the vampire genre by focusing upon women vampires living and killing in New
York City. The emergence of this cluster of independent vampire films
is linked to a heightened interest in independent cinema in this period
in New York. Robert Kolker explains that, in the early 1990s, a "studio
boycott" on mainstream filmmaking forced the "East Coast Council of
Movie Trade-Union Reps" to devise special low-budget film contracts
that deferred a percentage of the labor expense in favor of a percentage
of revenue. This led to a growth in the "city's modern local indie scene."[9]
According to film producer Christine Vachon, "New York remains the
epicenter of the American independent-film movement, with a large community of filmmakers committed to making serious films—not to picking
audiences' pockets."[10] The above vampire films were all made during this
particular boom.

The Indie Vampire Film

While the decision of both Michael Almereyda and Abel Ferrara to shoot
their vampire films, *Nadja* and *The Addiction* respectively, in black-and-
white suggests an intertextual reference to the classic Universal horror
films of the 1930s such as *Dracula*, it also, in relation to contemporary
filmmaking practices, indicates a film's destiny to be treated as an independent and art house product. It is commonly accepted in the mainstream industry that black-and-white film has come to symbolize classic
cinema, history, or art. These genres are perceived by many distributors
as lacking commercial viability as it is believed that audiences no longer have the patience for black-and-white, and that a film in black-and-
white will be "boring and difficult."[11] According to Almereyda, when he
approached various potential investors with his script, he was met with
enthusiasm for the film but also pressure to shoot it in color.[12] Similarly,
the cast and crew of *The Addiction* funded Ferrara's film so that they could
maintain control.[13] Many other directors have been faced with ultima-
tums from producers and financial backers about their artistic desires to
shoot in black-and-white. George Romero's film *Martin* was originally

conceived as a black-and-white film but was shot on color film stock in case the distributor saw a problem marketing it. The film was eventually released using a combination of color and black-and-white film.[14] The decision to shoot in black-and-white therefore has huge economic ramifications for any director.

Abel Ferrara's use of black-and-white suggests a connection to a legacy of horror films but it also draws upon an altogether different tradition of filmmaking. The film begins with a series of black-and-white still images of victims of a massacre in Vietnam accompanied by a voice-over that explains and condemns the atrocities. This opening evokes the conventions of the documentary tradition, despite the revelation that these images are actually part of a lecture taking place in a university philosophy course. The fact that the rest of the film is presented in black-and-white and contains a great deal of handheld camera work further inflects the film with the style of a documentary and the suggestion of authenticity. The film returns to such documentary footage and photographs twice more to confirm the connections between Ferrara's commentary about violence on the streets of New York and humanity's global crimes.

Coming from a different background than Ferrara, Almereyda earned his reputation for making a series of avant-garde short films with Pixelvision, a Fisher-Price toy video camera that he adapted specifically for his own use. Having received critical success with these films, Almereyda decided that he wanted to turn his attention to a more mainstream genre with *Nadja*. His approach to this genre was, however, anything but mainstream. In the first instance he was, like Ferrara, adamant that his film should be in black-and-white as it would be less expensive and therefore easier to achieve his ambitions for the project. Almereyda's use of black-and-white also draws upon the tradition of black-and-white surrealist filmmaking practices to which the film owes a great debt. Furthermore, Almereyda chose to shoot elements of the film in Pixelvision to express a poetic and surreal quality that was further enhanced by the film's discontinuous editing structure. Finally, his script for *Nadja* is an unusual cross-fertilization of mainstream horror and modernist art for it is both an unofficial remake of the classic Universal horror film *Dracula's Daughter* (1936) and strongly influenced by André Breton's surrealist novel *Nadja*.[15] Almereyda explains that the "book was a kind of starting point for me . . . There were lots of things about madness, love, chance, and identity in it that are related to what the movie is about. In Breton's book there's the feeling of a city having a separate life, and people being guided by and embracing chance."[16]

Figure 8.1. Urban reverie in *Nadja*.

The opening of the film demonstrates the influence of surrealism and the way Breton subjectively channeled meaning into empty locations. The film begins with an abstract image of smoke billowing out from the ground while streams of light fluctuate across the screen. A woman's voice is introduced as the film dissolves to a poetic image of the city, dreamily describing the experience of being in New York thusly: "Nights. Nights without sleep. Long nights in which the brain lights up like a big city." The camera tracks along a Manhattan street aimed up at the buildings. A close-up of Nadja, the title character, is superimposed over the street scene, while a further superimposition of moving streams of light adds texture and motion to the serene and thoughtful image. (Figure 8.1) The fusion of these three elements creates an association of meaning whereby the empty New York streets are infused with Nadja's presence and subjectivity.

This sequence cuts to a shot of Nadja, Dracula's daughter, describing why she is happiest in New York. She explains that "Europe is a village. Here you *feel* so many things rushing together. It even gets more exciting after midnight." Her comments suggest a synchronicity between the urban experience and the vampire's existence in which, as she says, "the brain lights up like a big city." The dreaminess of the opening montage of urban images overlain by her haunting voice establishes the atmosphere for the late night reverie of the urban vampire and the use of superimposition and seamless dissolves èquates Nadja with the city itself. This opening therefore serves to undermine one of the key characteristics of the book; while Breton's novel equates Nadja's madness with the unpredictability of the city, the story is told from the perspective of her male companion, using Nadja as a channel for his own experience of the city. The narration of Almereyda's film, however, has been handed over to Nadja.

Almereyda's Nadja is not simply drawn to any city. Her description demonstrates an affinity with the particular urban experience of New York. The opposition between the European village and the American city that she discusses suggests a much more significant evolution from the modernity of the European city to the even more modern American city—that is, Breton's Paris to Almereyda's New York. For Nadja, New York is truly the city that never sleeps. The streets are crowded and offer stimulus, choices, and a cloak of invisibility. Alfred Kazin suggests that it is the "accessibility to experience" that attracts writers to New York, and it is this same "accessibility to experience" that attracts the modern vampire as embodied by Nadja.[17] Evoking the legacy of New York as a central entry point from Europe, Breton's Nadja has emigrated to the New World and haunts the streets of New York instead of Paris. This shift from the modernity of Europe to the modernity of New York is further exhibited in *The Hunger* and *The Addiction*. These films also feature European vampires who have settled in New York and who, like Nadja, attempt to propagate this evolution by transforming a modern New York woman into a modern New York vampire.

The "accessibility to experience" that is possible in New York is central to these vampire films for it enables these independent women vampires to embrace the stimulus, excitement, and nightlife of the city. To these vampires, the feminist slogan "Take back the night" is a literal definition of their existence. They walk the streets at night with impunity, watching and absorbing the life around them rather than averting their eyes or retreating from it. The films emphasize the danger within the city but also the women's attraction to the city as a site of liberation, such as Nadja's liberation from Breton's narration. Vampirism in these films, as well as in novels like *The Hunger*, offers women the power to take back the night and claim their place within the urban space. Like Mina in *Dracula*, who comes to embody modernity through her absorption of new technologies, these vampires embody modernity by embracing the delirium that signifies modern New York.

This delirium has a long history for it is an outgrowth of New York's evolution as a modern city. Rem Koolhaas suggests that the iconic images of skyrises, electricity, and technology that have come to define Manhattan were shaped by the development of Coney Island, itself an icon of the modernizing twentieth century as well as a modern embodiment of Mikhail Bakhtin's notion of the carnival.[18] Bakhtin, in his analysis of the work of Rabelais, defines the carnival as a ritual spectacle engaged in by medieval folk culture as a form of "liberation from the prevailing truth and from the established order; it marked the suspension of all hierarchical rank, privileges, norms, and prohibitions."[19] It was a chance for all to be equal and for everyone to celebrate a release from the imposition of rules and regulations about public behavior. Unlike other forms of spectacle, Bakhtin argued that the carnival did not acknowledge any distinction between actors and audience. The people do not watch the carnival, "they live in it."[20]

The amusement park is the perfect modern embodiment of Bakhtin's carnival for it celebrates a release from rules and traditions. It blurs the distinction between audience and actor and, like the carnival, is the great equalizer of humanity. Coney Island's showcasing of towers, buildings, technology, speed, and energy mirrors the transformation of New York through its electric lights, skyscrapers, bridges, and transport, and highlights the carnivalesque quality of these technological developments.[21] It is this combination of fantasy, illusion, and delirium amidst efficiency, technology, and pragmatism that still informs how the city is read as a dichotomy between the imposed structures and systems of a metropolis and its carnivalesque underpinning. These two oppositional representations work together to create a truly modern space.

Many Hollywood filmmakers established the connection between the iconic nature of Coney Island and the emerging modernity of New York in the silent era, a time when the film industry was itself symbolic of modernity as well as consumed by a fascination with its trappings. Films like Thomas Edison's *Elephants Shooting the Chutes at Luna Park* (1904) and Fatty Arbuckle's *Coney Island* (1917) capitalize on the spectacle of the amusement park, while King Vidor's *The Crowd* (1927) explores both the wonder and the dangers of the modern city. The delirium and chaos inherent in these early representations of New York were transformed by Hollywood's conversion to films with sound and the development of the film musical into a romanticized site for emotion, passion, music, and dance. These musicals safely unleash the chaos that exists within New York through the order of a choreographed musical number.

By the 1970s and the rise of New Hollywood, the release of films such as *Midnight Cowboy* (1969), *Mean Streets* (1973), and *Taxi Driver* (1976) demonstrated that a particular strand of Hollywood filmmaking had emerged, precipitating a change in the representation of New York to a darker, more expressionistic experience of the city. This was partly influenced by the filmmakers' own subjective perception and experience of New York, rather than the optimistic fantasies of the earlier Hollywood films. While classical Hollywood reveled in the glorious new city and the endless possibilities it offered, New Hollywood was made up of filmmakers affected by the city's downward shift. New York was no longer a city of endless possibilities but rather a city on the brink of a severe economic crisis following revelations of municipal misspending.[22]

This dark vision of New York makes the city ideal for the appearance of a modern vampire. One of the distinguishing features of the New York vampire film is that the vampire is generally a woman. Women in the vampire genre, from Gloria Holden in *Dracula's Daughter* to Barbara Shelley in *Dracula: Prince of Darkness* (1965), have tended to be represented as wanton creatures whose destruction is a punishment for their sexual lasciviousness. They are portrayed as either mindless monsters ruled by a dominant male vampire or victims to be protected by strong vampire hunters, such as in *Brides of Dracula* (1960), *Count Yorga, Vampire* (1970), or *Dracula 2000* (2000). The freedom to revel in the power and intoxication of their vampirism and the accessibility to the experience of the city is usually withheld from the women and given only to the male vampires. Janet Wolff's attempt to locate a flâneuse within discussions and representations of the nineteenth-century city demonstrates that this absence is not without precedent. She argues that much of the literature about modernity describes the experiences of men and not women because in these discussions the experience of modernity is equated with the experience of public life and therefore fails to address the nineteenth-century female experience, which was largely relegated to the private sphere and therefore not evocative of the shock of modern urban life.[23]

She further suggests that women only appear in these works about modernity "through their relationships with men in the public sphere, and via their illegitimate or eccentric routes into this male arena—that is, in the role of whore, widow, or murder victim."[24] Women were, however, much more in tune with modernity and the city than these representations suggest. As I have already argued in relation to *Dracula*, the climate of new technologies and bureaucracy provided clear avenues for the introduction of single young women into the urban workforce, and therefore the modern experience. The place of the flâneuse may have been withheld from women, but their place within the crowd of urban dwellers is undeniable.[25] While it is easy to dichotomize the nineteenth-century woman into two categories, the virtuous and pure angel in the house and the streetwalking prostitute, women in fact began to play a wide range of urban roles that legitimately claimed a space for them on the street: from female philanthropist to department store assistant, from typewriter girl to suffragette. Mina in *Dracula* embodies the modern experience of space and time through her absorption of business technologies, which results in her vampirism.

It would seem likely that the role of women in the urban setting would have changed in the twentieth century, for women are no longer exclusively identified with the private sphere. As Jo Little, Linda Peake, and Pat Richardson have shown, the changing role of women in the postwar period has lead to a further reconfiguration of the "geography of everyday life" and the spatial role of men and women.[26] The work of filmmakers such as Martin Scorsese and Woody Allen, however, continues the tradition of denying the legitimate presence of women on the New York street. The women in Allen's films are generally either New York homemakers such as Mia Farrow in *Hannah and Her Sisters* (1986), or girls from out of town like Annie in *Annie Hall* (1977), all slightly at odds with Allen's conception of the city. In both *Taxi Driver* and *Bringing Out the Dead* (1999), Scorsese's heroes are torn between respectable, idealized women and the juvenile streetwalkers who haunt their urban reverie, while *After Hours* (1985) continues the tendency to pathologize those women who carve a niche for themselves in the urban milieu, "mak[ing] them fascinating characters, but the impression remains of a closed masculine view of women as radically other, as the inscrutable or the dangerous."[27] Clearly what defines them as "other," "inscrutable," and "dangerous" is their command of the nightmarish urban locale and the ease with which they negotiate it.

The representation of the female vampire in the New York vampire film not only enables her to embrace her vampirism but also to appropriate a place for herself, both within the urban landscape as well as in discourses around the modern flâneur. In *The Addiction*, Kathy's vampirism allows her to face the dangers and confrontations inherent in the urban setting and walk the streets of New York's East Village with confidence. At the beginning of the film, a sequence of Kathy walking through the East Village is partially shot with a handheld camera from her point of view, recording the actions of the people on the street. While this seems to suggest the potential for female flâneurism, watching the actions of the crowd from the crowd, it is clear from the direct looks into the camera

Figure 8.2. The vampire flâneuse in *Nadja*.

by those in the street that there is no anonymity in her gaze, for she is as much looked at as she is looking. This is supported by the objective counter shots of Kathy averting her gaze to avoid eye contact with the gangs who jeer at and harass her as she passes. After her transformation, she walks the same streets with her friend Jean and while Jean continues to avert her gaze, Kathy stops to directly face and challenge the men, warning that she will meet them again; she returns later to pick up one of the young men and kills him in a dark alley. This, of course, is a very basic form of empowerment and gender reversal, symptomatic of Ferrara's work since the controversial rape-revenge film *Ms. 45* (1981).

The opportunity to experience the pleasures of the city through the empowerment of vampirism is suggested in an early scene in *Nadja* when Nadja chooses to celebrate what she believes to be her new found freedom from her father by walking along the city streets in the middle of the night as snow falls around her. (Figure 8.2) To emphasize her freedom, the sequence is intercut with a series of euphoric images of her dancing alone in a nightclub. Unlike the women who figure in early works on modernity as described by Wolff, Nadja's presence in the city is not as a "whore, widow, or murder victim" nor is it dependent upon a relationship with a man. In fact, Nadja's emergence onto the Manhattan street at this point is directly a result of the severing of a relationship with her father.

Her walk along the street is her means of asserting her freedom and independence from his influence. This is a very self-conscious departure from Breton's novel where Nadja's presence on the street is exclusively conveyed by the male narrator. It is also a break from *Dracula's Daughter*, where Countess Zaleska celebrates what she thinks is her freedom from Dracula by staying at home until she realizes that her link to Dracula has not been severed at which point she is driven out into the street to hunt. Nadja does not have such a realization. Her sojourn onto the street is dictated by her own desire and while Zaleska's evening climaxes in an attack upon a man, Nadja's evening culminates in a consenting sexual encounter with a woman.

As the experience of the urban street is paramount to these films, they each offer a tangible and authentic representation of the actual streets of New York, a city that is easily identified by its landmarks.[28] Film director James Gray explains that the reason he shoots on location in New York is because "there's actually some texture to the neighborhoods . . . The extras have real faces here. The locations don't look like they belong in *Starsky and Hutch*. And the brutality of the weather is a great thing."[29] Martin Scorsese supports this perception of New York when he explains his attraction to shooting in New York: "There's always going to be an authenticity here . . . It's the look of the place, the streets, shooting at night—all of that makes a difference."[30]

Most of the films I have so far discussed were shot entirely or in large part on location in New York and place a great deal of emphasis upon the use of recognizable locations. *The Addiction* was shot in the areas of Greenwich Village surrounding Washington Square and New York University, as well as parts of the East Village. A great deal of the film was shot with a handheld camera following the protagonist as she negotiates her way through the city. Similarly, both *Nadja* and *The Hunger* were shot in large part on location and feature key sequences in which the vampire women must move through the urban streets as a rite of passage: Nadja when she celebrates her release from her father; Sarah as she undergoes her painful transformation into a vampire. The one exception to this tradition is *Vampire in Brooklyn*, which is the most studio-produced film of the group. It does, though, feature authentic establishing shots of the New York cityscape and the Brooklyn Bridge to affix a sense of place to the studio-shot material.

This emphasis upon the authenticity of the location scenes serves both to maintain the genre's association with the art film tradition, and to reinforce the importance of the creation of a female claim to the city streets and their absorption of the carnivalesque quality of the street. Elizabeth Wilson argues that "the city normalises the carnivalesque aspects of life," offering the city dweller a break from routine and ritual in the form of "pleasure, deviation, disruption."[31] While Wilson is talking about the city in general, her argument is particularly relevant to New York because of its own intrinsic embodiment of the carnivalesque since its earliest formation. The delirium and chaos, previously inscribed onto Coney Island and its representation on film as discussed earlier, now infuses a modern perception of New York and is made manifest in the aesthetics of contemporary New York vampire films. The delirium expressed in the musicals as urban celebration is transformed in these films to a haunting urban reverie, and it is the dreaminess of this representation that allows the films, like the earlier musicals, to tap into the city's chaotic, labyrinthine energies. I do not want to make an essentialist argument by equating delirium, hysteria, and chaos with femininity while social order is equated with masculinity. Rather, I would like to equate the manner in which New York's delirious energies circumvent society's attempt to rationalize the city space with how the presence of the female vampire on the urban street undermines the perceived incongruity between women and the city. In doing so, the New York vampire film creates a space upon which the expression of female urban voyeurism and desire can be projected. Furthermore, the delirium of the New York carnivalesque is indicative of the ever-changing face of modernity to which these modern vampires are attuned and through which they are able to appropriate the traditionally male-privileged role of the modern flâneur.

In *Vampire in Brooklyn* the dreaminess of the city is presented quite literally at first as Rita is haunted by nightmares and premonitions. Her first nightmare begins on her own street as the sounds and noises of the street gradually become more ominous and threatening. She escapes into her apartment building only to find that something, perhaps the city itself, is banging on the door behind her, almost bursting through. Gradually, however, the substance of Rita's nightmares begins to seep into her waking experience of the city, particularly as her vampire nature is awakened by the presence of Max, a Caribbean vampire searching for a partner. Her first two encounters with Max have the dreamlike suggestion of danger and vulnerability. The first encounter takes place in a Caribbean bar as a cobra manages to break through the glass of its aquarium only to be captured by Max as it is about to strike Rita. The second is a direct parallel with her first nightmare as Rita walks home in the evening, lost in thought, only to barely escape being run down by a speeding car appearing out of nowhere. The reverie of each these dreamy moments suggests the presence of energies or forces coexisting with the more rational imagery of the city.

Nadja also seeks to add a dreamlike reverie to the representation of the city, but where *Vampire in Brooklyn* achieves this predominantly through narrative and character development with a touch of expressionism, *Nadja* does it through the adoption of Almereyda's avant-garde visual style. Nadja's voice-over at the beginning of the film establishes the connection between nights in the city and a kind of sleepless reverie. To create the subjective perception of this reverie, "Almereyda shot sequences using 'Pixelvision,' which gives the image a blurry, out of focus quality as if they were seen through translucent glass."[32] Pixelvision is used expressively, combining the video footage with 35mm film to create a hallucinatory effect, here explained by Almereyda:

> The pixels shift and shimmer and seem to shed light as you watch, endowing everything the camera records with a distinct physicality, and a feel of floating weight and depth. It's unlike the flat, cold quality of ordinary video. I felt it would approximate this feeling the vampires have of being up all night. There's something very unsettling and hallucinatory about it.[33]

The effects of this technique have been described by Ray Pride of *Film-maker* magazine as "a shimmering black-and-white sleepwalking-reverie of New York's Lower East Side," while Nigel Floyd of *Time Out London* compared the effect of these sequences to "the classical silent tradition and feverish strangeness of F. W. Murnau's *Nosferatu*."[34] The use of this camera is primarily restricted to conveying Nadja's subjectivity, in order to present a vampire point of view. This feverish effect is accentuated in a scene when Nadja pursues her brother's nurse Cassandra into the streets. The sequence is a surreal combination of Pixelvision footage, slow motion, and rear projection as a means of alienating the events from the real locations in which they are set. As Nadja pursues Cassandra, Nadja is filmed walking down the street in slow motion in a medium-long shot. Two others, Lucy and Jim, pursue her. They are, however, deliberately separate from her as they are presented through rear projection and although they too run in slow motion, they move at a different film speed to Nadja. This disjunction between time and space transforms the all-too-familiar streets of New York into a location that seems both alien and supernatural.

To conclude my analysis of the New York vampire film, I will examine a lesser-known film by independent New York filmmaker Larry Fessenden entitled *Habit*. Although released after the more famous films I've discussed—*The Hunger, Nadja, The Addiction,* and *Vampire in Brooklyn*—Fessenden's film was conceived prior to them all. In 1980, Fessenden shot an early version of *Habit* while he was in film school at New York University. Then in 1994 he decided to rewrite and produce *Habit* for cinema release. Fessenden's film brings together all of the key characteristics of the New York vampire film that I have so far discussed with respect to budget, locations, visual style, the carnivalesque, and issues of gender. It captures in its tone and atmosphere the duality of the modern city that is both of the moment and ever-changing. The story is about a hopeless alcoholic, Sam, undergoing an emotional breakdown following the death of his father and the subsequent break-up with his girlfriend, presumably due to his excessive drinking and potential domestic abuse. The film follows him as he meets a mysterious, sexually aggressive, and possessive woman, Anna, who he discovers receives sexual gratification from drinking his blood while they make love.

An undeniably low-budget independent film, *Habit* was made on the streets of New York for less than $200,000 with each member of the small crew covering a multitude of roles in the film's production. In addition to writing, directing, editing, and starring in the film, Fessenden also handled makeup, wardrobe, and script supervision, while the producer Dayton Taylor acted as assistant director and recorded and mixed the sound.[35] The cast and crew went unpaid, many of the location sequences were shot without paying license fees, and the film was lit using available lighting sources—from Christmas lights to fluorescent lights purchased from their local hardware store and run off a car battery. It is this low-budget quality that gives the film the impression of authenticity traditionally associated with European filmmaking. Dayton Taylor explained that as they were making the film, he began to draw comparisons with their own production experiences and those of the Italian Neorealist filmmakers who, like the *Habit* crew, had to produce their films with little money, use borrowed equipment and whatever film stock they could find, and shoot amidst real life. Taylor suggests that "a huge part of the nature of the movie is its coexistence with reality."[36]

This emphasis on reality and the reliance on real locations is key to the film and places it within a tradition of art filmmaking practices rather than Hollywood studio production. Most of the film was shot using recognizable, almost iconic locations: from Battery Park to Central Park, from Little Italy to the Upper West Side, from Bridgehampton Beach on Long Island to the Long Island Expressway. The film, like *The Addiction*, is shot with a great deal of handheld photography and diegetic sound to capture a real sense of the crowded, hectic city streets. Fessenden, however, suggests that the film "is a meditation on the blurred lines between fantasy and reality, and [how] in New York, anything is possible: a bevy of opulent nude women might be standing on a marble stairway at any turn, there might even be wolves in the park. These are all images based on the reality of New York, where the surreal mingles with the everyday."[37] To capture this surreal quality, the film deliberately portrays New York at its most delirious and carnivalesque. Fessenden's intention in making this film was to emphasize the banality of Sam's everyday life and then gradually suggest the breakdown of that normality. As he explains, "*Habit* unfolds with great attention to the everyday details of Sam's life—changing cat litter, going to work, failing in romance—but through the blur of alcohol it becomes a story of insanity and the retreat to the supernatural."[38] However, before the film introduces the suggestion of insanity and the supernatural, the atmosphere of the supernatural is already evoked through the mise-en-scène and the association of New York with the carnivalesque.

Kenneth Turan of the *Los Angeles Times* claims that one of the strengths of the film is that Fessenden and his cinematographer Frank DeMarco "create an air of haunted and unsettling menace out of the rather pedestrian streets of Lower Manhattan."[39] For instance, the film begins with Sam going through his late father's belongings, looking at pictures of him as a child and on his excavations of ancient historical sites. The sequence is shot silently and quite statically, seeming to have an almost reverential attitude to the past and the dead. As Sam leaves the apartment and walks out onto the street, the tone of the film changes. It becomes apparent that it is Halloween and the city's population is issuing forth in macabre costumes and makeup. The sequence cuts to handheld footage of Sam walking along the crowded city street at sunset. The film is no longer silent but filled with urban street sounds and a loud contemporary music score. As Sam approaches an intersection, the film cuts to a series of shots, seemingly from Sam's point of view, of men, women, and children adorned in colorful costumes and preparing for Halloween. The film then cuts to a long shot of a child on the opposite corner dressed like the devil, seemingly staring back at him. Although the child is not moving, the motion of those around him shows that the footage has been shot in slow motion so as to create a slightly distorted image. This is accentuated by a jump cut to a medium shot of the boy still staring ahead. What begins as quite a realistic representation of the city streets gradually becomes infused with a degree of surrealism through the unusual sights, the splashes of color, and, as in *Nadja*, the subtle manipulation of time and space.

This surreal representation of the city continues throughout the film. For instance, when Sam and Anna walk through the city after having met at the San Gennaro Festival, the sequence is constructed around a montage of the two walking through the rather ominous city streets. The emptiness of the setting coupled with the disjunction between their voices, recorded separately and added in postproduction, creates a haunting tone that builds upon the uncanny atmosphere of the earlier Halloween images. As they walk through the financial district they come across a photographer taking pictures of a group of nude women sitting on the steps of one of the buildings—a recreation of Nelson Bakerman's Wall Street Nudes Project. Bakerman's project involved photographing rather Rubenesque women in front of financial district buildings, taking the photographer and his models from Wall Street to Chicago, Philadelphia, and Washington D. C. The re-creation of this image in *Habit* during Sam and Anna's late-night walk through the city lends a surreal quality to the nighttime world of New York and evokes an opposition between social order and the carnivalesque.[40] These sequences act as "signposts" that mark "Sam's descent into madness" but also his exposure to the delirious underpinning of the city. By staging Sam and Anna's seemingly coincidental meeting on the streets of the San Gennaro Festival in the heart of Little Italy, the film showcases the sanctioned break from the rationality of the city, allowing the carnivalesque to emerge. Similar to the representation of Coney Island in early cinema, the presence of this festival in the film presents a space where the established rules of behavior are allowed to be broken. As Sam walks through the crowd looking for his friends and later looking for Anna, the camera captures images of a couple kissing passionately, people cooking, eating, and drinking in the middle of the street. Sam and Anna carry this behavior beyond the boundaries of the festival when they have sex in Battery Park.

As the film progresses, what clearly distinguishes Anna from Sam is the manner in which she embraces the carnivalesque quality of the city. Increasingly, the surreal and delirious moments in the film are predicated upon Anna's actions or behavior. While Anna is at ease with these breaks from normality, Sam becomes overwhelmed and petrified. As Amy Taubin points out in her review of the film, Anna's aggressiveness is directly proportional to Sam's passivity.[41] For instance, Anna buys two tickets for the

Ferris wheel at the festival and as she tries to embrace him, Sam withdraws from her, seemingly frozen in fear either by her aggressiveness or the heights of the fair ride. Sam approaches their relationship in a calculated and formal manner by cooking for her, which is later revealed to be his usual courtship technique. Anna, on the other hand, takes Sam on a tour of the unexpected. When she arrives at his place for dinner she refuses to enter, dissuaded by the smell of the freshly chopped garlic, and produces a portable barbecue to be used on his rooftop. The film cuts to a shot of neighbors' windows as Anna's voice is heard asking, "Have you ever been naked on a New York rooftop?" Sam responds, "Not in this life," but follows her lead as she removes his clothes and climbs on top of him. Filmed in long shot and framed by the New York skyline, the sequence is both romantic and dreamlike as the film compresses time through a series of dissolves and romantic violin music mixed with the urban sounds of the street. The last shot is of Anna bending down over Sam, biting into his neck, and drinking his blood.

Later she unexpectedly turns up at the archaeological society where Sam is delivering a memorial speech for his father. She lures him away from this center for systematic learning and organized adventure and takes him into Central Park to show him the mysteries that lurk in their own backyard. Together they find a pack of wild dogs, urban descendants of the wolves that used to populate the park. They scurry through the shadows, lit in rather expressionistic pools of light, and howl at the moon. When a loud car crash is heard, reminding both Sam and Anna that the city is not that far away, the dogs spot Sam and Anna, and chase them out of the park. A montage of snarling fangs and blurred movement conveys the hysteria of their race out of the park. As they escape, they are met by the horrific scene of the car accident, water from a smashed fire hydrant spraying skyward, and two bodies strewn on the ground. While Sam hesitates, Anna swoops into the scene and picks up the body of an injured child. Sensing that his life is rushing out of him, she takes him to the hospital. The whirlwind of action is not over, for as soon as the child is treated, Anna whisks Sam into one of the examination rooms in order to have sex. This time however, Anna's blood drinking is far more aggressive and explicit as she tears into his wrist with her teeth in order to suck the blood, leaving a visible trace of blood on her face when they leave the room.

Anna embraces the adventure of the city, but Sam is overwhelmed by the intensity of their Central Park and hospital adventures, and runs from the hospital, jumping in a cab to go home alone. The vampire or half-vampire men in films such as *Habit* retreat from the street, while the vampire women claim the urban experience for themselves. This contrast demonstrates that, as Elizabeth Wilson suggests, "the city, a place of growing threat and paranoia to men, might be a place of liberation for women."[42] The city offers women freedom. Unlike their male counterparts, the vampire women in these New York films seem to embrace the "indeterminacy and labyrinthine uncentredness" of the city.[43] Nadja goes out into the streets to experience the city while her brother Edgar withdraws to the confines of his sickbed. Christopher Walken in *The Addiction* controls his addiction to blood and advocates restraint and normality, while Kathy abandons herself to the delirium in the climactic party scene as she leads her progeny in an orgy of bloodletting.

In *Habit*, Sam finds security within the confines of the taxi, which allows him to contemplate the city and experience its splendor without being touched by its chaos. The sequence is structured in stark contrast to his adventures with Anna as it is a slow montage of images of the city, viewed from the confines of the cab, and overlaid with a sound montage of Sam and Anna discussing their relationship. It is at this point that Sam decides to withdraw, not only from Anna's influence, but also from the carnivalesque quality of the city itself. Rather than be an active participant of the carnival, he becomes an observer of spectacles as he watches the city pass him by.

The portrayal of these vampire women may appear to be a further attempt to pathologize the presence of women in the urban space but these films are more subversive in their representation. Vampirism in these films works as a means of exploring female desire and "accessibility to urban experience," and the manner in which they maintain a subversive quality is through the prevalence of the vampire's point of view. For instance, unlike Breton's novel *Nadja*, which denies Nadja's point of view, Almereyda's film is completely informed by her perspective. Similarly *The Hunger*, *The Addiction*, and *Vampire in Brooklyn* privilege the female vampire's point of view either through subjective camera work, voice-over, or expressionistic visual style.

Unlike these films however, *Habit* is told from the point of view of the male hero and not the female vampire. In many ways this appears to be a return to the Scorsese-style New York films where women are coded as eccentric, unknowable, and dangerous, a projection of the men's own insecurities about sexuality and the urban experience. In many ways Sam's fear of Anna does act as a catalyst for his retreat from the world. Elizabeth Wilson has stated that the intrusion of the woman in the city suggested the potential release of sexual drives that defy the attempt at order and rationality that is part of the modern city. This is one of the reasons, according to Wilson, that women were not encouraged to identify with the city.[44] Films like *The Crowd* and *Coney Island* support this perception by presenting a trip to Coney Island's fun park as the suggestion of a girl, and each film bears witness to the man's rational undoing as a result. Anna's entrance into the city and into Sam's life seems to mirror these earlier films with even darker conclusions. Her presence in *Habit*, however, is much more ambiguously presented and Sam's point of view is not wholly to be trusted.

Deborah Parsons argues that in the literature of modernity there is one character who has been most often ignored in the discussions of the female flâneuse: the "passante" as addressed in Baudelaire's poem "To a Passer By."[45] In the poem, the woman walks the night city, dressed in mourning attire and shocks the narrator by returning his gaze. Parsons suggests that as a figure in the city, the passante is an ambiguous female presence as her mourning attire prevents identification of her as a prostitute and her gaze undermines the implications of a woman's "look."[46] She is ambiguous as she is not easily objectified or characterized. This form of ambiguity is present in the representation of Anna as a vampire. She defies any attempt to easily categorize her as widow, prostitute, or victim for she chooses to remain ambiguous. She won't explain why she won't eat, where she lives, why she only appears at night. She won't even tell Sam what she does for a living, explaining that "the less you know about me, the longer you'll stay interested." Fessenden argues that although the film focuses upon Sam's redemption through his resistance to Anna's influence and what she represents, Anna remains an enigma that can be read in a multitude of ways. He explains that "the film is not about her character arc; she is a metaphor embodied, an open book for the viewer to infuse with meaning. Temptress? Predator? Outsider? Scapegoat? Victim."[47] The film remains ambiguous as to whether or not Anna is actually a vampire.

Sam's belief that Anna is a vampire is directly related to her confidence and her command of the sexual energies of the city. Her presence in the film continually undermines accepted codes of behavior as she initiates each sexual encounter with Sam in increasingly public spaces. She pushes Sam to abandon his traditional ways of behaving and to open himself to the world around him. This release from convention both attracts him to Anna and eventually causes him to withdraw. Fessenden explains that "the essential difference between Sam and Anna is that she has transcended fear and Sam has not. She is free from worry and despair, she is a preda-tor."[48] For Sam, Anna's vampirism both explains her aggressiveness and ease within the city, and fuels Sam's need to retreat from her. He can run away because he views her as a monster. Unlike the women in *After Hours*, however, the representation of Anna in *Habit* is suitably ambiguous as to suggest a possible reading of her character as something beyond a mon-ster or simply eccentric and dangerous, and Sam's deteriorating mental state raises questions about his perception of her.

A deliriously oneiric film, it is often difficult to discern whether or not Anna's vampirism is real or a symptom of Sam's emotional state and drunken paranoia. As Fessenden suggests, "Maybe it is a movie about a drunk. It's designed to have a cumulative effect. It's about what you project onto it."[49] Fessenden does argue that when Sam retreats to the confines of the taxi, the film becomes engulfed in the "melancholy loneliness" that grips Sam.[50] This loneliness is transformed into a much broader sense of mourning for the past that clouds Sam's perception of Anna. While Anna's embrace of the modern is exhilarating, in the film there is also a fundamental nostalgia for the replaceable, for what has disappeared. For instance, the San Gennaro Festival evokes the carnivalesque Coney Island, but what distinguishes the two is that while Coney Island was presented as modern and technological, this festival represents the op-posite; it is old-fashioned and homegrown. The ethnic food being cooked and the location of the festival itself within Little Italy, harken back to a legacy of European immigration characteristic of New York's past. The Ferris wheel is no longer shiny and new, the essence of the speedy and efficient technology of the turn of the century, but old, rickety, and noisy. Fessenden points out that even since the film was released New York has changed, claiming that "the film already stands as a time capsule. Many of the locations have changed in the half-decade since we shot: the Ital-ian street fair is considerably less raucous now; there is no Ferris wheel anymore. Ludlow Street where Sam works is overrun with restaurants and shops now, and of course there are few homeless bums allowed to lie in Times Square."[51]

The film is haunted by feelings of loss, particularly expressed by Sam's friend Ray who is mourning for her deceased grandmother. Similarly Sam mourns for his father, and his father mourned for the dignity of the ancient cultures and relics. On Thanksgiving Day, Ray wears an antique dress that belonged to her grandmother, which is subsequently ruined in a rainstorm. All the icons of the past are destroyed or fade away. Sam's foray with Anna is his release from this sense of mourning for she embodies a break from the past. She tells Ray that she has "never liked antiques. I always like what is happening now." Sam's subsequent retreat from Anna is therefore a retreat from the modern back into the past and this retreat condemns him to die. "In a city like New York, in most cities, in most of culture—in fact in all things—the old is replaced by the new, and there is an inherent sadness to that simple truth, especially when we see ourselves becoming the replaceable."[52]

The ambiguity surrounding Anna's vampirism is compounded by her seemingly supernatural disappearance at the end of the film. Having plummeted from an upstairs apartment to the pavement below, Anna and Sam are shown lying on the ground. In the next shot, as the camera pans around the crowds arriving on the scene, Sam's body is alone. Is Anna really a vampire who fell from the window and then disappeared, or did the entire confrontation between Sam and Anna take place in Sam's head? The sudden disappearance of Anna could be indicative of her supernatural escape or signal the break from Sam's distorted point of view as he dies. Either way, Sam's inability to live in the moment like Anna has caused his death. Anna on the other hand, like Nadja, Kathy, Sarah, and Rita, is not forced to die or pay for her transgressions—in the manner of her Victorian predecessors Lucy Westenra and Carmilla—but is reborn. As Sam lies dead on the ground surrounded by friends and strangers, the film cuts to its final shot of a boat speeding away from New York Harbor suggesting Anna's escape just as the appearance of the ship at the beginning of the film suggests, like Dracula's arrival in Whitby, her arrival in New York.

Through the lone female vampire, the New York vampire film not only engages with the city's historical relationship with modernity, but reinvents that relationship by aligning the vampire with the notion of a flâneuse, a role previously denied to women in the literature of modernity. By living in the moment and embracing the carnivalesque quality of the city, the New York vampire is the essence of the flâneur and, like modernity itself, resists retreating into the past, but is reborn and revitalized. This final shot of *Habit* also reminds the audience that the modern vampire is no longer bound to a particular time and place, but through rebirth, the vampire is free to move on.

CHAPTER NINE

Vampire Road Movies: From Modernity to Postmodernity

> Near Dark *started because we wanted to do a western. But as no one will finance a western we thought, okay, how can we subvert the genre? Let's do a western but disguise it in such a way that it gets sold as something else. Then we thought, ha, a vampire western . . . Ours are modern vampires, American vampires, on the road.*
>
> KATHRYN BIGELOW ON *NEAR DARK*[1]

In an inversion of Jonathan Harker's memorable journey to meet Count Dracula, we now leave the East and enter the West. While Harker's journey chronicled a shift from the modern West to the premodern East, this journey through the American landscape will trace the modernization and Americanization of the vampire through its integration with the western and the road movie, two genres whose shared iconographies are indelibly linked to the formation of America. This new hybrid genre emerged in the 1980s as a means of reinventing the vampire film. Its hybridity makes the vampire road movie the perfect bridge between the modernist associations of New York and the fragmented identity of Los Angeles (to be discussed in Chapter 10). Through the clash of conventions and iconography, a range of discourses about modernity and postmodernity are suggested. By focusing upon the integration of the mythology of the vampire film with key imagery from the western and road movie, particularly such defining features as the frontier landscape, the car, and the highway, I will demonstrate how the vampire road movie explores the shifting terrain between the modern and the postmodern.

While the western genre served to transform the history of the American frontier into the myth of the formation of a nation, the road movie has emerged with the development of the American highway and the rise of the automobile. Both genres embrace the opposition between the vast, seemingly untamed frontier and the arrival of civilization. Jim Kitses has argued that the western genre is comprised of a series of binaries—West and East, wilderness and civilization, individual and community, freedom and restriction, nature and culture, purity and corruption, and past and future—"an ambiguous cluster of meanings and attitudes that provide the traditional thematic structure of the genre." Throughout the evolution of the western, the manner in which these binaries have been represented has served to either celebrate or mourn, oftentimes both, the taming of the frontier landscape.[2]

Similarly, the road movie embodies the escape from civilization into the freedom of the expansive landscape, usually in the form of a journey through what Steven Cohan and Ina Rae Hark describe as "an alternative space where isolation from the mainstream permits various transformative experiences."[3] The genre, however, also offers a continued reminder that the landscape has been tamed through the building of transnational highways, linking the frontier to the urban centers around the country. In 1957, the United States' highway development program was launched, an event that was viewed as both a blessing and a curse. While this program demonstrated a further commitment to the modernization of America that began with the development of the automobile, it also demonstrated the destructive nature of modernity through the imposition of technology on the natural landscape. Urban theorist, Lewis Mumford was highly critical of these developments, referring to the period as "the age of the bulldozer," precisely because it meant a massive assault being launched upon the natural and urban landscape.[4] The building of the highways and the resulting destruction of vast numbers of homes and communities were equated with the progress of modernity and were endemic of a spreading of urban circulation out of the city into the countryside. Together, therefore, the western and the road movie represent the creation and modernization of America. They are not necessarily contradictory but rather an extension of each other; the road movie often serves to modernize the western by transforming the horse, stagecoach, and railway (itself an icon of modernity in the western as it cuts through the frontier) into the automobile and the highway. The vampire film uses the iconography of both genres to reimagine the vampire through the language of modernization.

Most significantly, the expansive landscape of the western and the road movie undermines the visual characteristics of the Gothic. It is an open and sprawling space that spreads out as far as the eye can see, quite unlike the confined and enclosed spaces of conventional Gothic narratives, which include castles, coffins, graveyards, or even the small town of Braddock in *Martin*, the farmhouse in *Night of the Living Dead*, or the confined and labyrinthine urban streets of London or New York. As a result, this landscape often dictates the aesthetic design of the western and road movie, as noted by André Bazin who suggested that the western possesses a "predilection for vast horizons, all-encompassing shots that constantly bring to mind the conflict between man and nature. The western has virtually no use for the closeup, even for the medium shot, preferring by contrast the traveling shot and the pan which refuse to be limited by the frameline."[5] Furthermore, the frontier landscape is generally represented in the daylight and with particular emphasis upon the burning sun of the desert.

This landscape is fundamental to the vampire road movie as demonstrated in films such as *Near Dark* (1987), *From Dusk till Dawn* (1996), its sequels *From Dusk till Dawn 2: Texas Blood Money* (1999) and *From Dusk till Dawn 3: The Hangman's Daughter* (2000), *John Carpenter's Vampires* (1998), and *The Forsaken* (2001). For instance, Carpenter's film begins on a shot of the horizon as the sun begins to rise followed by a series of swooping camera shots over the barren desert landscape. To further emphasize the locale and the blazing sun, a filter is used to give everything an orange tinge. Conversely, *Near Dark* begins just as the sun is setting but like *Vampires* there is a visual emphasis upon the horizon. As the film's protagonist, Caleb, drives into town, his pickup truck is framed in long shot, dwarfed by the expanse of the surrounding landscape. This composition is repeated throughout the film as the vampires race along the highway against the rising sun. This emphasis upon the horizon serves to draw attention to both the landscape and the significance of the sun as it rises and sets. The Gothic is not absent from this landscape but instead is hidden within its shadows. By adopting this visual language, the vampire film is challenging its own Gothic heritage and inventing a new and indigenous aesthetic for the genre. As Sara Gwenllian Jones has claimed for *Near Dark*, the "gothic elements function like dark prisms, casting warped shadows across the western's bright geography," and the vampires in these road movies "seem to erupt not from the European past but from nature itself, from the unruly wilderness that lies just beneath the surface of the farmed and settled American Midwest."[6]

Furthermore, the vampires and their slayers are themselves recoded through the language of the western. In *Near Dark*, the vampires dress in the style of cowboys from past films. Jesse, the lead vampire, sports a duster in the style made famous in the spaghetti westerns of the sixties

Figure 9.1. Vlad the Impaler meets *The Wild Bunch* in *John Carpenter's Vampires.*

and seventies, Diamondback wears rider chaps, and Severin attaches spurs to his cowboy boots. Of greater significance, each of the vampires, with the exception of Mae, carry pistols, shotguns, and six-shooters. Caleb, the turned vampire and vampire slayer, is most clearly identified with the western as he sports a cowboy hat, rides a horse, and uses a lasso. In *Vampires*, John Carpenter has deliberately approached his film as a vampire western through its New Mexican desert landscape and citations in plot, character, and style of such notable western filmmakers as Howard Hawks, Sergio Leone, and Sam Peckinpah. Carpenter has even gone so far as to describe the film as "*The Wild Bunch* meets Vlad the Impaler,"[7] indicating that it is the vampire slayers who are particularly associated with the wild West as they embody what Noël Carroll, would describe as the professional western hero. (Figure 9.1) They are professional vampire slayers, mercenaries employed by the Vatican to hunt down and kill vampires. They possess specialist skills and knowledge and operate as a team. Their professional code is constantly reinforced as they remind each other throughout the film of the rules of their trade: "Rule number 7: Never bury a team member by yourself." "Rule number 10: You cannot kill a Master at night." "Rule number 1: If your partner is ever bitten by a vampire, never, ever let him live." This is taken further in *Vampires: Los Muertos* (2002) in which the slayers continue to work as professional guns for hire but this time their mission takes them into Mexico where they must save a small village from the vampires' nightly visitations. In this, the film is deliberately echoing the narrative of another professional western, *The Magnificent Seven* (1960), as both the vampires and the bandits drain the village of its life force and the professionals come to prioritize the needs of the village over their own monetary gain.[8]

Figure 9.2. The Gothic western in *Near Dark*.

Furthermore, the use of Mexico and New Mexico as a backdrop in most of these films also situates the vampire road movie within what Edward Buscombe and Roberta E. Pearson describe as "the South-Western," a subgenre that is "expressive of Hispanic cultural survival."[9]

Finally, the confrontation by the vampires and their vampire slayers are recoded as a western showdown. In *From Dusk till Dawn*, the surviving vampires and slayers literally stand in a line facing each other before the final fight. In *Near Dark*, when Caleb is effectively called to a showdown after the vampires abduct his sister, he must ride out on horseback to confront them at midnight rather than high noon. (Figures 9.2 and 9.3) The visual composition of the scene calls to mind countless western shootouts, both sides facing each other from opposite ends of a deserted highway.

If these films were simply a hybrid of the western and vampire film it would be easy to read them as representing the return of America's primitive past to disrupt the country's civilized identity to, as Sara Gwenllian Jones suggests, "expos[e] the illusory nature of the existing social order's security and permanency."[10] The use of the road movie and its iconography, however, further complicates the reinterpretation of the vampire myth. As I have argued with respect to *Dracula* and *Martin*, vampires are often associated with movement. Even in their most basic representations, vampires are usually outsiders who have recently arrived and settled into a new area. The lead vampire in *Fright Night* is a stranger who has moved into a derelict house in a suburban neighborhood; the vampires in *Blood Ties* (1992) are Carpathians who have emigrated to the United States;

Figure 9.3. A vampire showdown in *Near Dark*.

Marie in *Innocent Blood* is French and Anna in *Habit* arrives and leaves New York by boat from New York Harbor. Not only do both *Dracula* and *Martin*, like these other vampire films, begin with the vampire moving into a new city, but they also emphasize the circulation of the vampire through its new urban landscape. Released from the temporal and spatial confinement of classic Gothic, the vampire road movie extends this urban circulation beyond the boundaries of the city and onto the open road, enabling the vampire to become identified with the modernity of the highway and the automobile.

Near Dark is the story of a young farm boy, Caleb, who is abducted and turned by a group of vampires. The narrative follows Caleb's adventures with these vampires as they try to complete his transformation by making him accept his new lifestyle. The vampires are presented as a nomadic family who exist exclusively on the road, moving from one town to the next. They have no home but are bound to one another and follow the highway, leaving a trail of death and destruction in their wake. As Needeya Islam argues in her discussion of Kathryn Bigelow's first two features, both the bikers in *The Loveless* (1982) and the vampires in *Near Dark* "are figures of marginality who must keep moving, the road being absolutely essential to their definition. Both films contain repeated images not only of vehicles and movement, but of the road itself."[11]

The movement of the vampires along the Southwest highways of America in *Near Dark* demonstrates a freedom from the urban centers of *Dracula* and *Martin*. These vampires live on the fringes of society and are pictured almost exclusively on the open road or on the outskirts of cities, near railroad tracks, bus stations, and truck stops. Their movements are, however, an extension of the urban circulation of *Dracula* and *Martin*, as the roads they traverse crisscross America and bind the country's urban centers together. The vampires' nomadic lifestyle on these modern highways sets them in opposition to the rural lifestyle and professionalism exhibited by Caleb's family.[12] By associating the vampires with the car, the highway, and road movie genre, Bigelow has placed the vampires more in opposition to, than in league with, the western genre conventions that are evoked by the film's desert landscape. The fight for Caleb becomes the site for this tug of war. He seems to be undergoing this struggle even before he becomes engulfed in the nocturnal world of the vampires. As stated previously, Caleb is strongly identified with the western through his attire and surroundings. When he is introduced in the film, he is wearing a cowboy hat but is lying in the back of a modern pickup truck. Later, as he drives Mae back to a trailer park, he takes her on a detour to a farm to introduce her to his horse and then playfully uses his lasso to catch Mae. The horse balks at Mae's presence and runs away from her while Mae's vampiric strength enables her to escape Caleb's attempt to lasso her. These icons of the western genre—the hat, lasso, and horse—are very much placed in opposition to the modern icons such as the truck, the trailer park, and Mae herself. Caleb embodies the dichotomy between both worlds.

Throughout the film, Caleb's adventure with the family of vampires is equated with a teenager running away to the big city. When we are introduced to Caleb he is bored and looking for excitement. Despite the family loyalty he expresses later in the film, Caleb demonstrates a disdain for the ordered, conventional lifestyle of his family. He comes into town after dark, picks a fight with one of his friends, and then tries to pick up Mae, not exclusively because he is attracted to her, but also because she is from out of town and, to Caleb, represents an alternative to his present situation. After Mae bites him and runs off, Caleb heads home on foot, arriving just as the sun begins to rise. His father, a farm animal veterinarian, and sister are already up tending to the animals. Although the father seems slightly annoyed at his son's late arrival, he does not demonstrate any concern for Caleb, which suggests that this is a common occurrence. Caleb is an unruly teenager who is looking for an alternative to the responsible rural life his family is living. With the exception of Caleb's father, who witnessed his abduction, the adults in the film read Caleb's disappearance as a typical teenage runaway situation. The investigating sheriff assumes that

Caleb has "got mixed up with a bad bunch," while the police officer who finds Caleb at the bus station thinks that he is a potential troublemaker, a vagrant teenager showing symptoms of drug use. When Caleb and Mae hitch a ride, the truck driver similarly assumes that they are runaways, but does not try to turn them in because he understands that "sometimes home is bad."

Caleb's choice to either embrace or deny his vampirism is therefore not only a moral decision about killing or a question of love, but rather a choice between the nocturnal, urban lifestyle of the vampires and the diurnal, agrarian lifestyle of his family—in other words, the modern and the premodern. The bright open spaces of the daytime are continually set in opposition to the claustrophobic darkness of the interior of the vampires' automobiles or motel hideouts. Therefore the mixing of western, vampire, and road movie genres serves to play out this opposition to its fullest. As Pam Cook explains,

> *Near Dark* is almost as much Western as vampire movie, brilliantly using each genre to comment on the values of the other. When Caleb rides out, in the film's climactic sequence, to rescue his sister Sarah from the vampires' clutches, he is, like Ethan Edwards in *The Searchers*, fighting not only to preserve a lost dream of agrarian innocence, but also to overcome the barbaric, primitive impulses within himself.[13]

Caleb's attraction to the vampires is not exclusively caused by primitive impulses but rather propelled by modern ones. He is drawn to the vampires because of their embodiment of the open road and the urban landscape.

A key signifier of both of these elements is the car, a major narrative and thematic instigator in the road movie. As Steven Cohan and Ina Rae Hark have argued, the car suggests both a means of liberating oneself from the social constraints of civilization, as well as identifying with the key signifier of that civilization: its technology. The car from its very conception was associated with modernity and urban development as it was a feat of twentieth-century technological innovation produced through America's cutting-edge industrialization techniques, which also led to the modernization of America's cities, roads, and highways. Technology is what differentiates the genre from the western, as evidenced by the use of the car in *The Wild Bunch*, signifying the end of the west and the western hero. The road movie is therefore a celebration of how the car and the highway tamed the frontier through technological achievement. As Cohan and Hark suggest, "The road [movie] protagonist readily identifies with the means of mechanized transportation, the automobile or motorcycle, which 'becomes the only promise of self in a culture of mechanical reproduction,' to the point where it becomes 'transformed into a human or spiritual reality.'"[14]

By setting the film on the roads crossing the desert landscapes of the old west, Bigelow, who has stated that it was her intention to make a "vampire western," merges both the modern and the historical meanings of the setting. In her discussions of the film, she explains that she "wanted to take these people out of Gothic entrapments" for "the urban environment is immediately dangerous and primal. Setting *Near Dark* in the American heartland you don't expect horrific images."[15] As a result, the highway is the perfect location as it leads away from the urban landscape by moving through the vast expanse of the American rural landscape, but it also symbolizes an inability to escape the urban. The characters, in effect, bring the dangerous and dehumanizing qualities of the city with them. *Near Dark* therefore establishes an opposition between the frontier aspects of the landscape and the urban quality of the highway that moves through it. The highway upon which the vampires travel is itself technologically produced and reminds the audience that the western frontier no longer exists. It has been traversed, tamed, and redeveloped, and the highway now acts as a linchpin between the various urban settings.

While both the car and the highway suggest an association with modernity and the taming of the west through the imposition of technologies upon the face of its frontier landscape, these icons also embody what Marc Augé describes as postmodern non-places: "Space[s] which cannot be defined as relational, or historical, or concerned with identity."[16] He suggests that the non-place is the true measure of the twentieth century and is primarily embodied and quantified in the anonymous spaces in which we circulate and travel without engaging with any sense of place. These spaces do not invite identification and growth as they do not allow for personal interaction with the landscape through which we move. While much of the mise-en-scène of *Near Dark* is dominated by the expanse of the highway and the desert landscape, this landscape is counterpointed by the types of non-places described by Augé, such as the bus stations, truck stops, motels, and abandoned warehouses through which the vampires circulate.

Omayra Cruz and Ray Guins argue that the vampire road movie undermines the narratives of self-discovery and change traditionally associated with the genre, for their movement on the highway merely suggests the pursuit of life's necessities. In *Near Dark*, the road is the site of their nightly meal as each of the vampires uses the anonymity of the road to secure their victim. Jesse and Diamondback feed upon two hitchhikers who try to steal their car while Severin adopts the role of the dangerous hitchhiker when he murders the two women he seduces into giving him a ride. Homer gets a driver to stop by posing as an innocent child injured in a bike accident on the side of the road. Similarly in the *From Dusk till Dawn* series, the road brings the food to the vampires' door as they feed off the truck drivers, outlaws, and travelers who stop in their roadside bar, the Titty Twister. While they remain stationary at the bar, it is the endless motion of the road that facilitates their survival. As Cruz and Guins suggest, to survive, a vampire cannot "stray from the recurrent features of its existence: to travel, feed, and hide." In this way, the vampires are defined by movement while staying the same, therefore undermining the transformative experience of the road movie.[17]

In *Near Dark* the vampires don't grow or evolve but exist on an endless merry-go-round of highways, cars, motels, victims, and sunrises. As they drive along the highway, Jesse and Diamondback pass the side of the road where they first met, and laugh about how neither can remember when that was exactly. Later, when they book into a roadside motel, the motel clerk remarks that he has seen Jesse before. Jesse quips that he gets by there about every fifty years. The time span of the *From Dusk till Dawn* films similarly suggests that the vampires have survived on an endless cycle of nightly feeding since the nineteenth-century wild west. These films illustrate how the existence of the vampires on desert landscape is not predicated on a destination but rather the mindless repetition of actions and routes, night after night and year after year. This perception of the effects of the highway and automobile on the vampire mirrors the effects of all such non-places on the modern world. All travelers on the road are met with the same needs as the nomadic vampires and, to satisfy these needs, there is an endless series of identical highways, roadside restaurants, and motels in which we all travel, feed, and hide. We move but do not change for we are not touched by the landscape through which we travel but by an endless series of processed non-places.

Vampires further demonstrates how, through the vampire genre, the road movie has come to embody the shift from the modern to the postmodern. Like *Near Dark*, the film is also structured along the trajectory of the open road. The story follows a team of mercenaries who, on the

Vatican's payroll, hunt and destroy vampires across the United States. They live nomadically and simply move through the southwest following the trail of the vampires, locating their nests, and destroying them. The opening of the film immediately establishes a parallel between the vampires and their slayers. The lead vampire slayer Jack Crow looks through his binoculars at a derelict building in the middle of nowhere that he describes as "another New Mexican shithole. A perfect place for a nest." He and his team enter the presumed nest and systematically destroy each of the vampires. The vampires in this sequence are indistinguishable from each other and are easily dispatched.

This opening sequence is directly paralleled later in the film when the vampire Master Valek attacks the vampire slayers in a different kind of "New Mexican shithole," the Sun God Motel. Just as Crow tracked the vampires to their nest, Valek tracks the slayers to this location and systematically destroys each of them, leaving only the lead slayer Crow and his lieutenant, Montoya. Both the vampire nest and the Sun God Motel are presented as yet another in a long line of interchangeable locations through which the vampires and slayers travel, feed, and hide. Like the vampires, the slayers, with the exception of Crow and Montoya, are eminently interchangeable and are dispatched with ease. After his team is destroyed, Crow is instructed by the Vatican to return to his headquarters in Monterey and rebuild his team, beginning with a replacement for his priest. Similarly, Valek rebuilds his own team of vampires from the community of Santiago. On the road, vampires and slayers have become interchangeable.

In this film however, while the master vampires move through the anonymous landscape with purpose, the vampire slayers have come to truly embody the non-place and the essence of meaningless movement. Jack Crow shows his new apprentice priest a map that marks the location of each of the vampire and slayer encounters since the eighteenth century, and explains that the locations form a "logarithmic pattern that is ever widening." It is a search pattern and what the vampires are searching for is a religious artifact that will enable them to walk in the daylight. The vampire slayers, however, are no more than a tribe that moves through the landscape to follow the vampires like nomadic hunters follow the herd. These slayers have no home, simply a headquarters in Monterey, California, where the Vatican sends their payments. They exist solely on an indistinguishable road that does not touch them and that has no effect upon their lives.

The Forsaken is the ultimate vampire road movie. Its story takes place almost exclusively on the road as a trio of young vampire hunters stalk a group of nomadic vampires along the highway in their attempt to destroy the leader and subsequently cure their own vampire infection. The vampires haunt the highways and motels with no particular destination, simply feeding on the itinerant travellers they encounter. The slayers equally lack a destination as they simply act as the vampires' shadow on the road, following their trail of destruction. The distinction between slayer and vampire becomes increasingly blurred on the highway as they all move along the roads in an endless pursuit of one another and the hunters become the hunted.

Like the highway, the car acts as both an icon of modernity as well as the postmodern non-place. Leslie Dick has described the car in a road movie as a "place that is both secure (homelike) and dangerous. It can be a weapon, a means of suicide—or a coffin, a sarcophagus, a monument almost, as in the death scene in *Bonnie and Clyde*."[18] The cars in *Near Dark* and *The Forsaken* provide both a means to travel and security from the daylight. In *Near Dark* the vampires paint over the windows, while in *The Forsaken* they hide in the trunk of the car as their human familiar drives. In both films, the car symbolizes the vampire's abandonment of the spatial containment of the Gothic genre as well as the folklore tradition of vampires having to return to their coffins.[19] By replacing the coffin with a car, the vampire's mobility becomes all the more intrinsic to his or her lifestyle. Like the highway itself, however, the car lacks any true sense of identity or home, as it is simply one car in a long line of vehicles that they steal from identical used car lots across the country. These vehicles lack any sense of personal identity and connection to the space through which they travel. They are disposable.

In *Near Dark*, as soon as a car becomes identifiable, as when the one survivor of the barroom slaughter reports the vampires to the police, they escape and immediately steal a more anonymous vehicle. Similarly, in *Vampires*, while their vehicles are the only homes that the vampire slayers possess, they are anonymous and interchangeable and simply act as a space in which the slayers are stored. When Crow and Montoya approach the vampire nest at the opening of the film, they open up the back of the van to release the other slayers who are locked within. In *The Forsaken*, the vampires wear the car out before abandoning it and looking for a new one. While the car itself is of no consequence to the vampires, it does inherit their identity in the eyes of the vampire hunters who watch for the car on the road. Like the murderous trucks in *Duel* (1971), *Jeepers Creepers* (2001), and *Joy Ride* (2001), the car is attributed with a sense of menace suggesting the anonymous dangers of the road.

The constant movement drains the vampires of their individual identities and makes them the ultimate urban stranger, anonymous to everyone they encounter. As Leslie Dick suggests, "The potential fluidity of identity is a key element in the philosophical underpinnings of the road movie. On the road, nobody knows you—so you can be anybody, become anything. You can disappear," and you can make others disappear as well.[20] The stranger is a modern figure; in the metropolis all inhabitants are strangers, socially separate while physically proximate. The stranger is, however, also a symptom of the non-place, for on the highway, sealed within their cars, strangers are not even physically proximate. They are completely separate and unaffected by those who surround them.

Through the meeting of the desert and the highway—the western and the road movie—in this new form of vampire film, the vampire comes to embody the modern and the postmodern simultaneously. This is particularly suggested by Mae in *Near Dark* who defines her vampirism, like modernity, as the existence of the transitory moment within the eternal. She embraces her immortality by asserting that she will still be here when the light from a star finally reaches the earth in a billion years. She also tries to teach Caleb to recognize the magic of the aural and visual delights that surround them from moment to moment when she encourages him to look at and listen to the beauty of the night: "There is something I want to show you. The night. It's dark but also bright. It'll blind you. Listen. Listen closely. Do you hear it? The night. It's deafening. Listen hard." As Nina Auerbach explains, Mae's "attraction to vampirism has less to do with bloodthirst than with the thirst for immortality."[21]

The price of the simultaneous appreciation of the moment and the experience of eternity, however, is the nightly kill. Through the repetitive action of pursuing the life-sustaining need to drink blood Mae engages in the anonymous, superficial motions of the non-place. Mae instructs Caleb, "Don't think of it as killing. Don't think of it at all. It is just something that you have to do night after night." Similarly, while the vampires in Carpenter's film search for the Black Cross, a symbol of the failure of the Catholic Church, the slayers become numbed by their experiences until they all emulate the style and attitude of the chief vampire slayer, Jack Crow. At the end of the film, the apprentice priest has abandoned his faith in the church to become one of Jack's slayers, and to mirror the image of Jack himself. As the vampires and slayers in these vampire road movies move along the highway through the desert landscape, their identities become fragmented because they simultaneously embody the modernity of the East and the postmodernity of the West. In doing so they foreshadow the emergence of the vampire into the sparkling night of postmodern Los Angeles, where the vampire identity becomes even more fragmented until it takes on the superficial quality of the city in which it has emerged.

CHAPTER TEN

Los Angeles: Fangs, Gangs, and Vampireland

When Angel, the vampire with a soul, leaves Sunnydale and the television series of *Buffy the Vampire Slayer* to pursue his own destiny and television program, he is drawn to the city of Los Angeles and its diversity of victims and villains, humans and demons.[1] While Sunnydale was contained and unified, Los Angeles is sprawling and fragmented. Violence erupts onto the streets every night unnoticed, not because it is hidden but because the inhabitants of Los Angeles retreat behind closed doors and choose not to see it. "War Zone" (*Angel* 1:20) encapsulates one of the many themes of the Los Angeles vampire film, presenting this violence as a conflict of race, enacted upon the backstreets of the city through gang warfare. In this episode, Angel comes across two youth gangs segregated into distinct groups, vampire and human, fighting to maintain their turf and identity. Racially, the humans embody a diverse ethnic range of African, Asian, and Hispanic origins, while the vampires are presented as fascist skinheads looking to maintain the purity of the blood supply in the neighborhood. The battles they wage are in the open yet remain unseen. The fragmented nature of the city is summarized by Angel's assistant Cordelia when she laments, "Twenty minutes ride from billionaires and crab puffs, kids going to war."

As Angel proceeds on his mission, confronting different types of demons, vampires, victims, or villains, the serial nature of the program emphasizes the fragmentation of the city into distinct and often warring communities. Prior to Angel's arrival in Los Angeles, however, a diverse range of vampires already populated the city. Blacula and Count Yorga, two old-world vampires, from Africa and Europe respectively, relocated to Los Angeles in the 1970s. John Llewellyn Moxey followed up the success of *The Night Stalker* with *I, Desire* (1982), a made-for-television film about a young law student who becomes obsessed with hunting a vampire that is stalking contemporary Los Angeles. The city, however, became the locus for a subgenre of vampire films in the mid 1980s with the release of a group of teen-vampire films: *Fright Night* (1985), *Fright Night Part II* (1988), *The Lost Boys* (1987), *Beverly Hills Vamp* (1988), *Buffy the Vampire Slayer* (1992), followed by the less specifically teen-oriented vampire films *Blood Ties* (1992), *Blade* (1998), and *Revenant* (1999). The vampires in these films are a fragmented group, represented by a diversity of race, age, gender, and social makeup, and like the city itself, they are unified by their disunity. The movement from the New York vampire to the Los Angeles vampire along the highway of the vampire road movie, therefore, charts a shift from the specificity and locality embodied by New York to the absence of locale, the fragmentation of space and identity, and the prevalence of postmodern alienation that defines Los Angeles.

Greg Hise, Michael J. Dear, and H. Eric Schockman describe the disunity of the Los Angeles landscape as a form of "postmodern urbanism," arguing that the logic that previously "guided the urban process" has been altered and replaced by "multiple rationalities that do not cohere into a single logic of urbanization. In this sense, postmodern urbanism is about complexity and difference."[2] Edward Soja, a leading urban theorist, has suggested that the structure of Los Angeles is, by definition, a contradiction, as the freeways, which seemingly act as a linchpin to pull the city together, also act as barriers keeping it apart.[3] This fragmentation has led to the problem of identifying and reading the contemporary city.

The indecipherability of the real city of Los Angeles is reinforced by its primary window to the world: the film industry. As the home to Hollywood, Los Angeles is one of the most represented cities in the world. Los Angeles' city streets and buildings have been the backdrop of countless films, from the early days of silent cinema to the present, yet rarely are they presented in their own right. One of the reasons that the early filmmakers moved to Hollywood was because of the city's climate and malleability as a location.[4] From the beaches to the foothills, from the desert to the mountains, Los Angeles can pass for everywhere and nowhere, anytime and no time. As Jonathan Bell has argued, "the countless celluloid lies that have been born beneath the picture-perfect skies reflect a city of imitation, duplicity, simulation, and duplication."[5] Although we have seen it over and over again on film, it is very difficult to imagine the city itself.

Furthermore, the artificial worlds of the Hollywood backlots, as well as such theme parks as Disneyland and Universal Studios Hollywood, have been reproduced to replace the real Los Angeles. Mike Davis argues that with the rise of the entertainment and tourist industry in California, coupled with the tourists' hesitancy to venture into central Los Angeles, a form of "artificial Los Angeles" has gradually become confined in "fortress hotels and walled theme parks," offering "'easy, bite-sized pieces' [of the city] for consumption by tourists and residents who 'don't need the excitement of dodging bullets . . . in the Third World country' that Los Angeles has become."[6] Furthermore, according to Margaret Crawford, this form of architecture has ceased to be limited to consumerist locations such as malls, restaurants, hotels, and theme parks, and has crept into residential architecture as a marketing edge over other community developments.[7] Los Angeles has become a simulation. This supports Jean Baudrillard's argument that simulation blurs the distinction between true and false, real and imaginary, and as a result, that which is simulated ceases to exist in favor of the simulation.[8]

The manufactured and artificial quality of the contemporary Los Angeles landscape and its constituent communities and neighborhoods is evoked in the Los Angeles vampire films through their refusal to emphasize realism in favor of a more iconographic representation of space. These films present Los Angeles in fragments of images and signifiers, reproducing recognizable elements of the Los Angeles cityscape while also highlighting the artificiality of the setting's construction. The Los Angeles vampire films deny realistic space by filming on constructed sets in the studio or on the backlot. The image of Los Angeles in the film *Buffy the Vampire Slayer* (1992) is suggested by the presence of recognizable Valley Girls, and in *Fright Night* by the movie star vampire-killer Peter Vincent. While *The Lost Boys* is not literally set in Los Angeles but rather the fictional town of Santa Carla, based upon the real community of Santa Cruz, its use of icons such as beaches, gangs, motorcycles, and the homeless evokes the image of Los Angeles in a more succinct way than would be suggested by actual location shooting.

To situate its narrative within a very real and recognizable location, the studiobound New York film *Vampire in Brooklyn* opens with establishing shots of the New York cityscape and repeatedly returns to images of the Brooklyn Bridge. The Los Angeles vampire films avoid any such clearly identifiable establishing shots. *Buffy the Vampire Slayer* opens on a shot of an escalator in a mall with a caption reading "Southern California." *The Lost Boys* opens on a shot of a rollercoaster that serves to blur the distinction between the town of Santa Carla and the amusement park. *Fright Night* does not avoid the establishing shot but rather uses it to undermine any suggestion of reality. It emphasizes the artificiality of the filmic medium and its representation of place. The film opens on a long shot of the moon accompanied by the sound of a wolf howling. A man's voice inquires, "What was that?" to which a woman answers, "Just a child of the night, John." The traditional generic quality of this opening is undermined however by the slow tilt down of the camera onto an establishing shot of a cityscape whose bright lights and urban sprawl is reminiscent of Los Angeles. The film is therefore not taking place within a traditionally Gothic location as the soundtrack suggests, but in a contemporary setting. As the camera tracks right along a suburban street, the conversation continues in familiar fashion as the woman lures the man out onto a balcony and attempts to seduce him. The camera slows down slightly as it passes an old, decrepit house suggesting that this is perhaps the source of the voices, a seemingly suitable location because of its derelict and Gothic appearance. Once again, expectations are undermined as the camera continues to move on to a very traditional suburban house. The camera cranes up to the house and into a window to reveal that the source of the voices is a television playing an old vampire movie.

This opening shot establishes the key premises of the film. First, it suggests that the film will be about a traditional American suburb invaded by a generic Hollywood horror monster, a premise that is later supported by the starlike appearance of Jerry Dandridge and the impact he has on the community. Second, the opening shot's lateral movement along the suburban street emphasizes the surface of the backlot set and does not penetrate the facades of the buildings. Even when the camera cranes up to the window, all that is revealed is the two-dimensional surface of a television. Third, this sequence isolates each generic element of image and sound and manipulates how the audience might read the sequence based upon how they are juxtaposed together. This serves to establish an emphasis upon the textuality of the film and the superficiality of the genre's codes and conventions.

Blade presents a particularly ambiguous presentation of the urban landscape. The film opens in a hospital with a precredit sequence of Blade's birth and the subsequent death of his mother, who has been fatally bitten by a vampire. At the bottom of the screen appears a small caption reading "1967," though the geographic location of this scene is unclear. This is followed by the credit sequence and a series of time-lapse photography shots of the city, demonstrating the passage of day into night and also signaling a more general passage of time. That time has passed since Blade's birth is then indicated when the film cuts to a series of blurry shots of the street, taken from a moving vehicle as it speeds through the urban landscape over which another caption appears, simply stating "Now."

This second caption is deliberately ambiguous for it lacks any indication of the setting as well as leaves the time frame open to speculation. The film remains in the present but provides a conflicting set of images to represent the period. For instance, Blade's battle against the vampires is fought through the combination of advanced scientific and technological weaponry—such as vampire mace, ultraviolet light, and silver nitrate bullets—and the ritualized weapons of a samurai warrior. The production and maintenance of these weapons is set within the industrial landscape of an abandoned factory, while the vampires live in a postmodern high-rise. The vampires seem both ancient, as embodied by the noble House of Erebus, and modern, as suggested by Deacon Frost's vampire nightclub. The "now" of *Blade* is a curious mix of signifiers of the past, present, and future.

Further proof that the choice to not mention the location is deliberate comes when the epilogue to the film opens with the caption "Moscow" and features an iconic snowy image of the Russian capital. The specificity of this sequence stands in stark contrast to the ambiguity of the rest of the film, which is peppered with a wide range of conflicting urban icons. The sequences in the downtown area of the unnamed city emphasize the prevalence of skyscrapers, normally an iconic image of New York, and yet as Blade drives from his hideout in the industrial outskirts of the city, the film uses broad establishing shots that emphasize its sprawl. While the middle-aged, pure vampires of the House of Erebus, as represented by the German-born Udo Kier as Dragonetti, suggest a European heritage, Frost's followers of turned vampires, are a cultural mix of Caucasians, Africans, Japanese, and Chinese.

Giuliana Bruno, in her analysis of *Blade Runner* (1982) as a metaphor for the postmodern condition, suggests that the image of Los Angeles in the film presents the postindustrial city as a mix of temporal and spatial quotations ruled by the logic of recycling and pastiche. She argues that

> in *Blade Runner*, the visions of postindustrial decay are set in an inclusive, hybrid architectural design. The city is called Los Angeles, but it is an LA that looks very much like New York, Hong Kong, or Tokyo. We are not presented with a real geography, but an imaginary one: a synthesis of mental architectures, of *topoi*. Quoting from different real cities, postcards, advertising, movies, the text makes a point about the city of postindustrialism. It is a polyvalent, interchangeable structure, the product of geographical displacements and condensations.[9]

While *Blade* never says that it is set in Los Angeles, the manner in which it presents a set of deliberately conflicting impressions of time and space draws upon Bruno's description of the postmodern, postindustrial city in *Blade Runner*, effectively quoting *Blade Runner*'s spatial and temporal hybridity in its own representation of the city. The mise-en-scène of *Blade* suggests that its indecipherability is the postindustrial city's defining feature.

The manufactured quality of the Los Angeles vampire films is further emphasized by the manner in which the films are defined by the mechanisms of illusion. The product of mainstream Hollywood, these films have large budgets and showcase spectacular special effects. Significantly, while the New York subgenre and the vampire road movie are selective in their use of vampire conventions, the LA films more strictly adhere to the expectations of the genre. It is, however, its postmodern knowingness that distinguishes these films from the other urban vampire films. As Edward Buscombe argues, the notion of film genre "depends upon a combination of novelty and familiarity," for the genre film brings together the relationship between the genre and filmmaker, and the genre and audience.[10] This three-way relationship makes the genre film work so successfully; part of the pleasure of watching it is in recognizing its conventions intermixed with the thrill of the unexpected. For instance, anyone familiar with the vampire genre knows that one of the key weapons against a vampire is a crucifix, so when Peter Vincent holds a crucifix up before the vampire in *Fright Night*, the audience is confident in his attack. It is therefore a surprise that Vincent's gesture is met by hysterical laughter from the vampire. Suddenly the rules have changed and the audience's comfort in the security of the hero's protection against this monster has been pulled out from under them. If the crucifix doesn't work, what will?

Philip Brophy, however, has argued that the contemporary horror genre has seen a saturation of its conventions and an increasing awareness of itself as a genre.[11] While all genre films require a layer of self-awareness, the contemporary horror film began to textualize its conventions into its own discourse. This increase in the self-referentiality of the genre conventions matches Frederic Jameson's argument that the first and most obvious characteristic of postmodernism is "the emergence of a new kind of flatness or depthlessness, a new kind of superficiality in the most literal sense."[12] While modernism is generally associated with depth—demonstrated in Edward Buscombe's argument that the variation of the conventions of a genre film allows for changing narrative readings or thematic undercurrents—the postmodern horror film increasingly turns in on itself and makes its own conventions the subject of the film. As Brophy suggests, "The contemporary horror film knows that you've seen it before; it knows that you know what is about to happen; and it knows that you know it knows you know."[13]

This postmodern quality of the contemporary horror film is exemplified in the Los Angeles vampire films of the 1980s and 1990s. They draw their source and inspiration from popular culture, namely other vampire films, horror fiction, and comic books. For instance, in *Fright Night*, the fearless vampire-killer Peter Vincent, is actually a screen actor modeled upon two horror film masters: Hammer Studios' own Van Helsing, Peter Cushing, and the American horror star, Vincent Price. In *The Lost Boys*, the teen vampire-killers Edgar and Allen Frog are a composite of popular culture icons. Having worked in a comic book store, they use vampire comics as survival manuals. Their names evoke the master of American Gothic horror, Edgar Allan Poe, and their military attire presents them as military action-heroes from the 1980s. While their understanding and explanation of vampire mythology evokes Van Helsing from *Dracula*, their oath to "protect truth, justice, and the American Way" is inspired by *Superman*. Similarly, the original *Buffy the Vampire Slayer* movie was conceived as a hybrid of the vampire movie and the martial arts film and was, according to the film's director Fran Rubel Kuzui, inspired by the Hong Kong films of John Woo.[14] *Blade* is an adaptation of a comic book series, and furthermore the film's screenwriter, David Goyer, has cited the Hammer film *Captain Kronos: Vampire Hunter* (1972) as an influence.[15]

The films are rife with influences and allusions to popular culture and their structure is particularly defined by an awareness of vampire film tradition. Films like *The Lost Boys* and *Fright Night* feature a horror film fan as the supreme vampire-killer. In *The Lost Boys*, while the adults are blind to the strange and fatal occurrences around them, the teenage comic book aficionados Edgar and Allen Frog act as commando vampire-killers. They instruct Sam and Michael about how to protect themselves from the vampires, what weapons can be used, and how to save Michael from his transformation into a vampire. Similarly, in *Fright Night*, although Peter Vincent is a screen vampire-killer, teenager Charlie Brewster, a horror film fan, is first to overcome his modern common sense to believe that a vampire has moved in next-door. Furthermore, he goes to the outcast and monster-movie fan "Evil Ed" to receive instruction from him on the best ways to protect himself from the vampires. Long before the teenage heroes of Wes Craven's postmodern *Scream* (1996), the characters of *The Lost Boys* and *Fright Night* knew how to successfully survive a horror movie.

Figure 10.1. Vamping out in *The Lost Boys.*

The Los Angeles vampire film's emphasis upon surface-level appearances and performance styles further supports the genre's development of a postmodern aesthetic. While the New York vampires are grounded in a form of realism and surrealism and are portrayed without any supernatural accoutrements to prove that they are vampires, the Los Angeles vampires are primarily identified by their transformation into the monstrous visage of the vampire, achieved through spectacular special effects. In fact, the revelation of a vampire's true face is a significant generic moment in most Los Angeles vampire films. In *The Lost Boys*, Michael's initiation into vampirism occurs when he goes on the hunt and the vampires reveal their vampire faces. Up until this point, they have appeared quite human, but as they watch another group of young people party on the beach and prepare to attack, David turns from the shadows into the light to reveal his true visage. His vampiric image involves whitened, almost catlike eyes, and extended ratlike fangs. (Figure 10.1)

While the vampire face in *The Lost Boys* is a simple transformation from a human face, some other vampire films take this transformation much further, emphasizing the artificiality of the vampire. *Fright Night* is one such example. In this film, the vampire's image is completely artificial and dictated by the narrative expectation of him at different points in the film. In effect, he has a different face for different emotional moments. Charlie first realizes that his new next-door neighbor is a vampire when he watches him seduce a beautiful young woman. As Dandridge caresses her, he raises his head and opens his mouth to reveal two extended vampire fangs. Later, however, when Dandridge is trying to kill Charlie by pushing him out of a window, Charlie stabs him in the hand with a pencil, which results in Dandridge metamorphosing into a monstrous batlike creature. The transformation is achieved through prosthetic makeup and the revelation of his face is heightened by his slow turn to the camera as it tilts up from a close up of his injured hand to his monstrous face.

This sense of artificiality extends to Chris Sarandon's portrayal of the vampire, which shifts depending upon mood and nature of the scene. When Peter Vincent brings Charlie and his friends to Dandridge's house for the purpose of testing his vampiric nature, Dandridge stares meaningfully at Amy, takes her hand in his, slowly raises it to his lips to kiss it, looks into her eyes, and tells her he is "charmed" before turning to Charlie and asking, "Isn't that what vampires are supposed to do?" With this statement, Dandridge implies that he is simply playing the role that Charlie expects of him. Later, however, as he watches Charlie and Amy through his window, he mysteriously comments to his servant, "She [Amy] looks just like her, doesn't she?" and then turns away from the window and walks silently out of frame. Through the deliberate ambiguity of this statement, he adopts the role of the mysterious and threatening vampire, not for Charlie's benefit but for the audience's. By the end of the film, in his final confrontation with Charlie and Peter Vincent, Dandridge has stripped away the appearance of the mysterious vampire and replaced it with the face of a destructive monster. In *Fright Night*, the vampire's bite is presented as erotically as his kisses, while the revelation of his true vampire face involves a change of scene and makeup. When Dandridge reveals his monstrous side, the film presents this as a literal transformation through the use of specialized makeup.

Other characters in the film similarly exhibit an exaggerated resemblance to their traditional cinematic counterpart. Peter Vincent's decision to overcome his fear and help Charlie kill Dandridge is represented by his arrival at Dandridge's house having donned his full vampire-killer costume and toting his case of vampire-killing props. Amy is presented as the epitome of innocence. She giggles when she meets Dandridge and later describes him as "neat." Once she has been turned into a vampire, however, the release of her sexuality transforms her in to a voluptuous siren bearing little resemblance to her original appearance. While the vampire transformations of *The Addiction* and *Vampire in Brooklyn* cause a release of desire, in *Fright Night*, Amy's transformation is a purely physical one, for rather than releasing her repressed nature, she is merely transformed into someone else. (Figure 10.2) With an emphasis upon the surface level of the vampire genre through performance, special effects, intertextuality, and iconographic representation, the Los Angeles vampire films allegorize the superficiality of the postmodern city. While the New York

Figure 10.2. No more girl next door in *Fright Night.*

vampire embodies the depth that is suggested by the layered structure and carnivalesque image of the city, the Los Angeles vampire captures the city's superficial, fragmented theme park image.

The fragmentation of Los Angeles however is not exclusively embodied in the breakdown of the city into compartmentalized and themed communities, but also by the fragmentation of the city into cultural communities. Edward Soja argues that one of the causes of the increased fragmentation of Los Angeles is a movement towards increasing internationalization of the urban space. This internationalization has taken place through both the increasing rate of foreign investment leading to a renewal of the city center, and the wave of over "two million people from Third World countries" who have "moved into Los Angeles and extended their influence into virtually every aspect of the changing urban landscape and culture."[16]

Mike Davis, leading social historian of Los Angeles, has subsequently demonstrated that Los Angeles has, from the beginning, been defined by a range of different social groups, including European emigrés, socialists, Eastern intellectuals, Asian communities, and a growing population of Latino communities, merging within the city at different periods in its history to stake their own claim.[17] As the city continues to expand, the number of different communities continues to grow. From one perspective this is nothing new, for all cities are made up of neighborhoods and districts that contribute to the overall definition of the city. The satellite sprawl of Los Angeles, reinforced by the city's dependence upon the automobile and the highway over public transport, has, however, lead to these distinct neighborhoods being much more separate and fragmented than in other cities.[18]

This isolation and cultural fragmentation has been exacerbated by an increase in racial tension within the city. This tension of course is not a new phenomenon in Los Angeles or in the LA vampire film. As discussed in Chapter 4, the first black vampire, in *Blacula*, emerged in the community of Watts at a time of racial tension and riots. Since the Watts riots, Los Angeles has expanded—for example, the Hispanic population continues to grow, and the city is turning away from European influence and toward the Pacific Rim, which has led to an influx of Asian immigrants—and racial intolerance has increased.[19] All of this has contributed ethnic segregation to an already fragmented city and is a major contributor to the city's movement toward a thematic, artificial Los Angeles as people escape the urban reality of certain segments of the community in favor of a manufactured sense of security. Mike Davis argues that in recent years, inhabitants of Los Angeles are increasingly "liv[ing] in 'fortress cities' brutally divided between 'fortified cells' of affluent society and 'places of terror'"[20] and that this growing militarization of security within Los Angeles is leading to an acceleration of this "social polarization and spatial apartheid."[21] Where the modern metropolis was defined by crowded streets that caused individuals to be physically close though socially separate, the satellite sprawl of Los Angeles has, like the highway in the vampire road movie, removed the spatial proximity as well. Davis' observations, quoted above, were made a year prior to a series of events that once again placed issues of racism at the foreground of any discussion or representation of Los Angeles: the Rodney King beating in 1991, the acquittal of the police officers who were captured on video exhibiting unreasonable force, and the subsequent riots that engulfed the city. Since this Los Angeles uprising, Davis has asserted that the "social polarization and spatial apartheid are accelerating,"[22] while Ed Guerrero describes these events as "a consciousness-shaping moment for a whole new generation of Americans."[23]

This "consciousness-shaping moment" is fundamental to many post-riot Los Angeles films such as Kathryn Bigelow's *Strange Days* (1995) and Joel Schumacher's *Falling Down* (1992), both of which portray LA as a hotbed of racial tension, ready to erupt at a moment's notice. This tension informs the LA vampire film, particularly in what Nina Auerbach describes as the displacement of the nineteenth-century lone vampire by vampire gangs. She sees these new forms of vampires as "branded creatures, who are given their identity. Rather than masters who do the branding."[24] My analysis of the New York vampire, however, demonstrates that this is not quite the case. The New York female vampires discussed in Chapter 8 primarily remain lone figures as they self-consciously appropriate the image of the nineteenth-century male vampires Auerbach discusses. Furthermore, Anne Rice's vampires are more community- and family-based than ganglike. In the novel *The Queen of the Damned,* Rice goes to great lengths to trace the family tree of the vampire. Really only the Los Angeles vampire is depicted as ganglike. Gangs therefore become one of the few unifying characteristics of the Los Angeles vampires. While Sarah, Kathy, Nadja, Rita, and Anna find their own path along the urban streets of New York, the vampires in *The Lost Boys, Blood Ties, Blade,* and *Revenant* move through the city as a group.

Prior to making *Falling Down,* Joel Schumacher infused *The Lost Boys* with the presence of rival gangs and the theme that equates the transformation into a vampire with the initiation into a motorcycle gang. In this manner, *The Lost Boys* has much in common with later rites-of-passage hood films like *Boyz n the Hood* (1991) and *New Jack City* (1991). Like the young men in these films, the protagonist of *The Lost Boys,* Michael, must decide whether to join the gang or stand on his own. The presence of gangs is established in the opening of the film, which begins with a confrontation between rival gangs on a carousel in an amusement park. As one gang walks through the carousel, their leader David caresses the girlfriend of the leader of another gang, and a fight ensues until it is broken up by a security guard who kicks both groups off the boardwalk. The first gang is clearly the vampire gang, the Lost Boys of the film's title. They are further signified as a gang by the fact that they only appear together and their strength is dictated by group intimidation. These gangs, however, are more a tribute to the great cinematic rebels played by Marlon Brando in *The Wild Ones* (1953) and James Dean in *Rebel Without a Cause* (1955). The young vampires ride motorcycles with attitude like Marlon Brando, challenge Michael to a game of chicken on a cliff like the similar challenge in *Rebel Without a Cause,* and to further make the point, they decorate their underground lair with a poster of the Los Angeles-identified rock 'n' roll rebel Jim Morrison.

Made before the series of Los Angeles gangland films, from *Colors* (1988) to *Boyz n the Hood,* as well as Schumacher's own *Falling Down,* the gangs of *The Lost Boys* are not necessarily interested in race, turf, or colors, but rather with defying authority and the adults that surround them. The film is in fact completely peopled with children acting either in defiance to or in the place of their parents. The Frog brothers run their parents' comic store while simultaneously operating a vampire-killing business. Sam and Michael attempt to solve their vampire problem without seeking help from their mother and grandfather, both of whom seem oblivious to the dangers that surround them. Even the Lost Boys challenge their own father figure, Max, by entering his video store and intimidating his customers despite his warnings to stay away, as well as by terrorizing him at his home by hurling a monstrous bat-shaped kite onto his property and noisily circling his house on motorcycles. Furthermore, Michael is drawn to the Lost Boys as a means of escaping the responsibility imposed upon him by his recently divorced mother and his new role as man of the house. As David tells Michael, to be a vampire means to "never get old and never die," just like the Lost Boys in *Peter Pan*.

The Lost Boys may not address the issues of race that are associated with Los Angeles gangs and which Schumacher addresses in his later film *Falling Down*, but it does address the segregation of Los Angeles by making visible an urban space that has been traditionally invisible in Hollywood cinema. Paula J. Massood has argued with respect to African-American films about the hood that Hollywood has, through a process of inclusion and exclusion in its representation, "helped LA to nurture and reify a particular set of urban signs—palm trees, sun, abundance, paradise," and that the films about the hood have attempted to challenge this form of representation by focusing upon the utopian and dystopian dichotomy of the city.[25] The city in *The Lost Boys* is in many ways the embodiment of a very real urban milieu, what Mike Davis describes as the "free fire zone," the inner ring of Los Angeles. Davis claims that this inner ring is one of the most dangerous parts of the city, containing more homicides than any other part of the city and where the police can't even "keep track of all of the bodies on the street," let alone other crimes.[26] This description is mirrored in *The Lost Boys*, when Michael and Sam arrive in Santa Carla and Michael sees a sign covered in graffiti that reads "Santa Carla: Murder Capital of the World." When Michael asks his grandfather, a resident of Santa Carla, about it, the grandfather replies, "If all of the bodies that are buried around here were to stand up at once, we would have a hell of a population problem," evoking Davis' description of the inner ring of Los Angeles.

Furthermore, like the films about the hood, *The Lost Boys* concerns itself with life in the inner city and the effects of the urban landscape on the family by portraying Santa Carla as a community of outcasts and by immersing Michael, Sam, and their mother Sarah, who are as much outcasts as the others, within this community. Having left Phoenix after a messy and painful divorce, Sarah and her family are effectively homeless, penniless, and, like the other inhabitants of Santa Carla, hopeless. As the family arrives in the town, the film presents Santa Carla through a montage sequence introducing the city's population juxtaposed with the song "People Are Strange." This sequence establishes that although the film does not address issues of race and ethnicity, it is concerned with the unrepresented—the town is filled with society's outsiders, gangs of mods, goths, new romantics, ex-hippies, and a host of homeless children and adults. Within this mix, Sarah and her family are as strange as the rest.

In addition to the inner ring of Los Angeles, this presentation of Santa Carla also evokes Mike Davis' description of the city's Skid Row, a containment zone in which the homeless are forced to congregate. Santa Carla, like Skid Row, seems to be the official deposit zone for all of the country's outcasts. According to Davis, by condensing "the desperate and [the] helpless together in such a small space, and denying adequate housing, official policy has transformed Skid Row into probably the most dangerous ten blocks in the world—ruled by a grisly succession of 'Slashers,' 'Night Stalkers,' and more ordinary predators. Every night on Skid Row is Friday the 13th."[27] This is demonstrated in *The Lost Boys* by the walls of missing-person posters at the boardwalk. The vast number of these posters suggests that this community is a dangerous place, rife with crime, ignored by the outside world. In *The Lost Boys*, Davis' figurative "Night Stalkers" are transformed into literal night stalkers, vampires who feed off the lost and unseen. Through the fantasy narrative of vampire initiation this previously invisible face of Los Angeles is explored and made visible.

The Los Angeles gangs are, however, no longer restricted to the inner ring but, in some areas, have begun to move into the suburban parts of the city, suggesting yet another fragmentation of Los Angeles. This is clearly embodied by the gang of young vampires, the Shrikes, in *Blood Ties* (1991). Set in Los Angeles' Long Beach community, the narrative surrounds a wealthy group of Carpathian Americans trying to conceal their vampiric heritage and live among Americans. The Shrikes, however, are the next generation of vampires who have chosen to embrace the violence and bloodlust of their heritage, which they channel into gang activity. Where the Lost Boys are reminiscent of the cinematic rebels of 1950s cinema, the Shrikes have more in common with the gangs of the 1980s and 1990s hood films: the Lost Boys' vampirism is signified by their youth while the Shrikes' vampirism is signified by their ethnicity. While the adults in their families debate about Americanness, assimilation, and miscegenation, the Shrikes embrace their ethnicity and take their fight with humanity onto the street.

The Shrikes are immediately presented as a gang in the opening of the film when they are introduced riding their motorcycles into a parking garage at a courthouse where their leader Butch is on trial for the harassment and bodily harm of an elderly woman. In this instance, they are all dressed alike and pull up into the garage in perfect synchronization. When Butch's case is declared a mistrial the gang erupts into loud shrieks as they leap around the courtroom, ignoring the authority of the judge, and then lead Butch out into the street. They are next seen recklessly driving their motorcycles through the courtyard of the public building, forcing people to jump out of their way or be run over. In this they are not that different from the Lost Boys who similarly establish their authority through terrorizing the community around them. Throughout the film, the Shrikes are shown driving around the city, disrupting the peace, and marking walls with their colors, graffiti paintings of wolves, snarling animals, and bloodshed.

When initiating Cody, a young, country cousin unaware of his vampire heritage, into the gang, the others repeatedly call him "vamp." While this is a term their elders have sought to break away from, the Shrikes have reclaimed the word and wear it like an identity badge. Nina Auerbach sees the contemporary vampire as being given an identity and forced to wear it like a brand, but I would argue that the Shrikes appropriate the brand given to them by an unaccepting humanity and redefine it for themselves. When Cody asks Butch why he keeps calling him "vamp," Butch explains, "If I don't, they will. They won't ever let you forget what you are. You are one of us. Spawn of hell. Creatures from the dark side. Monsters. Fiends. You might as well get behind it because its your birthright." Butch and his gang of Shrikes do not cower from the names that they are called by Christian groups, but have embraced that heritage with the adage "If you've got the name you might as well have the game," a position that is shared by the gang of vampires led by Deacon Frost in the film *Blade*.

Blade, based upon the Marvel comic book series about a black superhuman vampire-killer, takes the ganglike opposition between vampire hunter and vampire, as well as the racial connotations of the films described above, much further. Created in 1972 by Marv Wolfman, the same year that saw the release of *Blacula*, the comic's initial appeal was, like the blaxploitation films of the period, its presentation of a strong, black, urban hero with whom audiences could identify placed at the center of an action-adventure narrative in which he would triumph in the end. The aim, according to Wolfman, was to present a "tougher character, with more of a street attitude" than other superheroes in this period.[28] The comic book unknowingly tapped into what Ed Guerrero describes as the lower-class blacks' increasing dissatisfaction with "the black bourgeois paradigm of upward mobility through assimilation," as embodied in the film work of Sidney Poitier, and it associated "the black experience with the defiant images and culture of the 'ghetto' and its hustling street life."[29]

It is therefore not surprising that as the Los Angeles vampires become increasingly ganglike in their representation, once again infusing the genre with issues of race, that the black vampire hunter emerges yet again. Just as one cannot disassociate *Blacula*'s emergence in 1972 from the Watts riots, *Blade* similarly carries the legacy of a post-Rodney King Los Angeles. The film is rife with associations with the King affair, and historically to the Watts riots, particularly in Blade's seeming opposition to the police force. Although Blade is the hero who fights on behalf of humanity, he is repeatedly shown to be working outside of the law and in opposition to a corrupt or ignorant police force. The film's opening scene in a vampire nightclub, in which Blade does battle with dozens of vampires, ends as Blade narrowly escapes the arrival of the police. As they enter the frame from screen right, Blade is seen crawling up the wall and out of the frame on screen left.

Later, when Blade arrives at the hospital to destroy a vampire, he must fight off a group of security guards and police officers who immediately begin shooting at him despite the fact that the real villain, the charred and regenerated vampire Quinn, has just attacked two members of the hospital staff and escaped the building. When Karen Jenson, the victim Blade saves from Quinn and who is now aware of the existence of vampires, says that she will go to the police, Blade's comrade Whistler informs her that the vampires own the police, a comment that suggests a culture of police corruption. This is proven to be true when the police officer, Krieger, arriving at Karen's apartment under the pretext of checking on her whereabouts, is revealed to be a vampire-familiar. Owned by Deacon Frost, Krieger acts as a messenger boy, shuttling shipments of blood between vampire hideouts within the security of his police car. However the most obvious suggestion of the Rodney King affair occurs when Blade is caught in Frost's apartment complex and is beaten into submission by a group of armed security guards whose black uniforms are reminiscent of the police force.

Like *Blacula*, however, the racial politics of *Blade* are far more complex than a simple opposition between the black vampire hunters—Blade and Karen—and the white, politically powerful, and corrupt vampires—Frost,

Quinn, and Officer Krieger. In the first instance, Blade exists somewhere between the human world and the vampire world, for his mother was bitten by a vampire while pregnant and the vampire blood was born into Blade, making him a curious hybrid of human and vampire. As a result, Blade's racial ambiguity makes him an outcast of both communities, and his own loathing of his vampire-self is condemned by Frost who views Blade as an assimilationist, denying his genuine heritage, and taking up the "Uncle Tom routine."

To further complicate the situation, Frost is presented as racially other, for the vampire world is itself plagued with racial prejudice and fears of miscegenation. Split into two camps, born vampires and turned vampires, a hierarchy is maintained by the noble House of Erebus who look down upon Frost and his gang of turned vampires, seen to be impure due to their mix of vampire and human blood, and treat him as a nuisance who disrupts their lifestyle and defies tradition. While the members of the House of Erebus are presented as the embodiment of authority and the establishment with their Armani suits, offshore accounts, and treaties with the humans, Frost and his friends are more ganglike. They are a mishmash of ages, nationalities, genders, and races, truly representing the racial mix of Los Angeles, and they congregate in groups, either in Frost's high-rise apartment or in one of Frost's vampire nightclubs. Like the Shrikes, who mark their turf with graffiti, the vampires in *Blade* mark their turf and property with glyphs, a combination of Asian characters and bar code. Frost's desire to bring about the vampire apocalypse through the invocation of the blood god La Magra is his rebellion against his imposed subjugation to humanity and the born vampires. When La Magra comes, everyone in its wake will be transformed into a vampire, wiping out humanity and the hierarchy of the born vampire. Frost's plan would do away with cultural segregation and separation by transforming Los Angeles into a unified city of homogenized vampire inhabitants. This plan does not come to fruition because Blade destroys Frost and, by refusing the cure that will take away his blood thirst and his superhuman strength, embraces the heterogeneity of his human-vampire existence and the Los Angeles urban landscape. While the vampire film represents, in its narratives and characterizations, the indecipherability of the city through its cultural and racial fragmentation, the generic structure of the Los Angeles vampire film captures the postmodern aestheticism of the city.

After the deconstruction of the vampire mythology in *Martin*, the vampire arrived in the 1980s a shattered genre in need of redefinition. Subsequently, the genre fragmented into a plethora of vampires that crisscrossed America through the decade and into the 1990s. The result of this fragmentation was the development of subgenres of vampire films based around their differing urban settings, drawing upon the discourses that define each city to construct the vampire's identity and representation. While the New York vampire film engages with a history of modernist representations of New York, tapping into the city's carnivalesque underpinning, the genre also reinterprets that representation by enabling the infiltration of the modern city by the female vampire and the reinterpretation of the language of modernity through the vampire's appropriation of urban flâneurism. The vampire road movie engages in a three-way discourse between the frontier, the modern, and the postmodern by using the hybridity of the road movie, western, and vampire genres to showcase the simultaneous reading of the American landscape as both modern and postmodern. The Los Angeles vampire films embody the fragmentation of the urban landscape by emphasizing the superficiality of the space, its association with the artificiality and stratification of the theme park, and the fragmentation of identity as a result of the city's decentralized structure. It also, however, embraces the plurality of microcities within the urban sprawl, offering glimpses of traditionally unseen spaces and cultures and using the vampire genre to explore the dynamics of racial tension within the city.

While the vampire films of the 1970s were engaged with a reinterpretation of the vampire mythology as seen through a shift in the perception of modernity, the films of the 1980s and 1990s demonstrate a complete fragmentation of the modern and postmodern landscapes and the emergent illegibility of the contemporary city. The reconstitution of the vampire film in this period mirrors the way in which American cities were forced to reinvent themselves following the economic and political crisis of the 1970s that resulted in America's transition from an industrial nation to a postindustrial one. As a result, the vampire films of New York, Los Angeles, and the road between them not only show the vampire redefining its mythology to suit its landscape, but also enter a dialogue with the newly constituted representation of the city.

PART FOUR

REDEFINING BOUNDARIES

CHAPTER ELEVEN

Vampire Cyborgs

They're everywhere. Vampires. The Hominus nocturna. *We hunt 'em, you see.*

WHISTLER TO DR. KAREN JENSON IN BLADE (1998)

Vampire Anatomy 101. Crosses and running water don't do dick, so forget what you've seen in the movies. You use a stake, silver, or sunlight. You know how to use one of these? [Hands her a gun.] The safety's off, round's already chambered—silver hollow point filled with garlic. You aim for the head or the heart. Anything else is your ass.

BLADE TO DR. KAREN JENSON IN BLADE (1998)

Hominus nocturna; virus; disease; genetic mutation; genetic experiment; a genetically engineered superrace. In the vampire films of the late 1990s and early twenty-first century, these terms have come to replace classic descriptions of the vampire: bloodsucker; revenant; succubus; shape-shifter; fiend. Vampirism is increasingly explained through the language of science, described as a disease, and in cases such as *Near Dark, The Forsaken, Vampire: Los Muertos*, and the *Blade* trilogy (*Blade* [1998], *Blade II* [2002], and *Blade Trinity* [2004]), a treatment or cure is discovered. This choice of language, however, goes beyond reading vampirism as a disease or specifically as an AIDS allegory. In particular, the *Blade* films, *Underworld* (2003), *Van Helsing* (2004), and *Underworld: Evolution* (2006) have contributed to a reconception of generic conventions and iconography that undermines the laws of religion and folklore in favor of the laws of science and technology. It is not simply the transmission of vampirism that is treated scientifically, but the methods of hunting and killing a vampire.

As such, this has led to a new understanding of the vampire body and its strengths and weaknesses. While the vampires in *John Carpenter's Vampires* and *Vampires: Los Muertos* turn to the church and its religious rituals to enable them to walk in the daylight, these later films show them using technology and developments in genetics to improve their physical condition. Furthermore, the manner in which the vampires embrace new technologies is mirrored in the way that these films have moved away from physical makeup effects in favor of computer-generated effects in their representation of the vampire. This change in technological method has equally contributed to the reconstitution of the vampire body on a representational level. They are no longer defined by the boundaries of their bodies but are often able to transcend and redefine them at their will. In this chapter, therefore, I will explore how, like in Stoker's *Dracula*, the vampire hunters embrace new technology while the vampires come to embody it, as they are transformed, both narratively and aesthetically, into vampire cyborgs.

John J. Jordan argues that *Blade* has reimagined vampire mythology through the lens of science by making Blade a vampire cyborg: "'A hybrid of machine and organism, a creature of social reality as well as a creature of fiction,' representing a mystical figure surrounded internally and externally by science."[1] Chris Hables Gray, Heidi J. Figueroa-Sarriera, and Steven Mentor see cyborgs as not simply the product of the physical fusion of machine and flesh, but as the product of a technologically-dependent society. "Even if many individuals in the industrial and postindustrial countries aren't full cyborgs, we certainly all live in a 'cyborg society.' Machines are intimately interfaced with humans on almost every level of existence not only in the West and Japan but among the elite in every country of the world."[2]

This technological dependency is conveyed in recent vampire films through the reinvention of the modern vampire-killer. First, their tools have changed. As Blade explains in the quotation that opens this chapter, the rules from old vampire films have been abandoned, and religious artifacts such as the crucifix, holy water, and holy wafer no longer have any effect on vampires. This alone is nothing new as, with the increasing secularization of society, films from *Martin* to *Near Dark* had already detached themselves from the codes of the church. What distinguishes these films is that scientific and technological tools have replaced the artifacts. In the *Blade* films, in addition to Blade's signature samurai sword, he and his fellow vampire hunters use modern weaponry such as technologically enhanced crossbows, shotguns, silver nitrate bullets, lasers, ultraviolet lamps, grenades and bombs, an anticoagulant superagent, and a biological weapon called Daystar. Similarly, in *Underworld*—a film that replaces the genre's conventional confrontation between the living and the undead, as described by Gregory A. Waller, with a centuries-old war between were-wolves and vampires—the werewolves develop ultraviolet ammunition to use against the vampires that explodes from within and is impossible to remove. In fact, the prevalence of UV-related weaponry in these films, including the nineteenth-century-set *Van Helsing*, strongly suggests that while many of the old rules from the movies have been abandoned, new conventions are being established. Furthermore, in the *Blade* films, even the effects of these weapons upon the vampires are often explained scientifically. For instance, they are allergic to garlic, described by its scientific name *Allium sativum*, which causes them to go into anaphylactic shock. They are similarly described as being "allergic" to silver and UV light, while the anticoagulant superagent and Daystar attack their systems on a cellular level.[3]

Second, the vampire-killer is now surrounded by scientists and/or a technological support team who develop the weapons necessary to fight the vampires. For instance, while *Van Helsing* may seem to return the vampire to its nineteenth-century *Dracula* origins, it does so with a modern twist. Van Helsing—now a young demon-killing adventurer employed by the Vatican rather than the learned doctor and lawyer of Stoker's novel—is accompanied on his trek to Transylvania by Friar Carl. Carl, clearly modeled on James Bond's "Q," is learned in folklore but is also an inventor and scientist who provides Van Helsing with the weapons and gadgetry required in his fight against demons. Through the character of Carl, this vampire film brings religion, folklore, science, and technology together as he provides Van Helsing with garlic, holy water, a crucifix, a silver stake, a semiautomatic crossbow, and a specially developed bomb that reproduces the light from the sun. Similarly, throughout the three *Blade* films, Blade collaborates with his weapons maker Whistler, hematologist Karen Jenson, mechanic Scud, and the Nightstalkers, a vampire-hunting team of scientists and weapons makers. Throughout the trilogy, the so-phistication of their technology evolves, climaxing with the Nightstalkers, who, largely due to their youth, embrace science and technology in every aspect of their vampire hunting and killing. Sommerfield and Hedges develop the cures and the weapons, while vampire hunters Abigail Whistler and Hannibal King embrace technology in the hunt, using enhanced UV weapons in the form of shotguns and lasers that can slice a vampire in two, while listening to techno on their MP3 players.

What is more, many of these characters are themselves represented as technology-human hybrids. Whistler wears a leg brace, while Scud has developed a mechanical crane that enables him to hover over and move around all of the machinery in his workshop. In *Blade Trinity*, Sommer-field, the scientist who develops the Daystar virus, is blind, but her use of computer technology reveals a fluid symbiosis with the technology that belies her disability. Furthermore, Karen in *Blade*, Whistler in *Blade II*, and Hannibal in *Blade Trinity* have each been cured of their vampirism through scientific intervention. To fight vampires in the *Blade* universe, therefore, is to embrace a cyborg existence.

Most importantly, the role of blood in the vampire film has evolved. Its original significance to the vampire myth was linked both to its mystical meaning as a life-giving force (menstrual blood symbolizes reproduction while the loss of blood can lead to death), and its Christian symbolism (the ritual of Holy Communion includes the symbolic drinking of Christ's blood).[4] Furthermore, as I've already discussed, recent films, from *Night of the Living Dead* to the present, have increasingly emphasized that the drinking of blood is a form of nourishment for the modern, secular vampire. In these later films, however, blood signifies the potential of modern genetics and the mysteries of DNA. Studies in genetics have in recent years become quite high profile in the media, most notably with the revelation in 1997 of Dolly, the first cloned sheep, and the completion of the Human Genome Project in 2003, in which all of the genes that make up a *Homo sapien* were sequenced and mapped. Additionally, the media regularly reports and comments upon the ethical issues raised by developments within genetics around such hot topics as genetically modified foods, gene therapy, stem cell research, "designer" babies, and most significantly, human cloning. The vast number of films that have recently explored these subjects from a range of perspectives, including *Jurassic Park* (cloning dinosaurs), *Alien Resurrection* (cloning aliens), *Sixth Day* (cloning humans), *Mimic* (genetic engineering), *Gattaca* (gene therapy or gene replacement techniques and genetic engineering), *Species* (genetic hybridity), as well as the recent superhero films such as *Spider-Man*, *Hulk*, *X-Men*, and *Fantastic Four* (genetic mutations), demonstrate this cultural preoccupation with both the science and the ethics of genetics and DNA.

Stephen Nottingham has suggested that while these films are prevalent, they do not necessarily represent a new genre. Rather, themes of "genetic engineering and clon[ing] have been spliced into existing horror and science fiction scenarios" enabling "old stories to be updated and modernised."[5] This is precisely the case with the modern vampire film that has reconceived the significance of blood as the source of vital DNA information and the building block for research. For instance, Blade is portrayed as a genetic hybrid between human and vampire; his mother was bitten by a vampire while pregnant, which, we are told in the first film of the trilogy, changed his DNA. It is his genetic hybridity that makes Blade so important to the vampires. In *Blade*, his blood is treated mystically, as the vital component of an ancient ritual to bring about the blood god, but in *Blade II*, the vampires opt to "harvest" Blade's blood in order to study it and find the key to his resistance to sunlight as part of their genetic experiments to improve the vampire constitution. In both cases he is bled to the point of near death. The first time it is in a stone sarcophagus from which the blood is siphoned down into an ancient chamber, while in the second, the mise-en-scène is changed to mirror the vampires' more scientific pursuit, as Blade is strapped to a gleaming, futuristic gurney with metal spikes used to puncture Blade's limbs and drain his blood. By *Blade Trinity*, Blade's blood is no longer of scientific interest, but the blood of the original vampire Dracula is sought by both the Nightstalkers, who want to use his DNA to construct a more powerful bioweapon against the vampires, and the vampires, who want to study his DNA to perfect their own.

Underworld similarly reconceives the role of blood in both the vampire and werewolf narrative through genetic science. This is made absolutely clear when Selene, the film's vampire heroine, is asked why a Lycan (a werewolf) would stalk a human if not for food. The film immediately cuts to a dilapidated lab where a Lycan scientist draws blood through a syringe from a human subject in order to perform tests. It is eventually revealed that the Lycans have been attempting to end the war between vampires and werewolves by experimenting with the bloodlines in order to create a genetic hybrid of the two species. The Lycans have been testing human blood as a means of isolating a particular DNA strand that is able to withstand the introduction of both the vampire and the werewolf DNA. Bloodlines in this film therefore signify both the heritage and the DNA of the two species. The scientization of blood within the genre extends beyond the lab environment when Lucian, the leader of the Lycans, bites the test subject Michael only to spit the blood into a test tube in order to attain a blood sample. His bite, however, also begins Michael's change into a werewolf, now reconceived through the language of science, as Selene describes the bite of an immortal as the transmission of a deadly virus. The vampire's bite completes the experiment when Selene chooses to bite Michael in order to initiate his genetic mutation as her DNA mixes with Lucian's in Michael's bloodstream.

While the iconography of the vampire film has been reconfigured to reflect a more technologically-oriented and -dependent society, the vampires in these films have embraced technology both internally and externally to become vampire cyborgs. In *Underworld*, the vampires develop synthetic blood to sustain their existence, while in *Van Helsing*, Dracula attempts to use Dr. Frankenstein's life-creating technology to infuse his dead offspring with electrically induced life, declaring that Frankenstein's "triumph of science over God" can now be usurped for his own devilish purposes. Vampirism, already representing an alternative to traditional reproduction methods, has been reinvented to represent the contemporary trends toward finding scientific alternatives to reproduction.[6]

The *Blade* trilogy, however, demonstrates the most complex reconception of vampirism through technology. John J. Jordan suggests in his discussion of the first *Blade* film that "Blade is shown to be most heroic when he relies on technology, and the villainous vampires are associated strictly with what is horrific and with the nonscientific."[7] This argument mistakenly assumes a clear-cut opposition between Blade and the other vampires—Blade is in fact a vampire who must suppress his bloodlust—and does not recognize the degree to which the vampires mirror Blade's cyborg nature, a fact that becomes increasingly apparent throughout the trilogy.

In the first film, both Blade and his archenemy Frost turn to science and technology to defy the limitations of the body. Frost, a turned vampire, struggles against a community that is divided between born vampires and turned vampires. As a result, those who are turned are treated as second-class citizens by purebloods, and the language of science is used to reduce them to a disease, a virus that can be cured. As previously mentioned, Blade is a genetic mix between human and vampire. He does not share their allergies to sunlight, silver, or garlic, but does possess their strength, regenerative powers, and thirst for blood. His war against the vampires therefore mirrors the war he is waging against the demands of his own body.

To wage this war, as Jordan argues, Blade adorns his body with the weapons and technology that are required to defeat the vampires, while internally he equally reconfigures himself through science with the injection of a serum to suppress his vampire thirst. This transforms him into what Mark Oehlert has described as a biotech integration cyborg.[8] For Blade, science and technology allow him to suppress the demands of his vampire body and transform him into a vampire-killing machine. Frost, however, turns to science and technology, not to suppress his nature but to eliminate the limitations of the vampire body. Frost is highly proficient

with new technology and, like Blade who has reinterpreted vampire mythology in scientific terms, Frost has adopted science and technology to
take the place of traditional vampire conventions. He uses a blood bank
for fresh blood supplies and has computerized timers to open the metal
shutters of his apartment's bay windows and his bed at sunset. When Dragonetti, the leader of the purebloods, finds Frost in the vampire archive
analyzing the ancient texts, Frost is presented sitting in the corner of
a clinical computer lab, listening to electronic techno music through
headphones. The music pulsates with the same rhythm as the computer
program flashing on the screen, linking Frost to the computerized trans-
lations through the music. Dragonetti claims that because Frost is not a
pureblood he could never understand the ancient texts, but Frost uses
a computer to translate the texts to his own language, one of modern
technologies.

Frost is regularly depicted in the film as communicating with the other
vampires through some form of computer or electronic technology. Blade
first faces Frost through a computer connection when he breaks into the
vampire archive to find Pearl the record keeper talking to Frost over a
digital link. Blade looks at the screen of the laptop to see Frost for the first
time, pictured on the monitor in close-up with looming high-rises behind
him. Later, when Blade returns to his hideout to find that Frost has captured his new ally, Dr. Karen Jenson, and brutally tortured his mentor,
Whistler, he once again comes face-to-face with Frost on a monitor as he
looks at a tape recording of Frost giving him the necessary instructions
to find Karen alive. When Blade follows those instructions and arrives
at Frost's high-rise command center, Frost communicates with his men
through a portable headpiece, coordinating the movements of his men in
their attempt to capture Blade. These communication technologies allow
Frost to extend himself beyond the boundaries of his own body to include
the actions and commands of hundreds of other vampires. This symbiosis
with technology is reinforced in the later *Blade* films.

In *Blade II*, Blade is forced to work with an elite team of vampires
called the Bloodpack, who have been trained as a unit to match Blade's
strength, skill, and technical hybridity. These vampires are overtly presented as mirror images of Blade's cyborg existence. Like Blade, they
dress in black leather, adorned with technological weaponry to enhance
their strength, stealth, and maneuverability. Like Frost, they are wired up
to radio microphones to facilitate efficient communication between the
team members. The Bloodpack first appears when two of their members
infiltrate Blade's hideout by silently leaping through the rafters of the

Figure 11.1. The Bloodpack in *Blade 2.*

warehouse like computerized trapeze artists. To protect themselves from Blade's ultraviolet lighting that reproduces the effects of sunlight, the vampires dress in black leather jumpsuits, with metallic masks covering their entire face. Mechanical, infrared goggles cover their eyes and allow them to see in the light. The costumes make the vampires appear completely robotic. The ensuing fight scene demonstrates that the vampires are able to flawlessly match Blade's fighting skill, as they smoothly dodge and parry each blow and turn somersaults and back flips through the air with ease. Like Blade, the Bloodpack is a fighting machine. (Figure 11.1)

These vampires stand in direct contrast to the vampire-patrons of the House of Pain, who take pleasure in the physicality of the body and the pain that can be derived from its mutilation. As the Bloodpack and Blade move through the nightclub, they look on in horror as they see vampires tattooing their bodies, injecting syringes into their tongues, slicing into each other's mouths with razor blades, and surgically removing layers of flesh and muscles. While the Bloodpack embody smooth and efficient blending of technology and the body, the rest of the vampire community continues to be equated with traditions of body modification and the physical pleasures of penetrating the skin and the flesh.

The Bloodpack are also contrasted with the Reapers, the object of their hunt. The Reapers are vampire mutants that are defined by the demands of their body. Like Frost's turned vampires, they are described as a disease, but rather than infecting humanity, they are a disease that runs rampant through the vampire system. Their metabolism runs faster than that of the average vampire, creating an insatiable hunger. If they do not drink blood every day, they eventually feed off their own body until they die. While seeming to suggest the vampire body run amok, it is eventually revealed that these mutations are the result of genetic experiments designed to improve the vampire race by scientifically altering their genetic makeup. During an autopsy, it is discovered that a tonguelike tentacle that latches onto a victim has replaced the traditional canine fangs. Their remaining fangs discharge a poison that anesthetizes the victim. These developments make the Reapers stronger and more effective, enabling them to drink the blood of vampires as well as of humans. The Reapers have also been designed to be impervious to harm from everything except the sunlight. The chest cavity has developed an armorlike cage made of bone that surrounds the heart and protects it from staking. The Reapers therefore embody science out of control: bodies that have become vampire machines.

Finally, the vampires in *Blade Trinity* are shown to comfortably use a range of technologies, including digital video cameras and computers. They are even developing a form of industrial human farm to sustain their blood supply after they have wiped out the free human race.[9] As in the previous films, technology is used to overcome their physical limitations, sensitivity to sunlight in particular. They are first shown arriving at an isolated location in the desert of Iraq, defying the danger of the sun, emerging from their helicopter covered from head to toe in light-resistant flight suits. In this opening, the sunblock and motorcycle helmets employed by Frost in the first film and the helmets and jumpsuits from *Blade II* are taken to their most extreme, as one vampire stares up at the burning desert sun and gives it the finger. More significantly, the film shows the vampires spearheading corporate scientific research, under the name Biomedica Enterprises, designed to destroy Blade and phase out their weaknesses through genetic engineering, taking the research of Damaskinos in *Blade II* to a global scale. Under the guise of this company, the vampires frame Blade for murder, manipulate the FBI, experiment upon animals to create a range of vampire dogs, and locate and study Dracula's DNA to improve their own. This image of a corrupt and self-serving vampire corporation reinforces Stephen Nottingham's argument that "genetic technology in the movies is often in the hands of giant corporations, acting unethically and beyond democratic control."[10]

While these uses of modern technologies and science allow the vampire to exceed the limitations of its body and embrace the modern age, it is through the use of computer-generated special effects rather than special makeup effects that the vampire is truly able to transcend its physical boundaries. In the 1970s and 1980s, while the horror film was preoccupied with body horror and physical special makeup effects, the science-fiction genre began to explore the potential of computer technologies to create new types of special effects that have subsequently come to dominate the industry.[11] Initially, when used within the horror genre, CGI achieved varying degrees of success. Films such as *The Relic* (1997), *Deep Rising* (1998), *Deep Blue Sea* (1999), and *Pitch Black* (2000) used CGI to create a wide range of spectacular monsters, some more convincing than others, while *The Frighteners* (1996), *The Haunting* (1999), *Stir of Echoes* (1999), and *What Lies Beneath* (2000) have more successfully used the technology to create a series of haunting specters. The smoothly animated quality of the technology lends itself to the translucent quality of ghosts.

   With the gradual introduction of computer-generated imagery into the horror genre, therefore, the relationship between the vampire and technology seems to have come full circle, as the way in which the technology is used suggests a return to the spectral presence of the vampire. When Buffy stakes a vampire in the television series *Buffy the Vampire Slayer,* it magically bursts into a sparkling cloud of dust, while the vampires in *Blade* are instantly turned to ash by the touch of Blade's sword. There is, however, a major distinction between the spectral effects of *Nosferatu* and those created by computers. When Schrek puts his hand in front of the projector in *Shadow of the Vampire*, the shadow that is projected is an image derived from his own body. Similarly, the demise of Orlok in *Nosferatu* is presented by fading out the real image of Orlok. The demise of each vampire in *Buffy*, however, is not drawn from life but created in a computer where, according to Stephen Prince, there is "no profilmic referent" to ground the image in reality.[12] Any illusion of reality in the digital image is created through the programming of a computer.

   Philip Rosen, however, argues that in trying to present computer and digital technologies as new and cutting-edge, computer designers, enthusiasts, and theorists have overplayed the technology's opposition to photographic realism and its indexicality. He suggests, however, that rather than being an opposition to previous media, digital technology involves a hybridity of the old and the new. The computer-generated effect often does have a profilmic referent; the digitized data that is subsequently interpreted by the computer and presented as an image. Similarly, this opposition is also based upon the perception that the indexicality of the photograph suggests a fixed quality to the image, but as I've already argued with regard to spirit photography, optical media, and early cinema, the photographic image has always been inherently malleable and that is part of its uncanny quality. Digital effects simply push this malleability beyond familiar boundaries, for, as Rosen explains, one of the characteristics of digitization is that it offers "practically infinite manipulability," which "implies that no image is necessarily stable, for any preexistent image is susceptible to an unending series of transformations."[13]

While special makeup effects showcase the manipulation and transformation of the body, they are always defined by physical boundaries. The computer-generated image, however, works toward redefining boundaries. It is able to take a seemingly realistic object and stretch, contort, and reshape it completely. Dennis Muren, the effects supervisor for *Terminator 2* (1991), one of the films that led the way in CGI technology, explains that once you've digitized an object, "you can do so many things with it, from pushing images around and making geometry, to re-lighting that image, to painting out artifacts that may show up." He explains how in one scene of *T2* they made the T-1000 appear to walk through prison bars by digitally manipulating the filmed image. "Everything on the screen in that shot is film—we didn't create anything, as we created the chrome guy in other shots. As much as we could, we twisted real film, because real film is so rich, and only when we had to did we make anything in the computer."[14] Stephen Norrington, director of *Blade*, sees these developments as a liberation from the filmed image and points out that

> we are at a point now where we can literally manipulate the context
> of a film to a degree that we couldn't have done only five or ten years
> ago, because we were locked in a film-frame mindset. Now, because we
> can create and adjust things digitally and photorealistically, the technol-
> ogy allows us to refine our stories with a lot more freedom.[15]

What is unsettling about the new technology has less to do with its lack of referent and more to do with the manner in which it can take an indexical image and effortlessly transform and reshape that image in ways far beyond the capabilities of photographic manipulation and effects.

The Visible Human Project (VHP), a digital anatomical atlas, takes the manipulation and transformation of the indexical to dramatic extremes and can be quite informative to a consideration of the impact of digital technology upon the representation of the vampire. Catherine Waldby explains that the project involved dissecting and digitizing a real human cadaver so that it could be displayed on the Web, either as a cross section of the inner workings of the body, or as "the segmented body can be reassembled, to define the body at every location in three-dimensional virtual space. This restacking capacity enables unlimited manipulation of the virtual corpse . . . [It] can also be animated, used to model human movement." Through the technological reanimation of the dead, Waldby argues, this technology creates an "indeterminacy between life and death, between living and dead bodies," for the technology does more than preserve the image of the dead but reanimates it, frees it from the restraints of eternal repetition that define the cinema. No longer doomed to this fate, the digital revenant has been liberated through the technology from the boundaries of the body and the distinction between life and death.[16] Through the use of computer-generated imagery, therefore, the vampire film has, like the VHP, evolved past the horror of the limitations of the body and the potential for its rupture, toward the seamless extension of the body, both in life and death, through technology.

In *Blade*, the possibility for a computer-generated vampire is manifested in Frost's transformation into La Magra, the blood god. The myth of the blood god purports to liberate vampires from the limitations of the body by transforming all in its path into vampires, therefore ending the distinction between purebloods and turned vampires. To begin this new world order, the blood god is called forth by mixing the blood of the Daywalker—Blade—with the spirits of the purebloods in the body of the turned vampire Frost; all are unified in one. Once Frost becomes La Magra, his body is transformed, but not on the surface. He still looks like Frost, but internally his entire constitution has changed. He becomes the embodiment of the computer-generated image, able to reshape and reconstitute himself at his own command in one fluid motion. When Blade cuts off Frost's arm, it reforms itself in a swirl of animated blood corpuscles and tissue shaping itself into an arm. Similarly, when Blade slices Frost through the middle, the two halves of his body fly through the air until they are drawn back together and reformed into a whole body. Frost is no longer confined by the boundaries of his body but rather has been redefined by the endless mathematical possibilities of the computer. The vampire has become eternally able to reshape and resurrect itself.

This ability is taken to its most extreme form in *Van Helsing*, the vampire film to date that most exploits the visual possibilities of computer-generated technology in the reconception of the vampire. Much like the representation of Van Helsing and his weapons, the film marks a return to a nineteenth-century Dracula, but this time the modern twist involves portraying Dracula and his brides as CGI cyborgs, a seamless blend between actor and special effect. This is achieved through the act of transformation. Unlike the contemporary vampires in *Blade*, *Underworld*, or

Figure 11.2. A CGI vampire in *Van Helsing*.

even *Buffy* and *Angel,* who are presented as a race with a differing physiognomy rather than supernatural powers, Sommers' *Van Helsing* once again presents Dracula as a shape-shifter able to metamorphose at will. This transformative ability however has been reinterpreted through CGI, which lends an unprecedented fluidity to the transformation and enables the vampire to contort and extend the boundaries of its body. For instance, when angered, the vampires' faces are made to appear to stretch beyond physical limits by photographing the actor's face and then digitally manipulating the image so that the jaws extend into an uncanny snakelike maw before returning to their "normal" shape. (Figure 11.2) Furthermore, like Frost in *Blade,* Dracula is able to regenerate with ease. When an explosion throws him into a fire, he emerges covered in burns, but unlike previous vampires in *Near Dark* or *Blade* who slowly regenerate their skin after being burned, Dracula walks out of the fire, in a shot reminiscent of the T-1000 cyborg similarly emerging from an explosion in *Terminator 2*, and instantaneously changes back to his human form.

Additionally, the vampires are able to transform from their human appearance into that of a bat, suggesting a true hybridity between the vampire and bat through the fluidity of the computer-generated effect. While the transformation sequences in such films as *Son of Dracula, House of Dracula*, and even *Bram Stoker's Dracula*—achieved through dissolves, stop-motion animation, and, in the case of Coppola's film, costuming— portray the vampire as bearing a connection to the animal world, the technological method of these transformations suggest that this is simply a tool of the vampire, serving almost as a disguise. In *Van Helsing*, however, the use of morphing effect, a technique "which allows [for] a very smooth transition between one form and another so that it looks continuous, making it impossible to detect where the boundary of one character finishes and the other begins," seems to blend the vampire and bat at cellular (or pixelated) level.[17] While the film's nineteenth-century setting prevents it from engaging in discussion of genetics in the manner of *Blade* and *Underworld*, its use of special effects visually presents the vampire as a genetic hybrid of human and bat. Their human faces are not simply a mask for their real vampire faces, as in films such as *The Lost Boys* or *Fright Night*, nor do they reflect a duality to their personality, as in *Buffy the Vampire Slayer* when a vampire's appearance is dictated by his or her social context (having vampire face when hunting and human face when socializing). In *Van Helsing*, it is impossible to tell which is their real face, as they effortless move between appearances, suggesting that their identity, like the T-1000, is defined by metamorphosis.

The hybridity of the vampires is reinforced by the technology used to create the effects of the vampires in bat form. Once transformed, the vampire brides turn into human-bat hybrids with large wings, clawed hands and feet, and an "emaciated, yet muscular physique,"[18] able to fly through the air. To achieve this effect, the technicians used a combination of actors and computer-generated characters created through motion capture. As Jody Duncan explains,

> Scott Squires [visual effects supervisor on *Van Helsing*] suggested a hybrid approach, in which ILM [Industrial Light and Magic] would track blue screen elements of the actresses' heads to CG bodies—thereby taking advantage of the photorealism of the real actress photography, while also taking advantage of the freedom of movement and stylization that could be attained with a computer-animated character.[19]

The vampire brides were, therefore, literally a hybrid of human and technology, a cyborg able to defy the limitations of the body.[20]

Like Orlok's death in *Nosferatu*, it is how the destruction of the vampire is presented, however, that reveals the degree to which the vampire has come to embody the spectral qualities of the new technology. In *Buffy*, *Angel*, the *Blade* trilogy, *Underworld*, and *Van Helsing* computer-generated graphics are used to create the spectacular demise of the vampire, and like Orlok, these vampires die in a manner that transcends their bodily limitations and suggests a supernatural demise. The spectral effect, however, no longer represents the uncanny quality of the photographic properties of film but rather of the computer. When vampires are staked, shot with silver bullets, or touched by the rays of the sun, the way in which their deaths are presented suggests that they do not simply fade away like Orlok, but rather they explode into minute particles. Matthew Justice, visual effects producer for *Blade*, describes the vampire's disintegration effect this way: "From the point of impact, the vampire's skin begins to burn, revealing ash below it. The skeleton is revealed beneath that, and the victim finally disseminates into particles and ash that leave a black stain in their wake." [21] The effect is achieved by digitally compositing each layer of the effect together to create a simple image of seemingly instantaneous physical disintegration. This explosion of the vampire into sparkling dust caused the special effects team on *Buffy* to rename the staking process as "dusting."

The spectacle of these effects is as much a part of the attraction of these new technologies as it was for optical transformations in the Phantasmagoria and other optical illusions. Graphic body horror effects are similarly based around spectacle, but the drive of that particular type of spectacle is to confront the audience with the horror and pain of transformation and the spectacle of the grotesque body in torment. Computer-generated images, like their spectral predecessors, create a sense of wonder and awe in the audience, derived as much from the fantasy being represented as from wondering how the effects were created. Michele Pierson argues that "the presentation of key computer-generated images," in such films as *The Abyss* (1989), *Terminator 2*, and *Jurassic Park* (1993),

> produces a distinct break in the action ... Effects sequences featuring CGI commonly exhibit a mode of spectatorial address that—with its tableau-style framing, longer takes, and strategic intercutting between shots of the computer-generated object and reaction shots of characters— solicits a contemplative viewing of the computer-generated image. [22]

When Buffy "dusts" the Master in "Prophecy Girl" (1:12), all of the action, fighting, and fast-paced cutting between parallel events stops as the Master dies. This is partly because this moment signals Buffy's triumph over the forces of evil, but also because it allows all involved to watch the Master's spectacular demise as his spirit, flesh, and blood are all transformed to dust and stripped from his skeleton in a shower of particles. It is a truly spectral moment.

In *Blade II*, the act of destroying the vampires has been made even more spectacular. In his first major fight sequence, Blade shoots a vampire with two silver bullets. The film follows the CGI bullets as they fly through the air in slow motion and enter the vampire from behind. The bullets cause mini explosions in the body that spread outward in concentric circles until the vampire is reduced to red ash that floats in the air. The deaths of the Reapers are presented as even more spectacularly violent. When exposed to sunlight, a white light emerges from within the Reaper and bursts outward, disintegrating the body in the process. To combat the Reapers, Blade's technical team develop ultraviolet grenades and a UV bomb to take into the sewers below the city where the Reapers are hiding. When surrounded by hundreds of Reapers, Blade detonates the bomb that sends a blast of UV light throughout the entire sewer system. The explosion has the effect of a nuclear bomb on the Reapers, as its bright light flashes through them like an x-ray and instantaneously vaporizes them, leaving behind cowering sculptures of ash.

While the special effects in these sequences present the deaths as physically violent, the deaths of Nyssa (the leader of the Bloodpack), and Nomak ("Patient Zero" of the Reaper strain), are presented as more tragic and spectral. This is emphasized by the contrast with the decidedly physical demise of Damaskinos, the leader of the vampires and the mastermind behind the Reaper genetic mutation. To destroy Damaskinos, Nomak bites him in the jugular vein and allows all of the vampire's lifeblood to drain away. Rather than bursting into a cloud of spectral dust, the vampire overlord collapses onto the floor, and as his life floods out of him, his body is turned to stone and breaks apart. Presented as an old-world vampire, visually reminiscent of *Nosferatu*, his death calls to mind the physical special effects of the 1980s. His lifeblood is a thick green liquid, much like the noxious liquids that spout forth from the vampires in *The Lost Boys* and *From Dusk till Dawn*, and his body crumbles to dust like the vampires in *The Hunger* and *Lifeforce*.

Nyssa and Nomak however, both of whom are victims of Damaskinos' treachery, choose spectral deaths rather than monstrous physical existence. In the climax of a hand-to-hand combat sequence between Blade and Nomak, Blade thrusts his sword through the Reaper's chest and into his heart. Rather than remove the sword, Nomak pauses briefly and then pushes the sword further into his chest. In slow motion, his body disintegrates into sparkling clouds of dust that float up into the air. Similarly, Nyssa is faced with a choice of transforming into a Reaper or dying while still a vampire. At her request, Blade takes Nyssa outside to see the sunrise. As Blade holds her and the sun comes up, Nyssa's skin begins to painlessly crack and peel and turn to dust as she peacefully disintegrates in

Figure 11.3. Nyssa's spectral death in *Blade 2*.

Blade's arms. (Figure 11.3) While Damaskinos is punished for his crimes by a physical death, the bodies of Nyssa and Nomak are transformed by the spectral technology into sparkling particles of dust suggesting that they transcend the pain of their physical existence and achieve a spiritual release. Their deaths are presented in a spectacle of modern special effects that reflects their place as ultramodern vampires.

The spectrality of the vampire is overtly acknowledged with the return of Dracula in an unusual episode of the television series *Buffy the Vampire Slayer*, "Buffy vs. Dracula" (5:1). In this episode, the seemingly anachronistic Count arrives in Sunnydale to confront the Slayer. While vampires in this series have been stripped of any supernatural powers, Dracula breaks all of the show's conventions by possessing the ability to transmogrify his body into mist, bats, and wolves. No longer achieved through optical or special makeup effects, Dracula's repertoire of "gypsy" tricks is achieved through his command of the digital image. He escapes Buffy's attacks by morphing into a cloud of mist or a bat and then reappearing elsewhere. His control of the effects is further demonstrated when Buffy finally stakes him through the heart and he bursts, like Nyssa and Nomak, into a cloud of dust. Rather than stay dead, however, Dracula alone realizes that within the dust is a cluster of computer pixels that can be reformed to facilitate his regeneration. After Buffy and her friends exit the castle, Dracula reforms only to be staked by Buffy again. These dustings are no longer final.[23] Like the Visible Human Project, the vampire has been released within the digital realm to regenerate at will. The ambiguity over

Dracula's demise in this episode captures the uncanniness of the virtual realm where the body no longer has meaning and death no longer seems final. While the filmic process is inherently vampiric by bringing the dead back to life, the computer frees the vampire from the torment of endless repetition and breathes new life into their undead existence.

From the Phantasmagoria to the Visible Human Project, the technological ability to present the illusion of life for the entertainment of audiences has consistently manifested itself in the illusion of the reanimation of the dead. Therefore, while the science-fiction genre and its futuristic narratives capture the wonders of new technologies, the horror genre foregrounds the technology's inherent uncanniness through its changing interpretation and representation of the undead. In *Nosferatu*, the vampire was presented as the embodiment of nineteenth-century ambiguity between the scientific and the supernatural by being equated with the photographic, temporal, and spatial properties of film itself. By the 1970s and 1980s, the fascination with the supernatural was replaced by an industrial reduction of the vampire to the confines of the body, technically reasserting what Martin advocated vocally, that there is no magic, only mechanical processes. The transition from the industrial to the postindustrial through the development of computer-generated images reinfuses the vampire with the spectral and releases the vampire from the confines of the body and into the virtual. The reinterpretation of the vampire through the language of cinema and its transforming technologies has enabled the vampire film to express the modern fascination with technology and the increasingly ambiguous role it plays in the definition and redefinition of the self.

CHAPTER TWELVE

Vampires in a Borderless World

From *Dracula* (1897) to *Blade* (1998) and its contemporaries, the cinematic vampire has undergone a process of liberation from the boundaries of space, time, and body and, as a result, embodies a legacy of transformation that expresses the experience of modernity. But where does the cinematic vampire go from here? As we move further into the twenty-first century, the vampire continues to show its presence in the cinema with such films as *Blade II* (2002), *Queen of the Damned* (2002), *The League of Extraordinary Gentlemen* (2003), *Underworld* (2003), *Van Helsing* (2004), *Blade Trinity* (2004), *Vampires: The Turning* (2005), *Night Watch* (2005), and *Underworld: Evolution* (2006). I have argued in this book that the link between the vampire and modernity has repeatedly forced the vampire to emerge in the heart of the modern world—London in the nineteenth century and America in the twentieth century—and yet it is noticeable that these recent films see the vampire largely return to its European origins. *Blade II*, *Underworld*, and its sequel *Underworld: Evolution* are set in Prague; *The League of Extraordinary Gentlemen* and *Van Helsing* follow their characters on their quests across Europe; *Night Watch* is set in Moscow; and the lead vampire of *Queen of the Damned*, Lestat, is no longer a modern American vampire like Martin or Deacon Frost, but an aristocratic French nobleman.[1] Rather than a return to a traditional, premodern vampire, however, these films suggest that the vampire in the twenty-first century continues to be a product of the changing modern world, this time by expanding its freedom of mobility beyond the borders of America. The modern vampire has gone global.

While the vampire has, in recent years, increasingly transcended its physical boundaries, world politics, communications, and economy have similarly been transcending national boundaries, favoring the global over the local. Zygmunt Bauman argues that boundaries in the contemporary world have become outmoded, suggesting that, in the past, "the divisions of continents and of the globe as a whole were the function of distances made once imposingly real thanks to the primitiveness of transport and the hardships of travel."[2] With the rise of new technologies and the potential for instantaneous communication, distances have not only been brought closer together, in the manner suggested by the telegraph and the telephone, but have been virtually eliminated through electronic messaging and the World Wide Web. As Chris Hables Gray, Heidi J. Figueroa-Sarriera, and Steven Mentor explain,

> We live in a world that is changing before our eyes. Corporations transcend particular countries and are now global, no longer really "centered" anywhere. Nations are breaking apart and reforming, and peoples are often far flung in diasporas across different continents . . . All these changes depend on and reflect new telecommunications technologies. As these larger "bodies"—or people, business, and government—are more closely tied to vast technologies, they too become cyborgs and we struggle to find ways to understand and predict how they are shifting.[3]

According to Michael Hardt and Antonio Negri, the power of the nation-state has, in recent years, declined, facilitating a freer flow of money, technology, people, and goods across national boundaries, all of which contribute to the strength of globalization.[4] The new global world market demands unhindered flow of capital in a deterritorialized market.[5]

But how does this relate to vampires? Franco Moretti has already established the relationship between vampires and capitalist consumption in his analysis of *Dracula*. Moretti saw a similarity in the manner in which capitalism squeezes the life out of its labor force and the way a vampire "manages to live thanks to the blood he sucks from the living. *Their* strength becomes *his* strength. The *stronger* the vampire becomes, the *weaker* the living become."[6] Confrontations between the zombies and humanity in an abandoned shopping mall in George Romero's *Dawn of the Dead* have also been read as an allegory for consumerism. The insatiable hunger of the zombies, who, like the humans, are drawn to the mall and aimlessly roam its corridors, is mirrored by the greed exhibited by the human survivors as they wallow in the consumer-excesses of the shopping mall. For Robin Wood, it is "through the realization of the ultimate consumer-society dream (the ready availability of every luxury, emblem and status-symbol of capitalist life, without the penalty of payment) [that] the anomalies and imbalances of human relationships under capitalism are exposed."[7] As Gregory A. Waller argues, the result of the survivors' leisurely life of unchecked consumption is that they become as dead as the zombies.[8] I would further argue that the intense physicalization of the zombies' hunger emphasizes how they physically embody these consumerist desires.

In the 1990s, the allegory of vampirism as consumer capitalism evolved from the embodied vampire to extended and disembodied vampire conglomerates. The pureblood vampires in *Blade* are respectable businessmen, while in the television series *Kindred: The Embraced*, the vampires are structured like the mafia with a vampire godfather overseeing the work of all the families. *Angel* featured a human-run law firm, Wolfram & Hart, who oversaw the illegal dealings and financial holdings of a range of vampire and demon clients, while the British television series *Ultraviolet* suggested the existence of a financial, scientific, and technological vampire conspiracy aiming for global control and the complete destruction of humanity.[9] These ambitions are shared by the more visibly corporate vampires in *Blade Trinity* who conduct their global machinations under the auspices of their medical research corporation, Biomedica Enterprises. It seems that the mob of vampires that emerged in the 1970s, from *Night of the Living Dead* and *Dawn of the Dead* to *Salem's Lot* and *Blacula*, organized themselves at the end of the twentieth century into vast corporations amassing large amounts of capital, stocks, and property as the means of extending their consumption beyond the human body to the modern world itself.

The return of the vampire to Europe, therefore, does not suggest a backward step toward primitivism and tradition, but rather is an extension of the modern vampire's existing relationship to capitalism. With the fall of the Berlin Wall in 1989 and the collapse of the Soviet Bloc, neoliberal capitalism was free to extend throughout these new markets. With rampant capitalism, therefore, came the image of the vampire continuing its quest for spatial liberation and freedom of movement, manifested in the transition from Dracula's constrained urban navigations to the freedom of the vampire to chart the shifting terrains of the postindustrial landscapes of America. Now, however, that spatial liberation extends across the globe and undermines national boundaries or identities. In *Blade*, Whistler explains that vampires are nomadic and that he and Blade move "from one city to the next city tracking their migrations." This is demonstrated in *Blade II* when Blade explains that he has been following the vampires through a chain of Eastern European cities from Moscow to Prague. The sense of space presented in the film, however, is increasingly vague and anonymous, reinforcing the idea that boundaries and distances no longer have meaning. While the hunt for the Reapers takes place in the Gothic underground of Prague, the corporate fortress of Caliban Industries is shown to be the heart of the vampire world. Unlike the vampire community in *Blade*, based within the heart of downtown Los Angeles, the company's precise location in relation to Prague is not made clear in *Blade II*. Journeys to and from this location are withheld from the narrative with the exception of one shot of Blade and his team being flown by helicopter to their meeting with Damaskinos.

While space is compressed in *Blade II* to suggest the breakdown of borders and national boundaries, *Queen of the Damned* is incredibly precise about the movements of its vampires. Each change of setting begins with a caption indicating the change of location over an elaborate establishing shot as the camera flies over the city and its surrounding landscape. As the vampires in this film are attributed with the power of flight, these sweeping camera movements evoke the ease and speed of vampire travel and the resulting meaninglessness of distance and global separation. Throughout the film, Lestat moves effortlessly between New Orleans, London, Glastonbury, Los Angeles, Death Valley, the Caribbean, and the Mohave Desert. This migrant lifestyle is reiterated by Lestat's business manager who informs two young fans who have been lured to Lestat's house that this is their home "this week. We move around a lot." When Akasha abducts Lestat and brings him to a quiet Caribbean island, she informs him, "We are home. We live everywhere and anywhere we choose. The world is our garden." As a result of this migrant lifestyle, national identity is obsolete in this new vampire world. While the human Lestat was of French noble birth, his transformation into a vampire suggests that he has equally been transformed into a member of a global elite, able to ignore national boundaries and travel across the globe with ease.

Zygmunt Bauman argues that this global freedom of mobility detaches the elite from any sense of locality, enabling them to ignore the consequences of their profit-driven decisions upon the community. They are motivated purely by economic factors.[10] He explains,

> Technologies which effectively do away with time and space need little time to denude and impoverish space. They render capital truly global; they make all those who neither follow nor arrest capital's new nomadic habits helplessly watch their livelihood fading and vanishing and wonder from where the blight might have come. The global travels of financial

resources are perhaps as immaterial as the electronic network they travel—but the local traces of their journeys are painfully tangible and real: qualitative depopulation, destruction of local economies once capable of sustaining their inhabitants.[11]

The vampire, in the form of Damaskinos in *Blade II* and Akasha in *Queen of the Damned*, has been infused with a global rapacity of consumer hunger that transcends the more physical hungers of the vampires who surround them. When Nyssa challenges Damaskinos about the nature of his genetic experiments and his betrayal of Nomak, his own creation, he explains that "bloodties mean nothing to me when compared to the ascendancy of our race." The needs of the corporation exceed the needs of the many who will die as a result of his experimentation. Akasha demonstrates a similar disdain for those who will suffer as she sates her hunger. When Lestat, now Queen Akasha's consort, awakens to find their island strewn with corpses, he challenges her assertion that this is their kingdom, "a kingdom of corpses," by asking, "Why?" She responds, "Why not?" Together these vampires embody the insatiable hunger and speed of execution of the global elite who care only for accumulating more capital and profit and not for the human consequences of their greed. Like capital itself, modern vampires effortlessly move across time and space, devouring all in their path.

In the twenty-first century, the cinematic vampire has emerged at yet another moment of intense social change as the world comes to terms with the consequences of globalization and shifts from the postindustrial to a global market economy. The vampires in these films are suitably transformed to capture the essence of this new age. Like Spike's destruction of the Anointed One in *Buffy* and Frost's destruction of Dragonetti in *Blade*, *Blade II* and *Queen of the Damned* feature the destruction of the master vampire by their progeny. *Underworld*, *Blade Trinity*, and *Underworld: Evolution* suggest an evolutionary leap for the vampire race, sparked by genetic intervention. These developments demonstrate that the vampire film continues to embrace the destructive violence of modernity by paving the way for the next wave of vampires. Perhaps just as the vampire came to embody the transition between the industrial and the postindustrial, the new vampire to emerge will again engage with these current debates and maintain its link with the spirit of "renewal and disintegration" that defines modernity by no longer being linked to the Old World or the New World, but rather embodying the global.

Notes

Introduction

1. It is worth noting that at the *Vampires: Myths and Metaphors of Enduring Evil* academic conference in Budapest (May 2003), there were six papers given on *Buffy the Vampire Slayer* as compared to five papers on *Dracula*.

2. The term "Gothic" has a multitude of meanings. It can also be applied to certain forms of medieval architecture, the paintings of Henry Fuseli and William Blake, and has continued to be used to describe various literary and cinematic traditions in the twentieth and twenty-first centuries.

3. Fred Botting, *Gothic* (London and New York: Routledge Publishing, 1996), 1–2.

4. David Punter, *The Literature of Terror*, Vol. 1, *The Gothic Tradition*. 2nd ed. (London and New York: Longman, 1996), 5.

5. Punter, *The Literature of Terror*, Vol. 1, *The Gothic Tradition*, 1.

6. Bram Stoker, *Dracula* (1897; Oxford: Oxford University Press, 1993), 28. All further references to *Dracula* will be made parenthetically and from this edition.

7. Brian W. Aldiss, foreword to *Blood Read: The Vampire as Metaphor in Contemporary Culture*, eds. Joan Gordon and Veronica Hollinger (Philadelphia: University of Pennsylvania Press, 1997), x.

8. Nina Auerbach, *Our Vampires, Ourselves* (Chicago: University of Chicago Press, 1995), 5.

9. Charles Baudelaire, *Painter of Modern Life and Other Essays*, trans. and ed. Jonathan Mayne (London: Phaidon Press, 1964), 13.

10. Georg Simmel, "The Metropolis and Mental Life," *Modernism: An Anthology of Sources and Documents*, ed. Vassiliki Kolocotroni, Jane Goldman, and Olga Taxidou (Edinburgh: Edinburgh University Press, 1998), 51–52.

11. Marshall Berman, *All That Is Solid Melts into Air: The Experience of Modernity* (London and New York: Verso, 1983), 15.

12. Anthony Giddens, *Modernity and Self-Identity: Self and Society in the Late Modern Age* (Cambridge: Polity Press, 1991), 17–18.

13. Auerbach, *Our Vampires, Ourselves*, 6.

14. Please see Chapter 3 for a more detailed discussion of Hollywood Gothic.

15. Dr. John Polidori, "The Vampyre," in *Vampyres: Lord Byron to Count Dracula*, ed. Christopher Frayling (1819; London: Faber and Faber, 1991), 108–125.

16. Sheridan LeFanu, "Carmilla," *In A Glass Darkly* (1872; Oxford: Oxford University Press, 1991), 243–319.

17. Giddens, *Modernity and Self-Identity*, 17.

18. Stephen Kern, *Culture of Time and Space 1880–1918* (Cambridge Mass.: Harvard University Press, 1983), 314.

19. Gregory A. Waller, *The Living and the Undead: From Stoker's "Dracula" to Romero's "Dawn of the Dead*," (Urbana and Chicago: University of Illinois Press, 1986), 29.

20. Waller, *The Living and the Undead*, 233–234.

21. Giddens, *Modernity and Self-Indentity*, 18.

22. Zygmunt Bauman, *Globalization: The Human Consequences* (Cambridge: Polity Press, 1998), 2.

Chapter One

1. Anne Rice, *Interview with the Vampire* (London: Futura, 1992), 206–207.

2. Paul Barber, *Vampires, Burial, and Death* (New Haven and New York: Yale University Press, 1988), 2.

3. Christopher Frayling, *Vampyres: Lord Byron to Count Dracula* (London and Boston: Faber and Faber, 1991), 6.

4. Julian Hawthorne, "Ken's Mystery," *Dracula's Brood: Rare Vampire Stories by Friends and Contemporaries of Bram Stoker*, ed. Richard Dalby (1888; Wellingborough, UK: Crucible, 1987), 92–110.

5. Hume Nisbet, "Vampire Maid," *Dracula's Brood: Rare Vampire Stories by Friends and Contemporaries of Bram Stoker*, ed. Richard Dalby (1900; Wellingborough, UK: Crucible, 1987), 217–221.

6. John Polidori, "The Vampyre," *Vampyres: Lord Byron to Count Dracula*, ed. Christopher Frayling (1819; London: Faber and Faber, 1991), 108–125.

7. Marshall Berman, *All That Is Solid Melts into Air: The Experience of Modernity* (London and New York: Verso, 1983), 15.

8. Elisée Reclus, "The Evolution of Cities," *Contemporary Review* (February 1895): 246.

9. Georg Simmel, "The Metropolis and Mental Life," *Modernism: An Anthology of Sources and Documents*, ed. Vassiliki Koloctroni, Jane Goldman, and Olga Taxidou (Edinburgh: Edinburgh University Press, 1998), 52.

10. Charles Baudelaire, *Painter of Modern Life and Other Essays*, trans. and ed. Jonathan Mayne (London: Phaidon Press, 1964), 9, 24.

11. Asa Briggs, *Victorian Cities* (London: Penguin Books, 1963), 312.

12. Reclus, "The Evolution of Cities," 263.

13. "Londoners at Home," *Quarterly Review* 182, no. 363 (1895): 59.

14. Baudelaire, *The Painter of Modern Life*, 9. Baudelaire's evocation of the "man of the crowd" was greatly influenced by Edgar Allen Poe's short story "Man of the Crowd," in *The Complete Poems and Stories of Edgar Allen Poe Vol. 1* (New York: Alfred A. Knopf, 1946), 308–314.

15. Fred Botting, *Gothic* (London and New York: Routledge, 1996), 114.

16. Judith R. Walkowitz, *City of Dreadful Delight: Narratives of Sexual Danger in Late-Victorian London* (London: Virago, 1992); Robert Louis Stevenson, *Dr. Jekyll and Mr. Hyde* (1886; London: Penguin, 1994); Arthur Machen, *The Three Impostors* (1895; London: Everyman, 1995); Richard Marsh, *The Beetle* (1897; London: Alan Sutton Publishing Limited, 1994).

17. Wolfgang Schivelbusch, *The Railway Journey: The Industrialization of Time and Space in the Nineteenth Century* (Leamington Spa, UK and New York: Berg Publishers, 1986), 59.

18. Schivelbusch, *The Railway Journey*, 61.

19. Roy Porter, *London: A Social History* (London: Hamish Hamilton, 1994), 229–231.

20. Schivelbusch, *The Railway Journey*, 63.

21. Machen, *The Three Impostors*, 15.

22. Baudelaire, *Painter of Modern Life*, 19.

23. Francis Ford Coppola's film adaptation, *Bram Stoker's Dracula* (1992), attempts to make the implicitly filmic quality of this sequence explicit by reinterpreting it and foregrounding the relationship between the vampire and early cinema. In the film, Dracula is observed stalking the daytime streets of London but this time it is not Jonathan or Mina who entrap him within their gaze but rather the objective eye of the cinematograph as Dracula is shot in the speeded up fashion of a hand-cranked early cinema camera.

24. Berman, *All That Is Solid Melts into Air*, 164.

25. Barbara Belford, *Bram Stoker: A Biography of the Author of "Dracula"* (London: Phoenix Giant, 1996), 77.

26. Porter, *London: A Social History*, 209.

27. Gregory A. Waller, *The Living and the Undead: From Stoker's "Dracula" to Romero's "Dawn of the Dead"* (Chicago and Urbana: University of Illinois Press, 1986), 35.

28. Max Weber, *From Max Weber: Essays in Sociology*, trans. and ed. H. H. Gerth and C. Wright Mills (London: Routledge and Kegan Paul, Ltd., 1948), 228.

29. W. J. Reader, *Professional Men: The Rise of the Professional Classes in Nineteenth-Century England* (London: Weidenfeld and Nicolson, 1966), 203.

30. Sheridan LeFanu, "Carmilla," in *In A Glass Darkly* (1872; Oxford: Oxford University Press, 1993), 243–319.

31. Stoker's preference for the professional class is further illustrated in his later novel *The Jewel of the Seven Stars* where a similar team of professionals are brought together to facilitate the resurrection of a mummified Egyptian Queen. Bram Stoker, *The Jewel of the Seven Stars* (1912; London: Arrow Books, 1975).

32. Gail B. Griffin, "'Your Girls That You All Love are Mine': *Dracula* and the Victorian Male Sexual Imagination," *International Journal of Women's Studies* 3, no. 5 (1980): 462.

33. Friedrich Kittler, "Dracula's Legacy," trans. William Stephen Davis, *Stanford Humanities Review* 1 (1989): 154–155.

34. Michel Foucault, *The Archaeology of Knowledge*, trans. A. M. Sheridan Smith (London: Tavistock Publishing, 1972), 129–130.

35. Bruce J. Hunt, "Doing Science in a Global Empire: Cable Telegraphy and Electrical Physics in Victorian Britain," *Victorian Science in Context*, ed. Bernard Lightman (Chicago: The University of Chicago Press, 1997), 319–320.

36. Berman, *All That Is Solid Melts into Air*, 345.

37. George Carl Mares, *The History of the Typewriter* (London: Guilbert Pitman, 1909), 13.

38. Jennifer Wicke, "Vampiric Typewriting: *Dracula* and Its Media," *ELH* 59 (1992): 471.

39. This reflects the nineteenth-century tendency to blur the distinction between the girl and the machine by calling typewriter girls "typewriters."

40. Pamela Thurschwell, *Literature, Technology and Magical Thinking 1880–1920* (Cambridge, UK: Cambridge University Press, 2001), 3.

41. William Lynd, *Edison and the Perfected Phonograph* (Tunbridge Wells: A. K. Baldwin, c. 1891), 11.

42. F. J. Garbit, "The Telephone—Edison's Speaking Phonograph, or 'Talking Machine,'" *Half Hour Recreations in Popular Science Series 2*, ed. Dana Este (Boston: Este and Lauriat, 1879), 235.

43. Garbit, "The Telephone—Edison's Speaking Phonograph, or 'Talking Machine,'" 217, 235.

44. Arthur Conan Doyle, "The Story of the Japanned Box," *The Strand Magazine* (January 1899): 9.

45. Steven Connor, *Dumbstruck: A Cultural History of Ventriloquism* (Oxford: Oxford University Press, 2000), 363.

46. These are different methods used by spirits to communicate, either directly by making knocking noises, or through a medium who serves as a recipient to the messages being channeled. Mediums transmit messages either by writing them down while in a trancelike state (automatic writing) or by allowing the spirit to speak through them (direct voice).

47. Connor, *Dumbstruck*, pp. 363–365.

48. Thomas S. Kuhn, *The Structure of Scientific Revolutions* (Chicago: University of Chicago Press, 1970), 5.

49. Kuhn, *The Structure of Scientific Revolutions*, 91.

50. Adrian Room, ed., *Brewer's Dictionary of Phrases and Fable*, 15th ed. (London: Cassell Publishers, 1997), 849; August Comte, *The Positive Philosophy of August Comte*, trans. Harriet Martineau (London: Kegan Paul, Trench, Trübner, and Co., 1893), 2.

51. John L. Greenway, "Seward's Folly: *Dracula* as a Critique of 'Normal Science,'" *Stanford Literature Review* 3, no. 2 (1986): 213.

52. John Allison, *Mesmerism: Its Pretensions as a Science Physiologically Considered* (London: Whittaker and Co., 1844).

53. Roger Luckhurst, "Trance-Gothic, 1882–1897," *Victorian Gothic: Literary and Cultural Manifestations in the Nineteenth Century*, eds. Ruth Robbins and Julian Wolfreys (Basingstoke, UK: Palgrave, 2000), 153, 164.

54. Dr. John Polidori, "The Vampyre."

55. William Gilbert, "The Last Lords of Gardenal," *Dracula's Brood: Rare Vampire Stories by Friends and Contemporaries of Bram Stoker*, ed. Richard Dalby (1867; Wellingborough, UK: Crucible, 1987).

56. Barber, *Vampires, Burial, and Death*, 29.

57. Garbit, "Telephone—Edison's Speaking Phonograph, or 'Talking Machine,'" 215.

58. W. T. Stead, "Suggestions from Science for Psychic Students: How Electricity Helps," *Borderland* 3, no. 4 (1896): 400.

59. Stead, "Suggestions from Science for Psychic Students," 400.

60. Edward C. Randall, *The Dead Have Never Died* (London: George Allen and Unwin, Ltd., 1918), 14.

61. *Modern Practise of the Electric Telegraph* (London: Sampson Low, Marston, and Co., 1891), 2.

62. W. T. Stead, "How We Intend to Study Borderland," *Borderland* 1, no. 1 (1894): 61.

63. Garbit, "Telephone—Edison's Speaking Phonograph, or 'Talking Machine,'" 198.

64. Walford Bodie, *The Bodie Book: Hypnotism, Electricity, Mental Suggestion, Magnetic Touch, Clairvoyance, Telepathy* (London: Caxton Press, 1905), 18.

65. Bodie, *The Bodie Book*, 112.

66. Randall, *The Dead Have Never Died*, 13.

67. Christopher Frayling, *Vampyres*, 64.

Chapter Two

1. The body of this chapter was originally published under the title "Spectral Vampires: *Nosferatu* in the Light of New Technology" in *Horror Film: Creating and Marketing Fear*, ed. Steffen Hantke (Jackson: University of Mississippi Press, 2004), 3–20. Special thanks to the editor and publishers for enabling me to reprint this chapter here.

2. Steve Neale, *Cinema and Technology: Image, Sound, and Colour* (London: Macmillan Education, 1985), 8.

3. Tom Gunning, interview by Adam Simon, *The American Nightmare*, 2000.

4. A Hungarian film made in 1921 entitled *Drakula* is purported to have been an adaptation of the novel, but as the film is lost and there is little information about its production, it is fair to consider *Nosferatu* the earliest existing version of *Dracula*.

5. The version of *Nosferatu* that I analyzed for this chapter is a restoration carried out by Filmmuseum Münchner and Cineteca del Commune di Bologna with the support of the Lumière Project, currently made available in the UK on DVD by Photoplay Productions and the British Film Institute. This version not only includes material previously excluded from other versions of the film, but also involved restoring the intertitles to their original phrasing and design. This resulted in a relocation of the bulk of the narrative from Bremen to Wisborg.

6. Terry Castle, "Phantasmagoria: Spectral Technology and the Metaphorics of Modern Reverie," *Critical Inquiry* (Autumn 1988): 27.

7. X. Theodore Barber, "Phantasmagorical Wonders: The Magic Lantern Ghost Show in Nineteenth-Century America," *Film History* 3, no. 2 (1989): 74–75.

8. Laurent Mannoni, *The Great Art of Light and Shadow: Archaeology of the Cinema*, ed. and trans. Richard Crangle (Exeter: University of Exeter Press, 2000), 143.

9. Mannoni, *The Great Art of Light and Shadow*, 136.

10. The transformation remains a staple convention of the horror film. It allows filmmakers to stop the narrative to showcase their new and wondrous technological capabilities, from dissolves, as used in Universal Studios' Wolf Man movies of the forties, to computer generated morphing effects as demonstrated by the T1000 in *Terminator 2* (1991). Transformation and spectacle through technological means continue to be significant elements that link vampire films from the 1920s to those of the present.

11. Henry Dircks, *The Ghost! As Produced in the Spectre Drama, Popularly Illustrating the Marvellous Optical Illusions Obtained by the Apparatus Called the Dircksian Phantasmagoria* (London: E & FN Spon, 1863), 40.

12. Castle, "Phantasmagoria," 36.

13. Quoted in Dircks, *The Ghost!*, 6.

14. Barber, "Phantasmagorical Wonders," 84.

15. Mannoni, *The Great Art of Light and Shadow*, 249.

16. Dircks, *The Ghost!*, 2.

17. Jennifer Tucker, "Photography as Witness, Detective, and Impostor: Visual Representation in Victorian Science," *Victorian Science in Context*, ed. B. Lightman (Chicago: Chicago University Press, 1997), 380.

18. André Bazin, *What is Cinema?* Vol. 1, trans. Hugh Gray (Los Angeles: University of California Press, 1967), 14.

19. This is demonstrated by photography's use in the study of meteorology and bacteria, the anthropological study of different cultures and traditions, psychological studies of the effects of dementia, and the classification of the signs of degeneracy. (Peter Hamilton and Roger Hargreaves, *The Beautiful and the Damned: The Creation of Identity in Nineteenth-Century Photography* [Aldershot, UK: Lund Humphries, 2001], 68, 79, 95, 96.) As a result of this seeming authenticity and mechanical reproduction, Walter Benjamin argued that photography and film were prevented from being perceived as a real art form. If it merely reproduced reality through technological means where was the space for creative expression? ("The Work of Art in the Age of Mechanical Reproduction," *Illuminations*, ed. Hannah Arendt and trans. Harry Zohn [New York: Schocken Books, 1969], 228.)

20. Tom Gunning, "Phantom Images and Modern Manifestations: Spirit Photography, Magic Theatre, Trick Films, and Photography's Uncanny," *Fugitive Images from Photography to Video*, ed. Petro Patrice (Bloomington and Indianapolis: Indiana University Press, 1995), 43.

21. James Coates, *Photographing the Invisible: Practical Studies in Spirit Photography, Spirit Portraiture, and Other Rare but Allied Phenomenon* (London: L. N. Fowler and Co., 1911), 2.

22. These properties could also be manipulated to produce false evidence of the afterlife by creating transparent images through double exposures or to create a ghostly double of the person being photographed if they moved before the exposure was complete. James Traill Taylor, editor of the *British Journal of Photography* and an expert photographer, was regularly called upon to prove or disprove the authenticity of supposed spirit photographs and, in his book *The Veil Lifted*,

cites numerous ways in which a spirit photograph could be faked. J. Traill Taylor, *The Veil Lifted: Modern Developments of Spirit Photography*, ed. Andrew Glendinning (London: Whittaker and Co., 1894), 14.

23. Tom Gunning, "'Primitive' Cinema: a Frame-up?; or, the Trick's on Us," *Early Cinema: Space, Frame, Narrative*, ed. Thomas Elsaesser (London: British Film Institute, 1990), 96.

24. Maxim Gorky, newspaper review of Lumière program at the Nizhni-Novgorod fair *Nizhegorodski listok* (4 July 1896), reprinted in *In the Kingdom of Shadows: A Companion to Early Cinema*, eds. Colin Harding and Simon Popple (London: Cygnus Arts, 1996), 5.

25. W. T. Stead, "Suggestions from Science for Psychic Students: The Kinetiscope of Nature," *Borderland* 3, no. 4 (1896): 400.

26. W. T. Stead, "The Kinetiscope of the Mind," *Borderland* 3, no. 4 (1896): 403.

27. Barber, "Phantasmagorical Wonders," 85.

28. Lewis Jacobs, "George Méliès: 'Artificially Arranged Scenes,'" *The Rise of the American Film: A Critical History* (1939; New York: Teacher's College Press, 1968): 23.

29. Jacobs, "George Méliès: 'Artificially Arrange Scenes,'" 24.

30. André Bazin, *What is Cinema?* Vol. 1, 27.

31. Thomas Elsaesser, "Secret Affinities," *Sight and Sound* 58, no. 1 (1989/90): 33.

32. Angela Dalle Vache, "Murnau's *Nosferatu:* Romantic Painting as Horror and Desire in Expressionist Cinema," *Post Script* 14, no. 3 (1995): 32.

33. David J. Skal, *Hollywood Gothic: The Tangled Web of "Dracula" from Novel to Stage to Screen* (New York and London: W. W. Norton and Company, 1990), 46.

34. Tom Gunning, interview by Adam Simon, *The American Nightmare*, 2000; Gorky, cited in *In the Kingdom of Shadows*, 5.

35. Gilberto Perez Guillermo, "Shadow and Substance: Murnau's *Nosferatu,*" *Sight and Sound* 36, no. 3 (1967): 159.

36. This is a characteristic picked up by Francis Ford Coppola in his adaptation of *Dracula* in the scene where Dracula's shadow, in homage to *Nosferatu*, actually knocks over a pot of ink while reaching for Mina's photo.

37. Mary Albert, "Towards a Theory of Slow Motion," (M. A. dissertation, British Film Institute/Birkbeck College, 1993), 1.

38. Albert, "Towards a Theory of Slow Motion," 4.

39. Barry Salt, *Film Style and Technology: History and Analysis* (London: Starword, 1983), 169.

40. David Bordwell, Janet Staiger, and Kristin Thompson, *Classical Hollywood Cinema: Film Style and Mode of Production to 1960* (London: Routledge, 1985), 48.

41. Stephen Kern, *The Culture of Time and Space, 1880–1918* (Cambridge, Mass.: Harvard University Press, 1983), 67–68.

42. Kern, *The Culture of Time and Space*, 68.

43. Tom Gunning, *The Films of Fritz Lang: Allegories of Vision and Modernity* (London: British Film Institute, 2000), 96.

44. Elsaesser, "Secret Affinities," 35.

45. Sylvia Pamboukian, "'Looking Radiant': Science, Photography, and the X-ray Craze of 1896," *Victorian Review* 27, no. 2 (2001): 56–74.

Chapter Three

1. David J. Skal, *Hollywood Gothic: The Tangled Web of "Dracula" from Novel to Stage to Screen* (New York and London: W. W. Norton and Company, 1990), 7.

2. Skal, *Hollywood Gothic*.

3. A great deal of work already exists on the development of the horror genre in both the United States and Great Britain. I have therefore focused my discussion in this chapter on the relationship of these vampire films to the theme of modernity. For further information on the early days of the American horror genre see *Hollywood Gothic* or *The Monster Show: A Cultural History of Horror* (London: Plexus Publishing Limited, 1993), both by David J. Skal. For a historical study of the development of the British horror genre, see David Pirie's *Heritage of Horror: The English Gothic Cinema 1946–1972* (London: Gordon Fraser, 1973); and for a historical and textual examination of the gothic tradition of Hammer Studios, see Peter Hutchings' *Hammer and Beyond: The British Horror Film* (Manchester, UK and New York: Manchester University Press, 1993) or *Dracula* (London and New York: I. B. Tauris, 2003).

4. Please note that this film is lost although Rick Schmidlin's photo reconstruction does give us an impression of what the film was originally like. This is available on the Region 1 DVD *The Lon Chaney Collection* (TCM Archives, 65791).

5. Charles Derry, *Dark Dreams: The Horror Film from "Psycho" to "Jaws"* (South Brunswick, N. J. and New York: A. S. Barnes and Company, 1977), 17; Robin Wood, *Hollywood from Vietnam to Reagan* (New York: Columbia University Press, 1986), 85.

6. The social milieu in which these characters circulate also seems to suggest the screwball comedy. The psychiatrist Dr. Garth is first introduced on a hunting holiday in Scotland, while his assistant Janet arrives in his office dressed in a stunning white evening gown that seems to extend beyond her means as a psychiatrist's assistant.

7. Chris Baldick, ed., *The Oxford Book of Gothic Tales* (Oxford: Oxford University Press, 1992), xv.

8. James B. Twitchell, *Dreadful Pleasures: An Anatomy of Modern Horror* (New York and Oxford: Oxford University Press, 1985), 146.

9. The British title was *Dracula*, while the American title was *Horror of Dracula*. For the sake of clarity I will refer to the Hammer production by its American title throughout this chapter, which will serve to distinguish this film from the Universal version.

10. Nina Auerbach, *Our Vampires, Ourselves* (Chicago: The University of Chicago Press, 1995), 117, 119.

11. Pirie, *A Heritage of Horror*, 87.

12. Hutchings, *Dracula*, 56.

13. Hutchings, *Dracula*, 66.

14. Gregory Waller, *The Living and the Undead From Stoker's "Dracula" to Romero's "Dawn of the Dead"* (Chicago and Urbana: University of Illinois Press, 1986), 127.

15. Andrew Tudor, *Monsters and Mad Scientists: A Cultural History of the Horror Movie* (Oxford: Basil Blackwell, 1989), 214. It should be noted that discussions of "invasion narratives" with respect to 1950s cinema are usually referring to such alien invasion films as *The Invasion of the Body Snatchers* (1956) and *The Thing from Another World* (1951). *The Return of Dracula* however stands out as a film that attempts to merge the preoccupations of earlier gothic horror with the invasion themes of 1950s science fiction/horror.

16. Skal, *Hollywood Gothic*, 7.

Chapter Four

1. Marshall Berman, *All That Is Solid Melts Into Air: The Experience of Modernity* (New York: Verso, 1983), 15.

2. Stephen Paul Miller, *The Seventies Now: Culture as Surveillance* (Durham and London: Duke University Press, 1999), 14.

3. Tod Gitlin, *The Sixties: Years of Hope, Days of Rage* (1987; New York: Bantam Books, 1993), 84.

4. Gitlin, *The Sixties*, 178.

5. Charles Derry, *Dark Dreams: The Horror Film from "Psycho" to "Jaws"* (South Brunswick, N.J. and New York: A. S. Barnes and Company, 1977), 18.

6. Gregory A. Waller ed., introduction to *American Horrors: Essays on the Modern American Horror Film* (Urbana and Chicago: University of Illinois Press, 1987), 5.

7. Gitlin, *The Sixties*, 316.

8. Fredric Jameson, "Periodising the Sixties," in *The Ideologies of Theory: Essays 1971–1986*, Vol. 2, *Syntax of History* (London: Routledge, 1988), 208.

9. Miller, *The Seventies Now*, 16.

10. Miller, *The Seventies Now*, 1.

11. Peter Wollen, *Raiding the Icebox* (New York: Verso, 1993), 36.

12. Robert F. Arnold, "Termination or Transformation: The *Terminator* Films and Recent Changes in the U.S. Auto Industry," *Film Quarterly* 52, no. 1 (1998): 23. See also Emma Rothschild, *Paradise Lost: The Decline of the Auto-Industrial Age* (London: Allen Land, 1984).

13. For a closer analysis of the studio system and their approach to film production, see David Bordwell, Kristin Thompson, and Janet Staiger's *The Classical Hollywood Cinema: Film Style and Mode of Production to 1960* (London: Routledge, 1985).

14. Thomas Schatz, "The New Hollywood," in *Film Theory Goes to the Movies*, ed. Jim Collins, Hilary Radner, and Ava Preacher Collins (New York and London: Routledge, 1993), 11.

15. Vincent Canby, "Is Hollywood in Hot Water?" *New York Times* (9 November 1969) in the *New York Times Encyclopedia of Film 1969–71*, ed. Gene Brown (New York: Times Books, 1984).

16. Leonard Sloane, "At Paramount, Real Financial Drama," *New York Times* (28 November 1969); Leonard Sloane, "M-G-M is Hopeful on Earnings," *New York Times* (16 January 1970); Mel Gussow, "Movies Leaving Hollywood Behind: Studio System Passé—Film Forges Ahead," *New York Times* (27 May 1970), all in the *New York Times Encyclopedia of Film 1969–71*, ed. Gene Brown (New York: Times Books, 1984).

17. Richard Matheson, *I Am Legend* (1954; London: Robinson Publishing, 1987).

18. Raymond T. McNally and Radu Florescu, *In Search of Dracula: The Enthralling History of Dracula and Vampires* (1972; London: Robson Books, 1994), ix.

19. Judith Weissman, "Women and Vampires: *Dracula* as a Victorian Novel," *Midwest Quarterly* 18 (1977).

20. Phyllis A. Roth, "Suddenly Sexual Women in Bram Stoker's *Dracula*," *Literature and Psychology* 27 (1977).

21. Fred Saberhagen, *The Dracula Tape* (New York: Ace Books, 1975); Stephen King, *Salem's Lot* (London: New English Library, 1976); Anne Rice, *Interview with the Vampire* (1976; London: Futura, 1992).

22. Waller, *American Horrors*, 4.

23. Derry, *Dark Dreams*, 17.

24. Robin Wood, *Hollywood from Vietnam to Reagan* (New York: Columbia University Press, 1986), 84.

25. Wood, *Hollywood from Vietnam to Reagan*, 75.

26. Nina Auerbach, *Our Vampires, Ourselves* (Chicago: University of Chicago Press, 1995), 117.

27. Mark Dawidziak, "*Dark Shadows:* The Supernatural Soap Opera That Fans Kept Alive Returns to TV in Prime Time," *Cinefantastique* 21, no. 3 (1990): 25.

28. *Dark Shadows* owes a debt to the innovations of Universal's *Dracula's Daughter* and *Son of Dracula*, clear precursors in their introduction of the reluctant vampire and American setting, respectively.

29. Jonathan Frid, "The Dark Shadows Connection," cited by Ted Edwards in *Buffy Xposed: The Unauthorized Biography of Sarah Michelle Geller and Her Onscreen Character* (Rocklin, Ca.: Prima Publishing, 1998), 162.

30. For a discussion of how the Gothic genre is defined by its containment within set boundaries, see Chris Baldick's introduction in *The Oxford Book of Gothic Tales* (Oxford: Oxford University Press, 1992).

31. For a closer analysis of *Blacula* in the context of racial representation, see George Lipsitz, "Genre Anxiety and Racial Representation in 1970s Cinema," in *Refiguring American Film Genres: Theory and History*, ed. Nick Browne (Berkeley and Los Angeles: University of California Press, 1985): 208–231.

32. Anthony Oberschall, "The Los Angeles Riot of August 1965," in *The Black Revolt: The Civil Rights Movement, Ghetto Uprisings, and Separatism*, ed. James A. Geschwender (New Jersey: Prentice Hall Inc., 1971), 274.

33. Leerom Medovoi, "Theorizing Historicity; or, The Many Meanings of *Blacula*," *Screen* 39, no. 1 (1998): 17–18.

34. *The Night Stalker* was the feature length pilot for the television series *Kolchak: The Night Stalker* (1974–1975).

22. Richard Matheson, *I Am Legend* (1954; London: Robinson Publishing, 1987), 130.

23. David Pirie, *The Vampire Cinema* (London: Hamlyn, 1977), 141.

24. George Romero, preface to *The Complete "Night of the Living Dead" Filmbook*, by John Russo (New York: Harmory Books, 1985), 6.

25. Wes Craven, "Last Housemates: Wes Craven and Sean Cunningham Reunite to Discuss Terrors Past and Future," interview by David A. Szulkin, *Fangoria*, no. 200 (2001): 58.

26. Romero, preface to *The Complete "Night of the Living Dead" Filmbook*, 7.

27. George Romero, *The American Nightmare*, interview by Adam Simon (2000).

28. John Russo, *The Complete "Night of the Living Dead" Filmbook*, 48.

29. Russo, *The Complete "Night of the Living Dead" Filmbook*, 55–56.

30. Romero, preface to *The Complete "Night of the Living Dead" Filmbook*, 7.

31. Anne Rice, *Interview with the Vampire* (1976; London: Futura, 1992), 82.

32. For a discussion of Anne Rice's *Interview with the Vampire* with respect to the relationship between Louis' desire to abstain from blood-drinking and the cult of dieting, see "Dieting and Damnation: Anne Rice's *Interview with the Vampire*" by Sandra Tomc in *Blood Read: The Vampire as Metaphor in Contemporary Culture*, ed. Joan Gordon and Veronica Hollinger (Philadelphia: University of Pennsylvania Press, 1997), 95–113.

33. As discussed in Chapter 3, the opposition between the black vampires and the predominantly white police officers in this film has strong racial undercurrents particularly as a large proportion of the film is set in Watts, the location for one of Los Angeles' most famous race riots.

34. Tom Savini, "Commentary," *Martin*, DVD, directed by George Romero, (1977; Troy, Mich.: Anchor Bay Entertainment, 2000).

35. For Hammer Studios, while Dracula tended to die by alternate means, brutal stakings did take place when staking female vampires, such as Barbara Shelley's death in *Dracula, Prince of Darkness*. These sequences tended to be, like Lucy's staking in the novel *Dracula*, intensely brutal, violent, and graphic.

36. Tom Savini, "Commentary," *Martin*, DVD, directed by George Romero, (1977; Troy, Mich.: Anchor Bay Entertainment, 2000).

Chapter Seven

1. Philip Brophy, "Horrality—The Textuality of Contemporary Horror Films," *Screen* 27, no. 1 (1986): 3.

2. Robert Kurtzman, "Special Makeup FX: The State of the Art," interview by Anthony C. Ferrante, *Fangoria* no. 200 (2001): 42.

3. Steve Johnson, cited by Antony Timpone in *Men, Makeup, and Monsters: Hollywood's Masters of Illusion and FX* (New York: St. Martin's Griffin, 1996), 5.

4. Yvonne Tasker, *Spectacular Bodies: Gender, Genre, and the Action Cinema* (London and New York: Routledge, 1993), 118.

5. Bryan S. Turner, *The Body and Society: Explorations of Social Theory*, 2nd ed. (London: Sage Publications, 1996), 5.

6. John Sweetman, "Only Skin Deep? Tattooing, Piercing, and the Transgressive Body," *The Body's Perilous Pleasures: Dangerous Desires and Contemporary Culture*, ed. Michele Aaron (Edinburgh: Edinburgh University Press, 1999), 166.

7. Sandra Tomc, "Dieting and Damnation: Anne Rice's *Interview with the Vampire*," *Blood Read: The Vampire as Metaphor in Contemporary Culture*, eds. Joan Gordon and Veronica Hollinger (Philadelphia: University of Pennsylvania Press, 1997), 109; Anthony Giddens, *Modernity and Self-Identity: Self and Society in the Late Modern Age* (Cambridge, UK: Polity Press, 1991), 105.

8. Paula A. Trehichler, "AIDS, Homophobia, and Biomedical Discourse: The Epidemic of Signification," *AIDS: Cultural Analysis/Cultural Activism*, ed. Douglas Crimp (London: MIT Press, 1989), 53.

9. Sweetman, "Only Skin Deep?" 177.

10. Steven Connor, "Integuments: The Scar, the Sheen, the Screen," *New Formations* 39 (1999): 52.

11. Pete Boss, "Vile Bodies and Bad Medicine," *Screen* 27, no. 1 (1986): 15.

12. Connor, "Integuments," 52.

13. Sweetman, "Only Skin Deep?" 167.

14. Brophy, "Horrality," 11.

15. Connor, "Integuments," 51.

16. James B. Twitchell, *Dreadful Pleasures: An Anatomy of Modern Horror* (New York and Oxford: Oxford University Press, 1985), 216.

17. Timpone, *Men, Makeup, and Monsters*, 3.

18. Boss, "Vile Bodies and Bad Medicine," 15.

19. Steve Neale, "'You've Got To Be Fucking Kidding!': Knowledge, Belief, and Judgement in Science Fiction," *Alien Zone: Cultural Theory and Contemporary Science Fiction Cinema*, ed. Annette Kuhn (London and New York: Verso, 1990), 160.

20. Neale, "'You've Got To Be Fucking Kidding!'" 161.

21. Brophy, "Horrality," 12.

22. Adam Eisenberg, "Vampires Next Door for *Fright Night*," *American Cinematographer* 66, no. 12 (1985): 61.

23. Ed Guerrero, "AIDS as Monster in Science Fiction and Horror Cinema," *Journal of Popular Film and Television* 18, no. 3 (1990): 87.

24. Another way of reading this transformation is as an allegory for drug addiction as the transfusion of blood takes place in the vein in her arm, and her symptoms, brought on by her refusal to give in to her blood lust, can be read as signs of withdrawal.

Chapter Eight

1. Alfred Kazin, "The New York Writer and His Landscapes," in *City Images: Perspectives from Literature, Philosophy, and Film*, ed. Mary Ann Caws (Langhorne, Pa.: Gordon and Breach, 1991), 137.

2. Larry Fessenden, e-mail to author, 2 May 2000.

3. For a comparison of the generic conventions of the New York and Los Angeles vampire film, please see Stacey Abbott, "Embracing the Metropolis: Urban

Vampires in American Cinema of the 1980s and 90s," in *Vampires: Myths and Metaphors of Enduring Evil*, ed. Peter Day (Amsterdam: Rodopi Press, 2006).

4. William Sharpe and Leonard Wallock, "From 'Great Town' to 'Non Place Urban Realm': Reading the Modern City," in *Visions of the Modern City: Essays in History, Art, and Literature*, ed. William Sharpe and Leonard Wallock (Baltimore and London: The Johns Hopkins University Press, 1987), 11.

5. Susan Elizabeth Lyman, *The Story of New York: An Informal History of the City* (New York: Crown Publishers, 1964), 232.

6. Hulbert Foutner, *New York: City of Cities* (London: J.B. Lippincott Company, 1937), 17–18.

7. This satirical equation of the consumer excesses of the period with violence and blood lust is conveyed most effectively in Bret Easton Ellis' *American Psycho* (London: Picador, 1991).

8. For more information on this aspect of New York filmmaking see Scott MacDonald, "The City as the Country: The New York City Symphony from Rudy Burckhardt to Spike Lee," *Film Quarterly* 51, no. 2 (1997–98): 2–20; Gregory Battock ed., *The New American Cinema* (New York: E.P. Dutton and Co., 1967).

9. Robert Kolker, "Screen Streets," *Time Out New York* (October 8–15, 1998): 16.

10. Christine Vachon, "How Low (Budget) Can You Go?" *Time Out New York* (October 8–15, 1998): 20.

11. Lynn M. Ermann, "The Facts in Black-and-white" *The Independent Film and Video Monthly* (January/February 1999): 26.

12. Michael Almereyda, "Vampire Girl: David Lynch Backs an Art Film Roger Corman Style," interview by Lawrence French, *Cinefantastique* 27, no. 2 (November 1995): 44.

13. Scott Macaulay, "Bloody Thoughts," *Filmmaker* 3, no. 2 (1995): 52–53.

14. Paul R. Gagne, *The Zombies That Ate Pittsburgh: The Films of George Romero* (New York: Dodd, Mead, and Company, 1987), 78.

15. André Breton, *Nadja*, trans. Richard Howard (1928; New York: Grove Weidenfeld, 1960).

16. Almereyda, "Vampire Girl," 44.

17. Kazin, "The New York Writer and His Landscapes," 143.

18. Rem Koolhaas, *Delirious New York*, (London: Academy Editions, 1978): 72.

19. Mikhail Bakhtin, *Rabelais and His World*, trans. Hélène Iswolsky (Bloomington: Indiana Univeristy Press, 1984), 10.

20. Bakhtin, *Rabelais and His World*, 7.

21. Koolhaas, *Delirious New York*, 72.

22. Martin Shefter, *Political Crisis/Fiscal Crisis: The Collapse and Revival of New York City* (New York: Basic Books Inc., 1985), xi.

23. Janet Wolff, "The Invisible Flâneuse: Women and the Literature of Modernity," *Theory, Culture, and Society* 2, no. 3 (1985): 37.

24. Wolff, "The Invisible Flâneuse," 44.

25. Judith Walkowitz, *City of Dreadful Delight: Narratives of Sexual Danger in Late Victorian London* (London: Virago Press, 1992), 20–21.

26. Jo Little, Linda Peake, and Pat Richardson, "Introduction: Geography and Gender in the Urban Environment," in *Women in Cities: Gender and the Urban Environment*, ed. Jo Little, Linda Peake, and Pat Richardson (Basingstoke, UK: Macmillan Education 1988), 10.

27. Bryan Bruce, "Scorsese: *After Hours*," *Cinéaction* no. 6 (1986): 31.

28. Sharpe and Wallock, "From 'Great Town' to 'Non-place Urban Realm,'" 14–15.

29. James Gray, "Screen Streets," cited by Robert Kolker, *Time Out New York* (October 8–15, 1998): 14.

30. Martin Scorsese, "Screen Streets," cited by Robert Kolker, 18.

31. Elizabeth Wilson, *The Sphinx in the City: Urban Life, the Control of Disorder, and Women*, (London: Virago, 1991), 7.

32. Lawrence French, "Vampire Girl," 45.

33. Michael Almereyda, "Vampire Girl," interview by Lawrence French, 45.

34. Ray Pride, "King of Infinite Space," *Filmmaker* 7, no. 2 (1999): 40; Nigel Floyd, review of *Nadja*, *Time Out London* (3–10 April 1996): 75.

35. Dayton Taylor, "A Crew Assembles to Blend Truth and Fiction," interview by Michael Ellenbogen, http://www.glasseyepix.com/html/interview.html (5 June 2002), 3.

36. Dayton Taylor, "A Crew Assembles to Blend Truth and Fiction," 4–5.

37. Fessenden, e-mail to author, 16 May 2000.

38. Fessenden, e-mail to author, 2 May 2000.

39. Kenneth Turan, "*Habit* Takes New Bite Out of An Old Tale," *Los Angeles Times* (29 October 1997).

40. Fessenden, e-mail to author, 16 May 2000.

41. Amy Taubin, "Blood Lust," *Village Voice* (18 November 1997): 85.

42. Wilson, *The Sphinx in the City*, 7.

43. Wilson, *The Sphinx in the City*, 7.

44. Wilson, *The Sphinx in the City*, 10.

45. Charles Baudelaire, "A une passante" in *Selected Poems from Les Fleurs du Mal*, trans. F. W. Leakey (Hexham, Northumberland, UK: FWL Publications, 1994), 100–101.

46. Deborah L. Parsons, *Streetwalking The Metropolis: Women, The City, and Modernity* (Oxford: Oxford University Press, 2000), 73.

47. Fessenden, e-mail to author, 16 May 2000.

48. Fessenden, e-mail to author, 5 May 2000.

49. Larry Fessenden, "New Blood," cited by Amy Taubin, *Village Voice* (10 June 1997): 74.

50. Fessenden, e-mail to author, 16 May 2000.

51. Fessenden, e-mail to author, 16 May 2000.

52. Fessenden, e-mail to author, 16 May 2000.

Chapter Nine

1. Kathryn Bigelow, interview by Ana Maria Bahiana, *Cinema Papers* 86 (January 1992), 33–34.

2. Jim Kitses, *Horizons West: Studies in Authorship within the Western* (London: BFI Publishing, 1969), 11.

3. Steven Cohan and Ina Rae Hark, *The Road Movie Book* (London: Routledge, 1997), 5.

4. Lewis Mumford, *The Highway and the City* (London: Secker and Warburg, 1964), 179.

5. André Bazin, "The Western: Or The American Film Par Excellence," in *What is Cinema?* Vol. 2, trans. Hugh Gray (Berkeley, Los Angeles, and London: University of California Press, 1971), 147.

6. Sara Gwenllian Jones, "Vampires, Indians, and the Queer Fantastic: Kathryn Bigelow's *Near Dark*," in *The Cinema of Kathryn Bigelow: Hollywood Transgressor*, ed. Deborah Jermyn and Sean Redmond (London: Wallflower Press, 2003): 60, 66.

7. John Carpenter, "Commentary," *John Carpenter's Vampires*, DVD, directed by John Carpenter (Culver City: Columbia Pictures, 1998).

8. For a further discussion of this subgenre of the western, see Noël Carroll, "The Professional Western: South of the Border," in *Back in the Saddle Again: New Essays on the Western*, ed. Edward Buscombe and Roberta E. Pearson (London: BFI Publishing, 1998), 46–62.

9. Edward Buscombe and Roberta E. Pearson, "Introduction," in *Back in the Saddle Again*, ed. Edward Buscombe and Roberta E. Pearson (London: BFI Publishing, 1998), 6.

10. Gwenllian Jones, "Vampires, Indians, and the Queer Fantastic," 61.

11. Needeya Islam, "I Wanted to Shoot People: Genre, Gender, and Action in the Films of Kathryn Bigelow," in *Kiss Me Deadly: Feminism and Cinema for the Moment*, ed. Laleen Jayamanne (Sydney: Power Publications, 1995), 104.

12. Sara Gwenllian Jones offers an alternative reading of the vampires in *Near Dark* by suggesting that they are equated with the Indian in the western for they are tribal, nomadic, instinct driven, and primitive. They also serve to disrupt Caleb's "idealized family." This is a convincing reading but does not recognize the hybridity of the western with the road movie which complicates the vampire representation. Gwenllian Jones, "Vampires, Indians, and the Queer Fantastic," 64.

13. Pam Cook, "Review of *Near Dark*," *Monthly Film Bulletin* 55, no. 648 (January 1988): 3.

14. Cohan and Hark, *The Road Movie Book*, 2.

15. Louise Gray, "Interview with Bigelow," *New Musical Express* (1 January 1988), 17.

16. Marc Augé, *Non-places: Introduction to an Anthropology of Supermodernity*, trans. John Howe (London: Verso, 1995), 77–78.

17. Omayra Cruz and Ray Guins, "Asphalt Veins: On and Off the Road with the Vampire," in *Lost Highways: An Illustrated History of Road Movies*, ed. Jack Sargeant and Stephanie Watson (London: Creation Books, 1999), 135.

18. Leslie Dick, "R: Road," *Sight and Sound* 7, no. 11 (1997): 25.

19. Chris Baldick, introduction to *The Oxford Book of Gothic Tales*, ed. Chris Baldick (Oxford: Oxford University Press, 1992): xv.

20. Dick, "R: Road," 25.

21. Nina Auerbach, *Our Vampires, Ourselves* (Chicago and London: University of Chicago Press, 1995), 190.

Chapter Ten

1. For further discussion of the significance of Los Angeles to the television series *Angel*, see Ben Jacob, "Los Angelus: City of Angel," 75–87; Stan Beeler, "Outing Lorne: Performance for the Performer," 88–100; Sara Upstone, "'LA's got it all': Hybridity and Otherness in *Angel*'s Postmodern City," 102–113, all in *Reading Angel: The TV Spin-Off with a Soul*, ed. Stacey Abbott (London: I. B. Tauris, 2005).

2. H. Eric Schockman, Greg Hise, and Michael J. Dear, "Rethinking Los Angeles," in *Rethinking Los Angeles*, ed. Michael J. Dear, H. Erick Schockman, and Greg Hise (Thousand Oaks, Calif. and London: Sage Publications, 1996), 9.

3. Edward Soja, *Postmodern Geographies: The Reassertion of Space in Critical Social Theory* (London: Verso, 1989), 243.

4. Eileen Bowser, *History of American Cinema*, Vol. 2, *The Transformation of Cinema, 1907–1915* (Berkeley, Los Angeles, and London: University of California Press, 1990), 150.

5. Jonathan Bell, "LA and the Architecture of Disaster," *Architecture and Film II* 70, no. 1 (January 2000): 51.

6. Mike Davis, *Beyond Blade Runner: Urban Control—The Ecology of Fear* (New Jersey: Open Media, 1992), 17, 18.

7. Margaret Crawford, "The Fifth Ecology: Fantasy, the Automobile, and Los Angeles," in *The Car and the City*, ed. Martin Wachs and Margaret Crawford (Ann Arbor: University of Michigan Press, 1991), 222.

8. Jean Baudrillard, *Simulations*, trans. Paul Foss, Paul Patton, Philip Beitchman (New York: Semiotext, 1983), 24.

9. Giuliana Bruno, "Ramble City: Postmodernism and *Blade Runner*," in *Alien Zone: Cultural Theory and Contemporary Fiction Cinema*, ed. Annette Kuhn (London and New York: Verso, 1990), 186.

10. Edward Buscombe, "The Idea of Genre," in *Film Genre Reader II*, ed. Barry Keith Grant (Austin: University of Texas Press: 1995), 21.

11. Philip Brophy, "Horrality—The Textuality of Contemporary Horror Films," *Screen* 27, no. 1 (Jan/Feb, 1986): 2–13.

12. Frederic Jameson, *Postmodernism, or The Cultural Logic of Late Capitalism* (London: Verso, 1991), 9.

13. Brophy, "Horrality," 5.

14. Mitch Persons, "Buffy Movie Director Fran Rubel Kuzui," *Cinefantastique* 25, no. 11 (March, 1998): 44

15. David Goyer, "*The Bloodtide* Documentary," *Blade*, DVD, prod. Susan Ricketts (New Line Home Video, 1998).

16. Soja, *Postmodern Geographies*, 215.

17. Mike Davis, *City of Quartz: Excavating the Future of Los Angeles* (New York: Vintage Books, 1990); Mike Davis, *Magical Urbanism: Latinos Reinvent the US City* (London and New York: Verso, 2000).

18. Robert Fishman, "Re-imagining Los Angeles," in *Rethinking Los Angeles*, eds. Michael Dear, H. Erik Schockman, and Greg Hise (Thousand Oaks, Calif. and London: Sage Publications, 1996), 254.

19. Soja, *Postmodern Geographies*, 217.

20. Davis, *City of Quartz*, 224.

21. Davis, *Beyond Blade Runner*, 17.

22. Davis, *Beyond Blade Runner*, 2.

23. Ed Guerrero, *Framing Blackness: The African-American Image in Film* (Philadelphia: Temple University Press, 1993), 162.

24. Nina Auerbach, "*The Bloodtide* Documentary," *Blade*, DVD, prod. Susan Ricketts (New Line Home Video, 1998).

25. Paula J. Massood, "Mapping the Hood: The Genealogy of City Space in *Boyz n the Hood* and *Menace II Society*," *Cinema Journal* 35, no. 2 (Winter 1996): 89.

26. Davis, *Beyond Blade Runner*, 6.

27. Davis, *City of Quartz*, 232–233.

28. Marv Wolfman, "*Blade* Comic Origin," interview by Dale Kutzera, *Cinefantastique* 29, no. 10 (Feb 1998): 25.

29. Guerrero, *Framing Blackness*, 89.

Chapter Eleven

1. John J. Jordan, "Vampire Cyborgs & Scientific Imperialism," *Journal of Popular Film and Television* 27, no. 2 (1999): 10.

2. Chris Hables Gray, Steven Mentor, and Heidi J. Figueroa-Sarriera, "Cyborgology: Constructing the Knowledge of Cybernetic Organisms," *The Cyborg Handbook*, ed. Chris Hables Gray (New York and London: Routledge, 1995), 3.

3. As I've written elsewhere, even the television series *Buffy the Vampire Slayer* and *Angel*—which have maintained traditional conventions of vampire mythology such as wooden stakes, holy water, the crucifix, and sunlight—portray these conventions as allergies or objects that cause physical pain rather than representing the spiritual confrontation between good and evil. See "A Little Less Ritual and a Little More Fun: The Modern Vampire in *Buffy the Vampire Slayer*," *Slayage: The Online International Journal of Buffy Studies* 3 (June 2001), available at http://slayageonline.com.

4. *Dracula 2000* very cleverly offers a modern rereading of the Dracula story to reinstate the significance of Christianity to the vampire myth.

5. Stephen Nottingham, *Screening DNA*, available at http://ourworld .compuserve.com/homepages/Stephen_Nottingham/DNAIntro.htm, accessed on 14 August 2005.

6. For further discussion of the theme of genetic reproduction in recent cinema see Susan A. George, "Not Exactly of Woman Born: Procreation and Creation in Recent Science Fiction Films," *Journal of Popular Film and Television* 28, no. 4 (Winter 2001): 176–183.

7. Jordan, "Vampire Cyborgs & Scientific Imperialism," 11.

8. Mark Oehlert, "From Captain America to Wolverine—Cyborgs in Comic Books: Alternative Images of Cybernetic Heroes and Villains," in *The Cyberculture*

Reader, ed. David Bell and Barbara M. Kennedy (London and New York: Routledge, 2000), 112–123.

9. The idea of the industrialization of the vampire blood supply is not new and has been suggested on a small scale in such films as *The Night Stalker* (1971) and *Thirst* (1979), and even in "The Wish," an episode of *Buffy the Vampire Slayer* (3:9). What *Blade Trinity* introduces to the idea is the seeming global scale of the plan. It is described as the vampire Final Solution.

10. Stephen Nottingham, *Screening DNA,* available at http://ourworld .compuserve.com/homepages/Stephen_Nottingham/DNAIntro.htm, accessed on 14 August 2005.

11. For more on the development of computer-generated effects in relation to developments within the science-fiction genre, see my article "Final Frontiers: Computer Generated Imagery and the Science Fiction Film," *Science Fiction Studies* 33 (March 2006): 89–108.

12. Stephen Prince, "True Lies: Perceptual Realism, Digital Images, and Film Theory," *Film Quarterly* 49, no. 3 (1996): 29.

13. Philip Rosen, *Change Mummified: Cinema, History, Theory* (Minneapolis and London: University of Minnesota Press, 2001), 347, 322.

14. Dennis Muren, "*Terminator 2:* For FX, The Future is Now," interview by George Turner, *American Cinematographer* 72, no. 12 (1991): 65.

15. Stephen Norrington, "Blade: Going for the Jugular," interview by Matthew J. MacDonald, *Cinefex* no. 75 (1998): 124.

16. Catherine Waldby, "Revenants: The Visible Human Project and the Digital Uncanny," *Body and Society* 3, no. 1 (1997): 2, 6. The ability of technology to blur the distinction between life and death is, however, not limited to virtual technologies. See Monica J. Casper's discussion of fetal-cyborgs, in which she outlines the procedure used for maintaining the life of a brain-dead mother through artificial life support in order to bring the fetus to full term. Both are alive through the intervention of technology, making them cyborgs. Like the VHP, these "technomoms" question the nature of the living and the dead in a cyborg world. Monica J. Casper, "Fetal Cyborgs and Technomoms on the Reproductive Frontier: Which Way to the Carnival?" in *The Cyborg Handbook,* ed. Chris Hables Gray (New York and London: Routledge, 1995), 183–202.

17. Robin Baker, "Computer Technology and Special Effects in Contemporary Cinema," in *Future Visions: New Technologies of the Screen,* eds. Philip Hayward and Tana Wollen (London: British Film Institute, 1993), 40.

18. Baker, "Computer Technology and Special Effects in Contemporary Cinema," 40.

19. Jody Duncan, "Man Made Monsters," *Cinefex* no. 98 (2004): 114.

20. For further discussion of CGI cyborgs, see my article "Final Frontiers: Computer Generated Imagery and the Science Fiction Film," *Science Fiction Studies* 33 (March, 2006): 89–108.

21. Matthew Justice, "*Blade:* Going for the Jugular," interview by Matthew J. MacDonald, *Cinefex* no. 75 (1998): 28.

22. Michele Pierson, "CGI Effects in Hollywood Science-fiction Cinema 1989–95: The Wonder Years," *Screen* 40, no. 2 (1999): 169.

23. This is reiterated in the final episode of *Buffy* ("Chosen," 7:22), when the vampire Spike sacrifices himself to save the world by burning up in the rays of the sun, achieved through a spectacular display of computer effects only to be reconstituted in the first episode of the following season of *Angel* ("Conviction," 5:1).

Chapter Twelve

1. While *Vampires: The Turning*, the second sequel to *John Carpenter's Vampires*, is set in Thailand and not Europe, it demonstrates a conscious break with the Americanization of the vampire by removing the iconography of the Wild West and replacing it with the iconography of the East, i.e. the martial arts film.

2. Zygmunt Bauman, *Globalization: The Human Consequences* (Cambridge: Polity Press, 1998), 12.

3. Chris Hables Gray, Heidi J. Figueroa-Sarriera, and Steven Mentor, "Cyborgology: Constructing the Knowledge of Cybernetic Organisms," *The Cyborg Handbook*, ed. Chris Hables Gray (London and New York: Routledge, 1995), 7.

4. Michael Hardt and Antonio Negri, *Empire* (Cambridge and London: Harvard University Press, 2000), xiv.

5. Hardt and Negri, *Empire*, 332.

6. Franco Moretti, *Signs Taken for Wonders: Essays in the Sociology of Literary Forms* (London: Verso, 1983), 93.

7. Robin Wood, "Apocalypse Now: Notes on the Living Dead," *American Nightmare*, eds. Robin Wood and Richard Lippe (Toronto: Festival of Festivals, 1979), 96.

8. Gregory A. Waller, *The Living and the Undead: From Stoker's "Dracula" to Romero's "Dawn of the Dead"* (Chicago and Urbana: University of Illinois Press, 1986), 314–315.

9. In the final season of *Angel*, the vampire Angel becomes CEO of Wolfram & Hart, further emphasizing this connection between vampirism and global corporations.

10. Bauman, *Globalization*, 9.

11. Bauman, *Globalization*, 75.

Selected Bibliography

Abbott, Stacey. "Embracing the Metropolis: Urban Vampires in American Cinema of the 1980s and 90s." In *Vampires: Myths and Metaphors of Enduring Evil*, edited by Peter Day. Amsterdam: Rodopi Press, 2006.

———. "Final Frontiers: Computer-Generated Imagery and the Science Fiction Film." *Science Fiction Studies* 33, no. 1 (2006): 89–108.

———, ed. *Reading "Angel": The TV Spin-Off with a Soul*. London: I. B. Tauris, 2005.

———. "Spectral Vampires: *Nosferatu* in the Light of New Technology." In *Horror Film: Creating and Marketing Fear*, edited by Steffen Hantke, 3–20. Jackson: University of Mississippi Press, 2004.

Arata, Stephen D. "The Occidental Tourist: *Dracula* and the Anxiety of Reverse Colonization." *Victorian Studies* 33, no. 4 (1990): 621–645.

Atkinson, Michael. "Crossing Frontiers." *Sight and Sound* 4, no. 1 (1994): 14–17.

———. "Vampire Variations." *Film Comment* 36, no. 6 (2000): 27–29.

Auerbach, Nina. *Our Vampires, Ourselves*. Chicago: University of Chicago Press, 1995.

Augé, Marc. *Non-Places: Introduction to an Anthropology of Supermodernity*. Translated by John Howe. London: Verso, 1995.

Baker, Robin. "Computer Technology and Special Effects in Contemporary Cinema." In *Future Visions: New Technologies of the Screen*, edited by Philip Hayward and Tana Wollen, 31–45. London: British Film Institute, 1993.

Bakhtin, Mikhail. *Rabelais and His World*. Translated by Hélène Iswolsky. Bloomington: Indiana University Press, 1984.

Baldick, Chris, ed. *The Oxford Book of Gothic Tales*. Oxford: Oxford University Press, 1992.

Barber, Paul. *Vampires, Burial, and Death*. New Haven and New York: Yale University Press, 1988.

Barber, X. Theodore. "Phantasmagorical Wonders: The Magic Lantern Ghost Show in Nineteenth-Century America." *Film History* 3, no. 2 (1989): 73–86.

Baudelaire, Charles. *Painter of Modern Life and Other Essays*. Translated and edited by Jonathan Mayne. London: Phaidon Press, 1964.

————. "A Une Passante." *Selected Poems from "Les Fleurs du Mal."* Translated by F. W. Leakey. Hexham, Northumberland: FWL Publications, 1994.

Baudrillard, Jean. *Simulations.* Translated by Paul Foss, Paul Patton, and Philip Beitchman. New York: Semiotext, 1983.

Bauman, Zygmunt. *Globalization: The Human Consequences.* Cambridge, UK: Polity Press, 1998.

Bazin, André. *What is Cinema?* Vol. 1. Translated by Hugh Gray. Los Angeles: University of California Press, 1967.

Belford, Barbara. *Bram Stoker: A Biography of the Author of "Dracula."* London: Phoenix Giant, 1996.

Benidt, Jennifer, and Janine Pourroy. "*Fright Night.*" *Cinefex* 25 (1986): 54–71.

Benjamin, Walter. *Charles Baudelaire: A Lyric Poet in the Era of High Capitalism.* Translated by Harry Zohn. London: NLB, 1973.

————. "The Work of Art in the Age of Mechanical Reproduction." In *Illuminations,* edited by Hannah Arendt, 217–251. Translated by Harry Zohn. New York: Schocken Books, 1969.

Berman, Mark. "Francis Ford Coppola on *Dracula.*" *Starburst,* no. 175 (1993).

Berman, Marshall. *All That Is Solid Melts into Air: The Experience of Modernity.* New York: Verso, 1983.

Boss, Pete. "Vile Bodies and Bad Medicine." *Screen* 27, no. 1 (1986): 14–26.

Botting, Fred. *Gothic.* London and New York: Routledge Publishing, 1996.

Breton, André. *Nadja.* Translated by Richard Howard. New York: Grove Weidenfeld, 1960.

Brophy, Philip. "Horrality—The Textuality of Contemporary Horror Films." *Screen* 27, no. 1 (1986): 2–13.

Bruno, Giuliana. "Ramble City: Postmodernism and *Blade Runner.*" In *Alien Zone: Cultural Theory and Contemporary Cinema,* edited by Annette Kuhn, 183–195. London and New York: Verso, 1996.

Buscombe, Edward, and Roberta E. Pearson, eds. *Back in the Saddle Again: New Essays on the Western.* London: BFI, 1998.

Carroll, Noël. *The Philosophy of Horror.* New York and London: Routledge, 1990.

Carter, Margaret L. *Dracula: The Vampire and the Critics.* Ann Arbor: UMI Research Press, 1988.

Casper, Monica J. "Fetal Cyborgs and Technomoms on the Reproductive Frontier: Which Way to the Carnival?" In *The Cyborg Handbook,* edited by Chris Hables Gray, 183–202. New York and London: Routledge, 1995.

Castle, Terry. "Phantasmagoria: Spectral Technology and the Metaphorics of Modern Reverie." *Critical Inquiry* (Autumn 1988): 26–61.

Charity, Tom. "Extra Sensory Projection." *Time Out,* 25 October 1995.

Charney, Leo. *Empty Moments: Cinema, Modernity, and Drift.* Durham and London: Duke University Press, 1998.

————, and Vanessa R. Schwartz. *Cinema and the Invention of Modern Life.* Berkeley: University of California Press, 1995.

Cohan, Steven, and Ina Rae Hark. *The Road Movie Book.* London: Routledge, 1997.

Comte, August. *The Positive Philosophy of August Comte.* Translated by Harriet Martineau. London: Kegan Paul, Trench, Trübner, and Co., 1875.

Connor, Steven. "The Impossibility of the Present: or, from the Contemporary to the Contemporal." In *Literature and the Contemporary: Fictions and Theories of the Present*, edited by Roger Luckhurst and Peter Marks, 15–35. Harlow: Longmans, 1999.

———. "Integuments: The Scar, the Sheen, the Screen." *New Formations* 39 (1999): 32–54.

———. *Dumbstruck: A Cultural History of Ventriloquism.* Oxford: Oxford University Press, 2000.

Cook, David A. *Lost Illusions: American Cinema in the Shadow of Watergate and Vietnam, 1970–1979.* History of American Cinema 9. New York: Charles Scribner's Sons, 2000.

Cook, Pam. Review of *Near Dark. Monthly Film Bulletin* 55, no. 648 (January 1988).

Craft, Christopher. "Kiss Me With Those Red Lips: Gender and Inversion in Stoker's *Dracula.*" *Representations* 8 (1984): 107–133.

Cranny-Francis, Anne. "Sexual Politics and Political Repression in Bram Stoker's *Dracula.*" In *Nineteenth Century Suspense: From Poe to Conan Doyle*, edited by Clive Bloom, Brian Docherty, Jane Gibb, and Keith Shand, 64–79. Basingstoke, UK: Macmillan Press, 1988.

Crary, Jonathan. *Techniques of the Observer: On Vision and Modernity in the Nineteenth Century.* Cambridge, Mass.: MIT Press, 1992.

Creed, Barbara. *The Monstrous-Feminine: Film, Feminism, Psychoanalysis.* London and New York: Routledge, 1993.

Croley, Laura-Sagolla. "The Rhetoric of Reform in Stoker's *Dracula:* Depravity, Decline, and the Fin-de-Siecle Residuum." *Criticism: A Quarterly for Literature and the Arts* 37, no. 1 (1995): 85–108.

Cruz, Omayra, and Ray Guins. "Asphalt Veins: On and Off the Road with the Vampire." In *Lost Highways: An Illustrated History of Road Movies*, edited by Jack Sargeant and Stephanie Watson, 129–146. London: Creation Books, 1999.

Curci, Loris. "George Romero." In *Shock Masters of the Cinema*, 118–127. Key West, Fla.: Fantasm Books, 1996.

Dalby, Richard, ed. *Dracula's Brood: Rare Vampire Stories by Friends and Contemporaries of Bram Stoker.* Wellingborough, UK: Crucible, 1987.

Daley, N. "Incorporated Bodies: *Dracula* and the Rise of Professionalism." *Texas Studies in Literature and Language* 39, no. 2 (1997): 181–203.

Davenport-Hines, Richard. *Gothic: 400 Years of Excess, Horror, Evil, and Ruin.* London: Fourth Estate Limited, 1998.

Davis, Mike. *City of Quartz: Excavating the Future in Los Angeles.* New York: Vintage Books, 1990.

———. *Beyond "Blade Runner": Urban Control/The Ecology of Fear.* New Jersey: Open Media, 1992.

———. *Magical Urbanism: Latinos Reinvent The US City.* London and New York: Verso, 2000.

Dawidziak, Mark. "*Dark Shadows:* The Supernatural Soap Opera That Fans Kept Alive Returns to TV in Prime Time." *Cinefantastique* 21, no. 3 (1990).

Dear, Michael J., H. Erik Schockman, and Greg Hise. *Rethinking Los Angeles.* Thousand Oaks, Calif. and London: Sage Publications, 1996.

Derry, Charles. *Dark Dreams: The Horror Film from "Psycho" to "Jaws."* South Brunswick, N.J. and New York: A. S. Barnes and Company, 1977.

Dick, Leslie. "R: Road." *Sight and Sound* 7, no. 11 (1997): 22–25.

Dickstein, Morris. "The Aesthetics of Fright." *American Film* 5, no. 10 (1980): 32–37, 56, 58–59.

Dillar, R. H. W. "*Night of the Living Dead:* 'It's Not Like Just a Wind That's Passing Through.'" In *American Horrors: Essays on the Modern American Horror Film,* edited by Gregory A. Waller, 14–29. Urbana and Chicago: University of Illinois Press, 1987.

Douglas, Mary. *Purity and Danger: An Analysis of the Concepts of Pollution and Taboo.* 1966. Reprint, London: Ark Paperbacks, 1984.

Dresser, Norine. *American Vampires: Fans, Victims, Practitioners.* New York: Vintage Books, 1989.

Duchovnay, Gerald. "Tony Buba: An Interview." *Post Script* 9, no. 1/2 (1989/90): 2–24.

Duncan, Jody. "Man Made Monsters." *Cinefex* 98 (July 2004): 98–124.

Dundes, Alan, ed. *The Vampire: A Casebook.* Madison: The University of Wisconsin Press, 1998.

Eisenberg, Adam. "Vampires Next Door for *Fright Night.*" *American Cinematographer* 66, no. 12 (1985): 58–65.

Eisner, Lotte. *Murnau.* London: Secker and Warburg, 1964.

Ellenbogen, Michael. "A Crew Assembles to Blend Truth and Fiction." *Glass Eye Pix.* http://www.glasseyepix.com/html/interview.html.

Elsaesser, Thomas. "Social Mobility and the Fantastic." *Sight and Sound* 36, no. 3 (1967): 14–25.

———. "Secret Affinities." *Sight and Sound* 58, no. 1 (1989/90): 33–39.

———. "Specularity and Engulfment: Francis Ford Coppola and *Bram Stoker's Dracula.*" In *Contemporary Hollywood Cinema,* edited by Steve Neale and Murray Smith, 191–208. London: Routledge, 1998.

Ermann, Lynn M. "The Facts in Black and White." *The Independent Film and Video Monthly,* January/February 1999.

Floyd, Nigel. Review of *Nadja,* directed by Michael Almereyda. *Time Out London,* 3–10 April 1996.

Flynn, J. K. *Cinematic Vampires: The Living Dead on Film and Television, from "The Devil's Castle" (1896) to "Bram Stoker's Dracula" (1992).* Jefferson, N.C. and London: MacFarland and Company, 1992.

Fontana, Ernest. "Lombroso's Criminal Man and Stoker's *Dracula.*" In *Dracula and its Critics,* edited by Margaret L. Carter, 159–165. Ann Arbor, Mich.: UMI Research Press, 1988.

Foucault, Michel. *The Archaeology of Knowledge.* Translated by A. M. Sheridan Smith. London: Tavistock Publications, 1972.

Francke, Lizzie. "Virtual Fears." *Sight and Sound* 5, no. 12 (1995): 6–9.

Frayling, Christopher. *Vampyres: Lord Byron to Count Dracula.* London and Boston: Faber and Faber, 1991.

———. *Nightmare: The Birth of Horror.* London: BBC Books, 1996.

Freeland, Cynthia. *The Naked and the Undead: Evil and the Appeal of Horror.* Boulder, Colo.: Westview Press, 2000.

French, Lawrence. "Vampire Girl: David Lynch Backs an Art Film Roger Corman Style." *Cinefantastique* 27, no. 2 (1995).

Friedland, Roger, and Deirdre Boden, eds. *NowHere: Space, Time, and Modernity*. Los Angeles: University of California Press, 1994.

Gagne, Paul R. *The Zombies That Ate Pittsburgh: The Films of George Romero*. New York: Dodd, Mead, and Company, 1987.

Gelder, Ken. *Reading the Vampire*. London: Routledge, 1994.

———, ed. *The Horror Reader*. London and New York: Routledge, 2000.

Giddens, Anthony. *Modernity and Self-Identity: Self and Society in the Late Modern Age*. Cambridge, UK: Polity Press, 1991.

Gitlin, Tod. *The Sixties: Years of Hope, Days of Rage*. 1987. Reprint, New York: Bantam Books, 1993.

Glover, David. *Vampires, Mummies, and Liberals: Bram Stoker and the Politics of Popular Fiction*. Durham and London: Duke University Press, 1996.

Gordon, Joan, and Veronica Hollinger, eds. *Blood Read: The Vampire as Metaphor in Contemporary Culture*. Philadelphia: University of Pennsylvania Press, 1997.

Grant, Barry Keith, ed. *Film Genre Reader II*. Austin: University of Texas Press, 1995.

———, ed. *Planks of Reason: Essays on the Horror Film*. Lanham, Md. and London: The Scarecrow Press, 1996.

———, ed. *The Dread of Difference: Gender and the Horror Film*. Austin: University of Texas Press, 1996.

Gray, Chris Hables, ed. *The Cyborg Handbook*. London and New York: Routledge, 1995.

Gray, Louise. "Interview with Bigelow." *New Musical Express*, 1 January 1988.

Greenway, John L. "Seward's Folly: *Dracula* as a Critique of 'Normal Science.'" *Stanford Literature Review* 3, no. 2 (1986): 213–230.

Griffin, Gail B. "'Your Girls That You All Love Are Mine': *Dracula* and the Victorian Male Sexual Imagination." *International Journal of Women's Studies* 3, no. 5 (1980): 454–465.

Guerrero, Ed. "AIDS as Monster in Science Fiction and Horror Cinema." *Journal of Popular Film and Television* 18, no. 3 (1990): 86–93.

———. *Framing Blackness: The African-American Image in Film*. Philadelphia: Temple University Press, 1993.

Guillermo, Gilberto Perez. "Shadow and Substance: Murnau's *Nosferatu*." *Sight and Sound* 36, no. 3 (1967): 150–153, 159.

Gunning, Tom. "'Primitive' Cinema: A Frame-up; or, the Trick's on Us." In *Early Cinema: Space, Frame, Narrative*, edited by Thomas Elsaesser, 95–103. London: British Film Institute, 1990.

———. "Phantom Images and Modern Manifestations: Spirit Photography, Magic Theatre, Trick Films, and Photography's Uncanny." In *Fugitive Images from Photography to Video*, edited by Petro Patrice, 42–71. Bloomington and Indianapolis: Indiana University Press, 1995.

———. *The Films of Fritz Lang: Allegories of Vision and Modernity*. London: British Film Institute, 2000.

Gwenllian Jones, Sara. "Vampires, Indians, and the Queer Fantastic: Kathryn Bigelow's *Near Dark*." In *The Cinema of Kathryn Bigelow: Hollywood Transgressor,* edited by Deborah Jermyn and Sean Redmond, 57–71. London: Wallflower Press, 2003.

Haining, Peter, ed. *The Dracula Scrapbook*. London: New English Library, 1976.

Halberstam, Judith. "Technologies of Monstrosity, *Bram Stoker's Dracula*." *Victorian Studies* 36, no. 3 (1993): 333–352.

Hall, Jasmine Yung. "Solicitors Soliciting: The Dangerous Circulation of Professionalism in *Dracula*." In *The New Nineteenth Century: Feminist Readings of Underread Victorian Fiction*, edited by Barbara Leah Harman and Susan Meyer, 97–116. New York: Garland Pub, 1996.

Hamilton, Peter, and Roger Hargreaves. *The Beautiful and the Damned: The Creation of Identity in Nineteenth-Century Photography*. Aldershot, UK: Lund Humphries, 2000.

Hantke, Steffen, ed. *Horror Film: Creating and Marketing Fear.* Jackson: University of Mississippi Press, 2004.

Harding, Colin, and Simon Popple. *In the Kingdom of Shadows: A Companion to Early Cinema*. London: Cygnus Arts, 1996.

Hardt, Michael, and Antonio Negri. *Empire*. Cambridge, Mass. and London: Harvard University Press, 2000.

Hunt, Bruce J. "Doing Science in a Global Empire: Cable Telegraphy and Electrical Physics in Victorian Britain." In *Victorian Science in Context*, edited by Bernard Lightman, 312–333. Chicago: The University of Chicago Press, 1997.

Hutchings, Peter. *Hammer and Beyond: The British Horror Film*. Manchester, UK and New York: Manchester University Press, 1993.

———. *Dracula*. London and New York: I. B. Tauris, 2003.

Islam, Needeya. "I Wanted to Shoot People: Genre, Gender, and Action in the Films of Kathryn Bigelow." In *Kiss Me Deadly: Feminism and Cinema for the Moment*, edited by Laleen Jayamanne, 91–125. Sydney: Power Publications, 1995.

Jameson, Fredric. *The Ideologies of Theory: Essays, 1971–1986*. Vol. 2, *Syntax of History*. London: Routledge, 1988.

———. *Postmodernism, or The Cultural Logic of Late Capitalism*. London: Verso, 1991.

Jankiewicz, Pat. "Innocent Vampires and American Werewolves." Special issue, *Starburst* (April 1993).

Jann, Rosemary. "Saved by Science? The Mixed Messages of Stoker's *Dracula*." *Texas Studies in Literature and Language* 31, no. 2 (1989): 273–287.

Jones, Stephen. *The Illustrated Vampire Movie Guide*. London: Titan Books, 1993.

Jordan, John J. "Vampire Cyborgs and Scientific Imperialism: A Reading of the Science-Mysticism Polemic in *Blade*." *Journal of Popular Film and Television* 27, no. 2 (1990): 4–15.

Kaminsky, Stuart M. "Kolchak: The Night Stalker." *Cinefantastique* 4, no. 1 (1975).

Katzman, Joshua. "Blood Lust." *Chicago Reader,* 21 March 1997.

Kazin, Alfred. "The New York Writer and His Landscapes." In *City Images: Perspectives from Literature, Philosophy, and Film*, edited by Mary Ann Caws, 129–143. Langhorne, Pa.: Gordon and Breach, 1991.

Keane, Colleen. "Director as 'Adrenaline Junkie': Commenting on Kathryn Bigelow's Genre Experiments, Thematic Interests, and Populism." *Metro*, no. 109 (1997): 22–27.

Kern, Stephen. *The Culture of Time and Space, 1880–1918.* Cambridge, Mass.: Harvard University Press, 1983.

King, Stephen. *Salem's Lot.* London: New English Library, 1976.

Kittler, Friedrich. *Discourse Networks 1800/1900.* Translated by Michael Metteer and Chris Cullens. Stanford: Stanford University Press, 1987.

———. "Dracula's Legacy." Translated by William Stephen Davis. *Stanford Humanities Review* 1 (1989): 143–173.

Koolhas, Rem. *Delirious New York.* London: Academy Editions, 1978.

Kristeva, Julia. *Power of Horror: An Essay on Abjection.* Translated by Leon S. Roudiez. New York: Columbia University Press, 1982.

Krum, P. "Metamorphosis as Metaphor in Bram Stoker's *Dracula.*" *Victorian Newsletter,* no. 88 (1995): 5–11.

Kuhn, Thomas S. *The Structure of Scientific Revolutions.* Chicago: University of Chicago Press, 1970.

Kutzera, Dale. "*Blade:* Marvel's Urban Anti-Vampire Assassin Jumps and Kicks His Way to the Big Screen." *Cinefantastique* 29, no. 10 (1998).

———. "*Blade* Comic Origin." *Cinefantastique* 29, no. 10 (1998).

Landon, Brooks. *The Aesthetics of Ambivalence: Rethinking Science Fiction in the Age of Electronic (Re) Production.* London: Greenwood Press, 1992.

Latham, Rob. *Consuming Youth: Vampires, Cyborgs, and the Culture of Consumption.* Chicago and London: The University of Chicago Press, 2002.

LeFanu, Sheridan. "Carmilla." In *In a Glass Darkly,* 243–319. 1872. Reprint, Oxford: Oxford University Press, 1993.

LeGates, Richard T., and Frederic Stout, eds. *The City Reader.* London and New York: Routledge, 1996.

Lippe, Richard. "The Horror of Martin." In *The American Nightmare,* edited by Robin Wood and Richard Lippe, 87–90. Toronto: Festival of Festivals, 1979.

Lipsitz, George. "Genre Anxiety and Racial Representation in 1970s Cinema." In *Refiguring American Film Genres: Theory and History,* edited by Nick Browne, 208–231. Berkeley and Los Angeles: University of California Press, 1985.

Little, Jo, Linda Peak, and Pat Richardson. *Women in Cities: Gender and the Urban Environment.* Basingstoke, UK: Macmillan Education 1988.

Luckhurst, Roger. "Trance-Gothic, 1882–1897." In *Victorian Gothic: Literary and Cultural Manifestations in the Nineteenth Century,* edited by Ruth Robbins and Julian Wolfreys, 148–167. Basingstoke, UK: Palgrave, 2000.

Macaulay, Scott. "Bloody Thoughts." *Filmmaker* 3, no. 2 (1995).

Macdonald, Andrew, and Gina Macdonald. "Before *The X-Files:* Kolchak and the Cassandra Complex." *Creative Screenwriting* 5, no. 5 (1998): 47–54.

MacDonald, Matthew. "*Blade:* Going for the Jugular." *Cinefex* 75 (1998): 26–30, 121–124.

Madison, Bob. "*Dracula*": *The First Hundred Years.* Baltimore: Midnight Marquee Press, 1997.

Magid, Ron. "Effects Add Bite to *Bram Stoker's Dracula.*" *American Cinematographer* 73, no. 12 (1992): 56–64.

———. "Dark Shadows." *American Cinematographer* 81, no. 12 (2000): 68–75.

Mandell, Paul R. "Make-up Effects for *The Hunger.*" *American Cinematographer* 64, no. 8 (1983): 50–53, 91–95.

Malina, Roger F. "Digital Image—Digital Cinema: The Work of Art in the Age of Post-Mechanical Reproduction." *Leonardo Digital Image—Digital Cinema Supplement* (1990): 35–38.

Mannoni, Laurent. *The Great Art of Light and Shadow: Archaeology of the Cinema.* Edited and translated by Richard Crangle. Exeter: University of Exeter, 2000.

Matheson, Richard. *I Am Legend.* 1954. Reprint, London: Robinson Publishing, 1987.

McCammon, Robert R. *They Thirst.* London: Sphere Books Limited, 1981.

McCarty, John. *Splatter Movies: Breaking the Last Taboo.* Kent: Columbus Books, 1984.

———. *The Official Splatter Movie Guide.* New York: St. Martin's Press, 1989.

———. *The Modern Horror Film.* New York: Carol Publishing Group, 1990.

———. *John McCarty's Official Splatter Movie Guide.* Vol 2. New York: St. Martin's Press, 1992.

McNally, Raymond T., and Radu Florescu. *In Search of Dracula: The Enthralling History of Dracula and Vampires.* 1972. Reprint, Robson Books, 1994.

Medovi, Leerom. "Theorizing Historicity, or The Many Meanings of *Blacula*." *Screen* 39, no. 1 (1998): 1–23.

Melton, J. Gordon. *Video Hound's Vampires on Video.* Detroit: Visible Ink, 1997.

Miller, Elizabeth, ed. *Dracula: The Shade and the Shadow.* Westcliff-on-Sea, UK: Desert Island Books, 1998.

Miller, Stephen Paul. *The Seventies Now: Culture as Surveillance.* Durham and London: Duke University Press, 1999.

Monaco, James. "AAAAEEEAARGGH!" *Sight and Sound* 49, no. 2 (1980): 80–82.

Moretti, Franco. *Signs Taken for Wonders: Essays in the Sociology of Literary Forms.* London: Verso, 1988.

Mulvey-Roberts, Marie. *The Handbook of Gothic Literature.* London: Macmillan Press, 1998.

Neale, Steve. *Cinema and Technology: Image, Sound, and Colour.* London: Macmillan Education, 1985.

———. "'You've Got to Be Fucking Kidding!': Knowledge, Belief, and Judgement in Science Fiction." In *Alien Zone: Cultural Theory and Contemporary Science Fiction Cinema.* Edited by Annette Kuhn, 160–168. London and New York: Verso, 1990.

———. *Genre and Hollywood.* London and New York: Routledge, 2000.

Newman, Kim. "Dracula Has Risen from the Grave . . . Again." *Monthly Film Bulletin* 55, no. 648 (1988).

———. *Nightmare Movies: A Critical Guide to Contemporary Horror Films.* New York: Harmony Books, 1988.

Nye, David E. *Electrifying America: Social Meanings of a New Technology, 1880–1940.* Cambridge, Mass.: MIT Press, 1990.

———. *Narratives and Spaces: Technology and the Construction of American Culture.* Exeter: University of Exeter Press, 1997.

Orr, John. *Cinema and Modernity.* Cambridge, UK: Polity Press, 1993.

Pamboukian, Sylvia. "'Looking Radiant': Science, Photography, and the X-ray Craze of 1896." *Victorian Review* 27, no. 2 (2001): 56–74.

Parsons, Deborah L. *Streetwalking the Metropolis: Women, the City, and Modernity.* Oxford: Oxford University Press, 2000.

Perkin, Harold. *The Rise of Professional Society: England Since 1880.* London and New York: Routledge, 1989.

Phillips, Mike. "Chic and Beyond." *Sight and Sound* 6, no. 8 (1996): 25–27.

Pick, Daniel. "Terror of the Night: *Dracula* and Degeneration." *Critical Quarterly* 30 (1984): 71–87.

Pierson, Michele. "CGI Effects In Hollywood Science-Fiction Cinema 1989–95: The Wonder Years." *Screen* 40, no. 2 (1999): 158–176.

Pirie, David. *Heritage of Horror: The English Gothic Cinema 1946–1972.* London: Gordon Fraser, 1973.

———. *The Vampire Cinema.* London: Hamlyn, 1977.

Polidori, John. "The Vampyre." In *Vampyres: Lord Byron to Count Dracula,* edited by Christopher Frayling, 108–125. London: Faber and Faber, 1991.

Porter, Roy. *London: A Social History.* London: Hamish Hamilton, 1994.

Powell, Anna. "Blood on the Borders—*Near Dark* and *Blue Steel*." *Screen* 35, no. 2 (1994): 136–156.

Pride, Ray. "King of Infinite Space." *Filmmaker* 7, no. 2 (1999).

Prince, Stephen. "True Lies: Perceptual Realism, Digital Images, and Film Theory." *Film Quarterly* 49, no. 3 (1996): 27–37.

Punter, David. *The Literature of Terror.* Vol. 1, *The Gothic Tradition.* 2nd ed. London and New York: Longman, 1996.

———. *The Literature of Terror.* Vol. 2, *The Modern Gothic.* 2nd ed. London and New York: Longman, 1996.

Reader, W. J. *Professional Men: The Rise of the Professional Classes in Nineteenth Century England.* London: Weidenfeld and Nicolson, 1966.

Rhymer, John. *Varney the Vampire, or The Feast of Blood.* London: E. Lloyd, 1847.

Rice, Anne. *Interview with the Vampire.* 1976. Reprint, London: Futura, 1992.

———. *The Vampire Lestat.* 1985. Reprint, London: Futura, 1993.

———. *The Queen of the Damned.* 1988. Reprint, London: Futura, 1990.

Rosen, Philip. *Change Mummified: Cinema, History, Theory.* Minneapolis and London: University of Minnesota Press, 2001.

Roth, Phyllis A. "Suddenly Sexual Women in *Bram Stoker's Dracula*." *Literature and Psychology* 27 (1977): 57–67.

Russo, John. *The Complete "Night of the Living Dead" Filmbook.* New York: Harmory Books, 1985.

Saberhagen, Fred. *The Dracula Tape.* New York: Ace Books, 1975.

Sage, Victor, and Allan Lloyd Smith, eds. *Modern Gothic: A Reader.* Manchester, UK and New York: Manchester University Press, 1996.

Salt, Barry. *Film Style and Technology: History and Analysis.* London: Starword, 1983.

Sargeant, Jack, and Stephanie Watson, eds. *Lost Highways: An Illustrated History of Road Movies.* London: Creation Books, 1999.

Sarris, Andrew. "Out, Out, Damned Demon!" *The Village Voice,* 3 January 1974.

Scandura, Jani. "Deadly Professions: *Dracula,* Undertakers, and the Embalmed Corpse." *Victorian Studies* (Autumn 1996): 1–30.

Schivelbusch, Wolfgang. *The Railway Journey: The Industrialization of Time and Space in the Nineteenth Century.* Leamington Spa, UK and New York: Berg Publishers, 1986.

Schneider, Stephen Jay. "'Suck . . . Don't Suck': Framing Ideology in Kathryn Bigelow's *Near Dark*." In *The Cinema of Kathryn Bigelow: Hollywood Transgressor,* edited by Deborah Jermyn and Sean Redmond, 72–90. London: Wallflower Press, 2003.

Schneider, Tassilo. "Generic Overdetermination and Textual Excess: Notes on *The Lost Boys.*" *Spectator* 13, no. 2 (1993): 60–69.

Senf, Carol A. "*Dracula:* Stoker's Response to the New Woman." *Victorian Studies* (Autumn 1982): 33–49.

———. *Dracula: Between Tradition and Modernism.* New York: Twayne Publishers, 1998.

Sharpe, William, and Leonard Wollock, eds. *Visions of the Modern City: Essays in History, Art, and Literature.* Baltimore and London: Johns Hopkins University Press, 1987.

Shapiro, Steven. "Contagious Allegories: George Romero." In *The Cinematic Body*, 82–104. Minneapolis: Minnesota University Press, 1993.

Shelley, Jim. "The Abel Guy." *Neon*, May 1997.

Silver, Alain, and James Ursini. *The Vampire Film: From "Nosferatu" to "Interview with the Vampire."* 3rd ed. New York: Limelight Editions, 1997.

———, eds. *Horror Film Reader.* New York: Limelight Editions, 2000.

Simmel, Georg. "The Metropolis and Mental Life." In *Modernism: An Anthology of Sources and Documents.* Translated by Edward A. Shils. Edited by Vassiliki Koloctroni, Jane Goldman, and Olga Taxidou, 51–60. Edinburgh: Edinburgh University Press, 1998.

Skal, David J. *Hollywood Gothic: The Tangled Web of "Dracula" from Novel to Stage to Screen.* New York and London: W. W. Norton and Company, 1990.

———. *The Monster Show: A Cultural History of Horror.* London: Plexus Publishing Limited, 1993.

———. *V is For Vampires: The A–Z Guide to Everything Undead.* New York: Plume Books, 1996.

———, and Nina Auerbach. *"Dracula": Authoritative Text, Contexts, Reviews and Reactions, Dramatic and Film Variations, Criticism.* New York and London: W. W. Norton and Company, 1997.

Smith, Gavin. "Momentum and Design: Kathryn Bigelow interviewed by Gavin Smith." *Film Comment* 31, no. 5 (1995): 46–60.

Soja, Edward. *Postmodern Geographies: The Reassertion of Space in Critical Social Theory.* London: Verso, 1989.

Spenser, K. "Purity and Danger: *Dracula*, the Urban Gothic, and Late Victorian Degeneracy." *ELH* 59 (1992): 197–225.

Steensland, Mark. "The Chill Atmosphere of *Fright Night.*" *American Cinematographer* 66, no. 10 (1985): 68–72.

Stoker, Bram. *Dracula.* 1897. Reprint, London: Oxford University Press, 1996.

———. *Famous Impostors.* London: Sidgwick and Jackson Ltd., 1910.

———. *The Jewel of the Seven Stars.* 1912. Reprint, London: Arrow Books, 1975.

Summers, Montague. *The Vampire in Europe.* 1929. Reprint, London: Bracken Books, 1996.

Szulkin, David A. "Last Housemates: Wes Craven and Sean Cunningham Reunite to Discuss Terrors Past and Future." *Fangoria* no. 200 (2001).

Tasker, Yvonne. *Spectacular Bodies: Gender, Genre, and the Action Cinema.* London and New York: Routledge, 1993.

———. "Bigger Than Life: Kathryn Bigelow Brought Intimacy to the Action Movie, but Will She Get the Chance to Reinvent Another Genre?" *Sight and Sound* 9, no. 5 (1999): 12–15.

Taubin, Amy. "New Blood." *Village Voice* (10 June 1997).

———. "Blood Lust." *Village Voice* (18 November 1997).

Telotte, J. P. *Replications: A Robotic History of the Science Fiction Film.* Urbana and Chicago: University of Illinois Press, 1995.

Tester, Keith, ed. *The Flâneur.* London and New York: Routledge, 1994.

Thurschwell, Pamela. *Literature, Technology, and Magical Thinking, 1880–1920.* Cambridge, UK: Cambridge University Press, 2001.

Timpone, Anthony. *Men, Makeup, and Monsters: Hollywood's Masters of Illusion and FX.* New York: St. Martin's Griffin, 1996.

Tomc, Sandra. "Dieting and Damnation: Anne Rice's *Interview with the Vampire.*" In *Blood Read: The Vampire as Metaphor in Contemporary Culture*, edited by Joan Gordon and Veronica Hollinger, 95–113. Philadelphia: University of Pennsylvania Press, 1997.

Toufic, Jalal. *(Vampires): An Uneasy Essay On The Undead In Film.* New York: Station Hill Press, 1993.

Tropp, Martin. *Images of Fear: How Horror Stories Helped Shape Modern Culture (1818–1918).* Jefferson, N.C. and London: McFarland and Company, 1990.

Tudor, Andrew. *Monsters and Mad Scientists: A Cultural History of the Horror Movie.* Oxford: Basil Blackwell, 1989.

Turan, Kenneth. "*Habit* Takes New Bite Out of Old Tale." Review of *Habit*, directed by Larry Fessenden. *Los Angeles Times*, 29 October 1997.

Turner, Bryan S. *The Body and Society: Explorations of Social Theory.* 2nd ed. London: Sage Publications, 1996.

Turner, George. "The Two Faces of *Dracula.*" *American Cinematographer* 69, no. 5 (1988): 34–42.

———. "*Terminator 2*: For FX, The Future is Now" *American Cinematographer* 72, no. 12 (1991): 62–69.

———. "*Bram Stoker's Dracula*: A Happening Vampire." *American Cinematographer* 73, no. 11 (1992): 36–45.

Twitchell, James B. *The Living Dead: A Study of the Vampire in Romantic Literature.* Durham: Duke University Press, 1980.

———. *Dreadful Pleasures: An Anatomy of Modern Horror.* New York and Oxford: Oxford University Press, 1985.

Vacche, Angela Dalle. "Murnau's *Nosferatu*: Romantic Painting as Horror and Desire in Expressionist Cinema." *Post Script* 14, no. 3 (1995): 26–36.

Vachon, Christine. "How Low (Budget) Can You Go?" *Time Out New York*, 8–15 October 1998.

Vié, Caroline. "To Cast a *Shadow of the Vampire.*" *Fangoria* no. 198 (2001).

Waldby, Catherine. "Revenants: The Visible Human Project and the Digital Uncanny." *Body and Society* 3, no. 1 (1997): 1–16.

Walkowitz, Judith R. *City of Dreadful Delight: Narratives of Sexual Danger in Late-Victorian London.* London: Virago, 1992.

Waller, Gregory A. *The Living and the Undead: From Stoker's "Dracula" to Romero's "Dawn of the Dead."* Chicago and Urbana: University of Illinois Press, 1986.

————, ed. *American Nightmares: Essays in the Modern American Horror Film*. Urbana and Chicago: University of Illinois Press, 1987.

Warren, Bill. "Reflections on Horror." Pts. 1 and 2. *Fangoria* no. 200 (2001).

Weber, Max. *From Max Weber: Essays in Sociology*. Translated and edited by H. H. Gerth and C. Wright Mills. London: Routledge and Kegan Paul, Ltd., 1948.

Weiss, Andrea. *Vampires and Violets: Lesbians in the Cinema*. London: Capre, 1992.

Weissman, Judith. "Women and Vampires: *Dracula* as a Victorian Novel." *Midwest Quarterly* 18 (1977): 69–77.

Wicke, Jennifer. "Vampiric Typewriting: *Dracula* and Its Media." *ELH* 59 (1992): 467–493.

Williams, Ruth. "A Virus Is Only Doing Its Job." *Sight and Sound* 3, no. 5 (1993): 31–35.

Williams, Tony. *The Cinema of George Romero: Knight of the Living Dead*. London: Wallflower Press, 2003.

Wilson, Elizabeth. *The Sphinx in the City: Urban Life, the Control of Disorder, and Women*. London: Virago, 1991.

Winter, Douglas E. "Whatever Happened to the Class of 1979?" *Fangoria*, no. 150 (1996).

Wolff, Janet. "The Invisible Flâneuse: Women and the Literature of Modernity." *Theory, Culture, and Society* 2, no. 3 (1985): 37–46.

Wollen, Peter. *Raiding the Icebox*. London: Verso, 1993.

Wood, Robin. *Hollywood from Vietnam to Reagan*. New York: Columbia University Press, 1986.

————. "Apocalypse Now: Notes from the Living Dead." In *The American Nightmare*, edited by Robin Wood and Richard Lippe, 91–97. Toronto: Festival of Festivals, 1979.

Yakir, Dan. "Morning Becomes Romero." *Film Comment* 15, no. 3 (1979): 60–65.

Filmography

Films

Addiction, The (1995), dir. Abel Ferrara, US
Alabama's Ghost (1972), dir. Fredric Hobbs, US
Because the Dawn (1988), dir. Amy Goldstein, US, short film
Blacula (1972), dir. William Crain, US
Blade (1998), dir. Stephen Norrington, US
Blade II (2002), dir. Guillermo Del Toro, US
Blade Trinity (2004), dir. David Goyer, US
Blood and Donuts (1996), dir. Holly Dale, Cananda
Blood and Donuts (2000), dir. Jeffrey Schwarz, US, short film
Blood for Dracula (1973), dir. Paul Morrissey, Italy/France
Bloodstone: Subspecies II (1992), dir. Ted Nicolaou, Romania/US
Bloodlust: Subspecies III (1993), dir. Ted Nicolaou, Romania/US
Bram Stoker's Dracula (1992), dir. Francis Ford Coppola, US
Breed, The (2001), dir. Michael Oblowitz, US/Hungary
Brides of Dracula (1960), dir. Terence Fisher, UK
Buffy the Vampire Slayer (1992), dir. Fran Rubel Kuzui, US
Captain Kronos (1972), dir. Brian Clemens, UK
Cronos (1992), dir. Guillermo Del Toro, Mexico
Count Yorga, Vampire (1970), dir. Bob Kelljan, US
Daughters of Darkness (1971), dir. Harry Kumel, Belgium/France/Germany
Dawn of the Dead (1979), dir. George Romero, US
Day of the Dead (1985), dir. George Romero, US
Deathdream (1974), dir. Bob Clark, US
Deathmaster, The (1972), dir. Ray Danton, US
Dracula (1931), dir. Tod Browning, US
Dracula (1979), dir. John Badham, US
Dracula A.D. 1972 (1972), dir. Alan Gibson, UK
Dracula and Son (1976), dir. Edouard Molinaro, France
Dracula: Dead and Loving It (1995), dir. Mel Brooks, US
Dracula's Daughter (1936), dir. Lambert Hillyer, US

Dracula's Dog (1977), dir. Albert Band, UK
Dracula: Pages from a Virgin's Diary (2002), dir. Guy Maddin, Canada
Dracula: Prince of Darkness (1965), dir. Terence Fisher, UK
Dracula 2000 (2000), dir. Patrick Lussier, US
Drakula (1921), dir. Károly Lajthay, Hungary, lost film
Fearless Vampire Killers, The (a.k.a *Dance of the Vampires*) (1967), dir. Roman Polanski, UK
Forsaken, The (2001), dir. J. S. Cardone, US
Fright Night (1985), dir. Tom Holland, US
Fright Night II (1988), dir. Tommy Lee Wallace, US
From Dusk till Dawn (1996), dir. Robert Rodriguez, US
From Dusk till Dawn II: Texas Blood Money (1999), dir. Scott Spiegel, US
From Dusk till Dawn III: The Hangman's Daughter (2000), dir. P. J. Pesce, US
Ganja and Hess (1973), dir. Bill Gunn, US
Graveyard Shift (1986), dir. Gerard Ciccoritti, Canada
Habit (1997), dir. Larry Fessenden, US
Horror of Dracula (1958), dir. Terence Fisher, UK
House of Dark Shadows (1970), dir. Dan Curtis, US
House of Dracula (1945), dir. Erle C. Kenton, US
House of Frankenstein (1944), dir. Erle C. Kenton, US
Hunger, The (1983), dir. Tony Scott, US
I Bought a Vampire Motorcycle (1990), dir. Dirk Campbell, UK
Innocent Blood (1992), dir. John Landis, US
Interview with the Vampire (1994), dir. Neil Jordan, US
Kiss of the Vampire (1962), dir. Don Sharp, UK
Lady Dracula (1977), dir. Franz Joseph Gottlieb, Germany
Land of the Dead (2005), dir. George Romero, US
League of Extraordinary Gentlemen, The (2003), dir. Stephen Norrington, US
Lifeforce (1985), dir. Tobe Hooper, US
London After Midnight (1927), dir. Tod Browning, US, lost film
Lost Boys, The (1987), dir. Joel Schumacher, US
Love at First Bite (1979), dir. Stan Dragoti, US
Lust for a Vampire (1970), dir. Jimmy Sangster, UK
Manoir du diable (1896), dir. George Méliès, France
Mark of the Vampire (1935), dir. Tod Browning, US
Martin (1977), dir. George Romero, US
My Grandfather is a Vampire (a.k.a. *Moonrise*) (1991), dir. David Blyth, New Zealand
Nadja (1994), dir. Michael Almereyda, US
Near Dark (1987), dir. Kathryn Bigelow, US
Night of the Living Dead (1968), dir. George Romero, US
Night Watch (2004), dir. Timur Bekmambetov, Russia
Nocturna, Granddaughter Of Dracula (1979), dir. Harry Tampa, US
Nosferatu (1922), dir. F. W. Murnau, Germany
Nosferatu, the Vampyre (1979), dir. Werner Herzog, Germany
Once Bitten (1985), dir. Howard Storm, US
Queen of the Damned (2002), dir. Michael Rymer, US
Rabid (1976), dir. David Cronenberg, Canada

Red Blooded American Girl (1990), dir. David Blyth, Canada
Red Lips (1995), dir. Donald Farmer, US
Requiem for a Vampire (1971), dir. Jean Rollin, France
Return of Count Yorga (1971), dir. Bob Kelljan, US
Return of Dracula, The (1957), dir. Paul Landres, US
Return of the Vampire, The (1943), dir. Lew Landers, US
Return to Salem's Lot (1987), dir. Larry Cohen, US
Revenant (1999), dir. Richard Elfman, US
Satanic Rites of Dracula (1973), dir. Alan Gibson, UK
Scream Blacula Scream (1973), dir. Bob Kelljan, US
Shadow of the Vampire (2000), dir. E. Elias Merhige, US
Son of Dracula (1943), dir. Robert Siodmak, US
Subspecies (1990), dir. Ted Nicolaou, Romania/US
Subspecies 4: Bloodstorm (1998), dir. Ted Nicolaou, US/Hungary
Tale of a Vampire (1992), dir. Shimako Sato, UK
Taste of Blood, A (1967), dir. Herschell Gordon Lewis, US
Taste the Blood of Dracula (1969), dir. Peter Sandy, UK
Thing from Another World, The (1951), dir. Christian Nyby, US
Thirst (1979), dir. Rod Hardy, Australia
Twins of Evil (1971), dir. John Hough, UK
Underworld (2003), dir. Len Wiseman, US
Underworld: Evolution (2006), dir. Len Wiseman, US
Undying Love (1991), dir. Greg Lambertson, US
Vamp (1986), dir. Richard Wenk, US
Vampira (1974), dir. Clive Donner, UK
Vampire Bat, The (1933), dir. Frank Strayer, US
Vampire in Brooklyn (1995), dir. Wes Craven, US
Vampire in Venice (1988), dir. Augusto Caminito, Italy
Vampire Lovers (1970), dir. Roy Ward Baker, UK
Vampire's Kiss (1988), dir. Robert Bierman, US
Vampires (1998), dir. John Carpenter, US
Vampires: Los Muertos (2002), dir. Tommy Lee Wallace, US
Vampires: The Turning (2005), dir. Marty Weiss, US
Vampyr (1931), dir. Carl Theodor Dreyer, France/Germany
Van Helsing (2004), dir. Stephen Sommers, US
Velvet Vampire (1971), dir. Stephanie Rothman, US
Wisdom of Crocodiles (1998), dir. Po-Chih Leong, UK

Television Films and Series

Angel (1999–2004), prod. Joss Whedon and David Greenwalt, US, series
Blood Ties (1992), dir. Jim McBride, US, film—pilot for series
Buffy the Vampire Slayer (1997–2003), prod. Joss Whedon, US, series
Dark Shadows (1966–1971), prod. Dan Curtis, US, series
Dark Shadows (1991), prod. and dir. Rob Bowman and Dan Curtis, US, series
Dracula (1968), dir. Patrick Dromgoole, UK, film

Dracula (1973), dir. Jack Nixon Brown, Canada, film
Dracula (1974), dir. Dan Curtis, US/UK, film
Dracula (1977), dir. Philip Saville, UK, film
Forever Knight (1992–1996), prod. and dir. Barney Cohen and James D. Parriott, Canada, series
I, Desire (1982), dir. John Llewellyn Moxey, US, film—pilot for series
Kindred: The Embraced (1996), prod. Peter Medak, US, series
Nick Knight (1989), dir. Farhad Mann, US, film—pilot for series *Forever Knight*
Night Stalker, The (1971), dir. John Llwellyn Moxey, prod. Dan Curtis, US, film—pilot for series
Salem's Lot (1979), dir. Tobe Hooper, US, miniseries
Salem's Lot (2004), dir. Mikael Salomon, US, miniseries
Ultraviolet (1998), dir. Joe Ahearne, UK, series
Vampire (1979), dir. E.W. Swackhamer, film—pilot for series
Vampire High (2000–2002), prod. Garry Blye and Mark Shekter, Canada, series

Index